Psychological Aspects
of
International Conflict

CONTEMPORARY PSYCHOLOGY SERIES

Edward L. Walker, Editor

Psychological Aspects of International Conflict
Ross Stagner, Wayne State University

An Anatomy for Conformity
Edward L. Walker,
The University of Michigan
and Roger W. Heyns,
University of California, Berkeley

BROOKS/COLE Publishing Company,
Belmont, California

A Division of Wadsworth
Publishing Company, Inc.

Psychological Aspects
of
International Conflict

ROSS STAGNER

Wayne State University

BROOKS / COLE Publishing Company
Belmont, California
A Division of Wadsworth Publishing Company, Inc.

4 5 6 7 8 9 10   74 73 72 71 70

Acknowledgment: Harper & Row, Publishers, Inc.,
for permission to reprint passages from **War, Peace
and Change** by John Foster Dulles.

L. C. Cat. Card No.: 67-25148
Printed in the United States of America

Preface

Nations begin in the minds of men. It was human effort, energized by desires for security and for power, that converted France from a gaggle of brawling duchies and petty kingdoms into a society within which people gave allegiance to a unified nation and submitted to national authority. The same was true of Great Britain, of Italy, and of other western nations. Men transformed the feuding American colonies into a united nation—although it took a bitter Civil War to establish the supremacy of the central government in the face of lingering regional loyalties. And, even now, some politicians still show a nostalgia for local tribalism as against national unity.

Nations are also transformed by men. Hitler in Germany and Lenin in Russia violently destroyed old institutions and laid the foundations for new systems. Franklin D. Roosevelt presided over a major change, fortunately peaceful, in the American nation. While recognizing the importance of institutional forms and traditions, we must be alert to the human dynamics which disrupt old patterns and mold new national forms.

Conflict between nations also begins with human emotions, desires, ideas, and aspirations. Controversies over tariffs, strategic military outposts, and territorial boundaries arise when men (identified with different nations) seek to gain what is perceived as an advantage for them or for their group.

This book offers an approach to the behavior of nations—and especially to conflict between nations— in terms of the decision-making processes of individuals, leaders and citizens. It seeks to illuminate some dark areas of international relations by casting the light of modern psychological concepts and theories onto political events.

This book necessarily encounters some intricate questions. I have tried to provide answers to these in a straightforward and comprehensible manner. While recognizing the technical complexities involved, I have endeavored to avoid esoteric jargon and to emphasize fundamental processes. Perhaps some of my colleagues, specialists in one or another field, will feel that this is an oversimplified version of the truth. To such a comment I can say only that it is sometimes necessary to chop away some underbrush in order to provide a clear view of the forest.

Acknowledgments are due to many persons whose ideas, comments, and criticisms of various versions of this book have modified its form. Especially I would like to mention the SPSSI * Committee on Peace and War, of which I was chairman from 1937 to 1941, and its members, J. F. Brown, Ralph H. Gundlach, and Ralph K. White. The present statement of my ideas has profited from detailed critiques by S. E. Asch and T. M. Newcomb. Needless to say, I must accept responsibility for any errors or inadequacies remaining in the published version.

Ross Stagner

* Society for the Psychological Study of Social Issues.

Contents

Psychological Aspects
of
International Conflict

1
Men Make
Policy Decisions

The casual observer is likely to be impressed
with the detachment, the almost mechanical
impersonality, of national policy decisions.
This is because he does not take a close
look. These decisions are — and hopefully
will continue to be — made by men. The
President of the United States, senators,
Cabinet members, and bureaucrats are all
human. Likewise, their counterparts —
prime ministers, Presidium members, and
commissars — are human.

Is this too banal to be said? I think
not. The observation is important precisely
because so many people neglect it. There is
a widespread notion that human frailties do
not affect national policy decisions, despite
the literally mountainous evidence to the
contrary. Perhaps because we idealize our
leaders, perhaps because we erroneously
think of the nation as having an existence
apart from the people who comprise it, we
assume that our leaders make decisions
which are somehow free of the biases and
errors of ordinary humans. This is an inde-
fensible view of our own nation, and it has
important implications for our view of other
countries as well.

1

To err is human. There is nothing about the process of accepting the role of national leader which suddenly endows a man with supernatural wisdom. The Bay of Pigs fiasco can remind Americans of this fallibility in national policy decisions; and the fascinating account by Schlesinger[1] of the various bits of distorted or biased information sent to President Kennedy on that occasion could serve as an introduction to this volume. The Russians are now willing to admit that policy errors were made during the Stalin regime (although they are unwilling to admit that the objective conditions of communist rule inevitably gave rise to such a regime). It will probably be some time before the Chinese Communists will dare admit that the Great Leap Forward was an all-too-human error, but most observers suspect that it was.

There are at least two reasons why it is important to remember that national policies can be in error. First, if we remind ourselves that these decisions were, after all, made by human beings, they lose some of their artificial sanctity and become fair game for critical comments. We can accept the necessity for unified support of a national policy, once adopted, without abandoning our right to search for and criticize errors.

A second point has more extensive implications. Once we concede that national decisions are of human origin, we must accept the relevance of a vast body of psychological research on learning, thinking, and problem solving to national affairs and international relations. Over twenty years ago the framers of the UNESCO charter coined the phrase: "Wars begin in the minds of men." Regrettably little effort has since been applied to a systematic exploration of the human mind and its role in exacerbating international tensions.

The purpose of this little book is to identify some features of human thinking, emotions, motives, and attitudes, which seem to contribute significantly to the occurrence of international conflict. It is not a book about how to wage peace. It is not even a self-defense manual for keeping out of wars. Rather, it offers a way of thinking about nations, about national leaders, and about citizens, which can throw unexpected illumination into dark corners of policy making and policy execution. The proposition is set forth that we need to anticipate, and to try to forestall, major sources of error in making decisions. We now have enough solid information about how human thought processes operate, that discussion of these influences is no longer a mere semantic exercise.

This approach does not amount to the naive treatment of a nation as a somehow magnified individual. My concern is with the behavior of national leaders and national citizens. Under certain conditions one may deal with the nation as if it were a true unit; and, indeed, under

---

Notes are listed at the back of the book.

most circumstances a national policy decision does lead to coordinated action. Even under these conditions, some citizens may refuse to cooperate; and, in the democracies, large blocs may actively oppose a policy decision while overtly conforming to it. It therefore becomes necessary to say that a nation is composed entirely and exclusively of human beings, and simultaneously to say that nations have distinctive attributes apart from their human components.

The nation, considered as an operating unit, becomes the proper object of study by political scientists, who are concerned with legislative, administrative, and judicial processes. Nations unquestionably differ in the way they handle these functions, and no psychologist would propose that we substitute research on individual congressmen for observations of how Congress operates. I shall, however, insist that additional insight into congressional maneuvering can be achieved by exploring some of the psychological events which occur as a congressman makes up his mind on a particular issue. We can also benefit by considering whether specific institutional patterns increase the probability that persons of a given psychological makeup will achieve positions of national leadership.

Many political scientists, writing about nations, unconsciously attribute human characteristics to these impersonal aggregates.[2] A nation *as such* does not cherish sovereignty, national honor, or expansion of territory; but leaders of the nation can and do. The revolutionary changes wrought by Hitler in Germany, by Lenin in Russia, and by other powerful leaders should remind us that *national institutions are subject to an overriding human control.* It would be a grave error to become so fascinated by the complex mechanism of representative democracy as to forget that this was molded by men and can be transformed out of recognition by men.

Finally, it is important to note that the behavior of a man in national office will differ from that of the same man as a citizen. The thinking of executives, judges, and legislators is modified by their social roles. A chief of state can quite honestly say: "I must do this for my country, even though it is against my principles." (It is unlikely that the Nuremberg trials have modified this pattern.) We must therefore avoid the error of assuming that decisions by citizens adequately duplicate decisions by leaders — at the same time recognizing that decisions by citizens may have considerable weight in influencing decisions of leaders. We must take account of the individual's *national role* as a factor influencing how he perceives reality and how he chooses among courses of action.

The nation is not a person, a psychological unit; and this book does not pretend that psychological science can displace economics, sociology, and political science as major disciplines contributing to an understanding of international affairs. Consider the role of economic processes. The people of a nation, in the grip of delusions of national grandeur, may declare their ability to move from primitive agriculture to complex industrialization without outside assistance. However, if the resources are not there, the effort is doomed to failure. Even in a nation with rich mineral deposits, the organization of a suitable technology requires much time, effort, and guidance. No amount of perceptual distortion can compensate for the absence of an organized industrial base.

Psychology is likewise no substitute for geographical reality or for military strength. The French in 1939 apparently were under the delusion that they held great military power, but the German attack in the spring of 1940 proved otherwise. Thus, misperceptions in some areas may lead to overconfidence, as when delusions of national grandeur gloss over disorganization and poor morale in the military forces.

The same generalization holds for sociological and other realities.[3] A nation like India, riddled with religious, linguistic, and caste hostilities, has problems which will not be suddenly solved by clever internal propaganda. It is correct to argue that the real damage in such a situation results from the refusal of individuals to cooperate efficiently with groups seen as hostile, but these detrimental perceptions are supported by an intricate network of group affiliations and group sanctions. What happens to a lower-caste individual who violates caste rules on behalf of the national welfare? He will encounter a great deal of unpleasantness both from higher castes and from his own group. It does little good in such cases for Indian leaders to make speeches about the mystical unity of the Indian people.

In the 1960 rebellion in the Congo, the Simbas carried magic amulets which would, they believed, protect them from the white men's guns. Large numbers died as a result; probably such beliefs even contributed to the failure of the rebellion, since the white mercenaries had an easier time than with typical guerrilla tactics. Thus, psychological distortions can play a role in a social movement, but they cannot bypass the harder realities of technology.

This warning about nonpsychological realities must not be interpreted as a statement that the psychological side can safely be ignored. How the Russians perceive us may be grievously in error as compared with reality measured by scientific means. Nevertheless, they must act on reality as they see it; and if in their view we are about to attack them, they may resort to a nuclear first strike as a preventive device — as, indeed, many American strategists feel that we might make a preventive strike. In either case, we shall all be just as dead, whether the perceived readiness to attack was justified or not.

NATIONAL POLICY AND INDIVIDUAL PERCEPTION

Nations come into conflict because they have adopted policies directed toward goals which are incompatible. Hitler in 1939 wanted territorial acquisitions and economic control of Europe; Britain and France resisted this. But on neither side was the leadership group unanimous. Many advisers opposed Hitler's aggressive nationalism as long as they dared, and many western leaders feared to take active military steps in opposition to the powerful nazi machine. The decision *not* to fight in 1938 (when Czechoslovakia was dismembered) and to fight in 1939 (when Poland was invaded) can be taken as an example. In 1938 most of the western leaders saw their own military weakness and feared to challenge Nazi Germany; in 1939 some improvement was noted and they saw some chance of success if war ensued.

One arrives at a policy decision by assessing the facts as they appear at a moment in time. The Japanese leaders in 1941 examined the international situation and "saw" facts which seemed to indicate an opportunity for national expansion. Their "facts" turned out to be dangerously erroneous, with catastrophic results for their nation.

Psychologists, philosophers, and even physicists now agree that every fact is relative to an observer. The naive notion that man has direct knowledge of reality must be abandoned. What man has to guide him in his daily behavior is the evidence of his senses — all notoriously fallible. Automobile drivers often misperceive facts on the highway, with results sometimes fatal. Businessmen base policy decisions on reports from observers, and these often are unreliable and invalid. The President of the United States cannot *know* the real facts about Russia, or China, or France; he gets reports that are filtered through the eyes of observers who are biased in various ways. Hopefully, he gets enough of a range of biases that he can cancel most of them out; but he can never be absolutely sure. In this world, I can never be certain of the thoughts and intentions of a man sitting next to me; how much less then, can I expect to be sure of the plans of a leader of another nation.

Diplomatic representatives listen and observe, trying to gather information; but they listen to only a few citizens of their host country. Spies are employed to ferret out concealed activities, but they are often concerned to relay only reports which will keep them on the payroll. Even unpaid informants are likely to be seeking psychological gratification by their actions and, therefore, to be representing only their own biases.

A psychologist, recently returned from Russia, made an observation which seems to me most important. When he spoke with his hosts (he

DISTORTIONS OF PERCEPTION

What is a clearly visible "fact" to one observer may appear quite different to another viewer. It is essential to keep in mind the role of biases in the perception of international conflicts. (Cartoon by Seibel, in *The Richmond Times-Dispatch*. Reprinted by permission of Fred O. Seibel.)

is fluent in their language), he was impressed by their tendency to parrot the Voice of America criticisms of Russia and arguments for the American position. And those who sought him out, he noted, also fell into this pattern. On the other hand, when he went out and contacted people on his own, men and women who could not have known in advance that an American would speak to them, he found much more support for the Russian regime. He suspected that our reporters and diplomats in the USSR had been misled by the discontented souls who came to them with complaints about the government. Biased information could lead to a totally incorrect expectation as to the likelihood of revolt or of strong pressure on the regime for a change in policy. The hazards of such errors are obvious.

WHY IS PERCEPTION UNRELIABLE?

Action must be guided by perception. But perception can give us only an approximation, an estimate, of what is "out there." (I, like most people, assume that *something* is out there but that my senses give me only limited information about it.) One gets visual, auditory, tactual, and other sensory inputs and, from these, constructs a picture of the probable object.

These images on which we act are unreliable for many reasons. The human being receives certain information through his eyes, ears, nose, skin, and other sensitive organs. In many cases, the information does not come by direct contact with an object but depends on light waves, sound waves, chemicals, etc. From these, the human being makes *inferences* about "real" objects. But even in the case of touch, which we trust most, we know that we are often fooled.

Modern physics suggests that we must be cautious even in making assumptions about the nature of an object. If I look at my desk, it seems solid; it feels quite comfortingly real. But the physicist says it is really a bunch of electrons and protons in rapid vibration, with mostly empty space between. What happens to my solid desk? Is it really an illusion? Our senses are limited. You cannot know whether a block of metal in your hand is destroying your flesh by radioactive emanations, because you have no sense-organs which are sensitive to such energies. That is why men in atomic installations must wear exposure badges.

But this kind of weakness in learning about physical reality is trivial in comparison with the problems in acquiring knowledge about people. Our daily activities require judgments of people as to their honesty, integrity, skill, intelligence, and so on. Yet, we have no sense-organs that identify such attributes. Further, the person observed may be trying to transmit misleading information as to what he is really

SPLIT PERSONALITY

The cartoonist refers here to the primitive character of
world statesmanship, as compared to world
science. More precisely, the split is between our
rational understanding of issues and our primitive
emotional response when valued symbols, for example,
the nation, are attacked. (Cartoon by Mauldin,
in the *St. Louis Post-Dispatch*. Reprinted by permission.)

like. It may be to his advantage to deceive you as to his intentions. Most important of all, human prejudices and emotions prevent us from gathering as much information as is available about another person or group.

When a young man falls in love, he is quite likely to exaggerate, in a manner obvious to detached observers, the beauty, intelligence, and other attributes of his sweetheart. While this perceptual distortion undoubtedly helps to get a marriage off to a good start, it may not be desirable in the long run. Families in which husband and wife can still enjoy each other without being unrealistic about personal qualities probably manage better. Novelists like Somerset Maugham (*Of Human Bondage*) have delineated the tragedies which can result from unrealistic perceptions in marriage.

Most citizens also love their nation; and while this relationship is less intimate than marriage, it is not always less important. We must therefore be concerned about the extent to which such emotions as patriotism cause citizens to misperceive the qualities of their nation. Exaggeration of national power probably contributed to the decision of the Japanese leaders to go to war in 1941. Loving parents cannot see the errors of their children; passionate patriots are usually blind to errors of their national leaders. The devoted communist cannot admit that his party could be in error; he can always invent rationalizations to show that party policy was correct. Obviously such attitudes do not help to rectify mistakes or to stabilize realistic policy orientations.

THE CRUCIAL ROLE OF PERCEPTION

Why are psychologists so much concerned about perception? Should we not — one might ask — concentrate on the facts and ignore these subjective, emotion-gilded perceptions? How pleasant, and how much simpler, life would be if this question could be answered in the affirmative.

The real dilemma for policy makers arises from the scarcity of objective facts. There are some data, items which can be counted, on which virtually universal agreement can be achieved: It is a fact, we may say, that the USA now has 190 million inhabitants. Even this is somewhat lacking in precision, however, since births, deaths, and migration change the total momentarily. But it is highly objective as compared with, for example, whether it is a *fact* that the Diem government was the legitimate government of South Vietnam. The USA elevated this to the status of a fact by giving diplomatic recognition; but the Diem government had far less control of its territory than did the Chinese Communist government, which we refused to recognize.

The problem can be grasped more easily if we take a smaller scale example — one from industry. Consider the case of a large American corporation which I visited a few years ago. There was clear evidence that sales had' dropped on a certain product; it was possible to count these sales, so the data were fairly objective. There were, however, numerous explanations (facts), which aroused sharp disagreement. Some executives said it was a fact that production costs were too high. Others claimed that the important fact was that marketing had been neglected. The remedies were likewise diverse: One group wanted to spend money for new production facilities and automated machinery, the other for advertising and market promotions. It will surprise no one that the first solution was pressed by the vice-president for production and the second by the vice-president for sales.

Each man had the best interests of the corporation at heart. Each genuinely believed that his proposal was the right policy for the company to follow. But — quite obviously — each was exaggerating the evidence favoring more money and more power for *his own department*, while ignoring evidence pointing to added appropriations for the other executive. The perception of facts is often biased by personal considerations such as power and profit.

This phenomenon is common in national decision making. Heads of government departments and bureaus see the facts which justify their continuance and expansion; each tends to ignore facts which would suggest elimination of his empire. Thus, when Defense and State collide with differing views of the facts, this should not be interpreted as treason (as fanatics occasionally do). Each department secretary sees the facts which support him — those which have been reported to him by staff members sharing the same bias. Each fails to see the facts cited by the opposition. Both men are patriotic; both are honest. Each sees the situation through spectacles which magnify some items, minimize others. This subtle, usually unconscious process is crucial to an understanding of conflicts within national governments.

The same generalization holds even more strongly for international conflicts. The spokesman for a nation is under powerful emotional pressure to see only the facts which make a good case for his side. The Russian leader, for example, defends a separate UN vote for the Ukrainian republic by asserting that it is truly a separate government. Americans scoff at this claim. But when asked by Russians why Washington does not protect the lives of visitors to Mississippi, we point to the status of the government of Mississippi as, in some respects, independent of federal control. One can spot fragments of reality in each argument, but the amount of defensive exaggeration on each side is substantial.

Perception plays a crucial role in these debates precisely because it can, almost on command, provide the evidence to support a position. Actually, as my thesis will run, the perception precedes the policy decision and shapes it. If we perceive our missiles as purely defensive, we cannot see any reason why the Russians should complain about them. And if the Russians see their ICBM force as purely defensive, they are equally puzzled by our protests. Most men prefer not to be cynical liars. While it may be true, as the old Latin proverb goes, that "an ambassador is a brave man sent abroad to lie for his country," it is easier on the conscience if the lying is unconscious. Distortion of perception makes this possible.

IMAGE AND REALITY

When psychologists start discussing the way people look at reality — specifically, how they view their own nation and other, competing nations, there is an implicit assumption that such perceptions are relevant to the course of national policy decisions. Many political scientists argue that public opinion carries no weight in the formation of policy in international affairs. Others disagree. The following considerations seem appropriate in thinking about this question:

1. Public attitudes determine what kind of candidate will be elected (in democratic nations) or will survive in the power struggle (in totalitarian regimes). A candidate for Congress who advocates protection of American jobs, no matter what effect this has overseas, usually gets more votes than one who favors tariff reduction. The presidential candidate who promises a tough line against our perceived enemies—or our friends—has an advantage over one who is seen as "soft" on the opposition. Even in the rough-and-tumble variety of politics in the Kremlin, there are clearly considerations of groups within the Communist party and the kinds of policies they will support.

2. As a corollary of this, it appears from both public statements and private memoirs that holders of public office make policy decisions with one eye on the voter reaction. One often sees the statement, "It would be political suicide for the president to take this step." Whether the observer is correct or not, the president may see matters in the same way and refrain from the act, even though logic might have favored it. (In this respect, the leaders of communist countries seem to have more real freedom of decision than do those in the democracies.)

3. Studies of the average citizen and his attitudes have some relevance simply as examples of the population from which leaders are drawn.

Emotional appeals which are effective with the public are probably effective with leadership elites, although the latter are influenced by a much wider array of stimuli. General laws of thinking and action, however, hold for leaders simply because they are human. The tendency to shut out unpleasant information, for example, does not diminish just because a man becomes a high official. He may be forced to look at it, but he can still misinterpret it. (The psychotic breakdown of Secretary of Defense Forrestal[4] is a warning of the extent to which public policy decisions may be affected by emotional abnormalities; the actions of Josef Stalin and Adolf Hitler remind us that men not overtly insane may, if in power positions, devastate whole nations.)

We cannot know reality, either physical or human, in a direct fashion. We know the evidence of our senses, but they are easily deceived. We make inferences about people from their words and actions, but these inferences are often wrong. We shall never know what the Russians are *really* like.

We know *images*. Each person has an image of himself (and, alas, may find that others have quite a different image). Often I find that my picture of a certain individual, even after long observation, is erroneous in some major detail.

Americans do not know Russia; they know an image of Russia, subject to many errors and misconceptions. In fact, they do not know America, but only an image thereof; and it is sometimes amazing to find how we differ among ourselves as to the attributes of our nation. Certainly, the national image is not the same for Barry Goldwater and Lyndon Johnson, or for Harry S Truman and Dwight D. Eisenhower.

These images become distorted in various ways. Typically, one grossly overestimates the virtue of his own group and the villainy of opposing groups. This is true with regard to groups inside the nation and also with regard to groups outside the nation. Images become distorted because of emotions such as love or hate, fear and anxiety; they are also twisted by biased information (censorship, propaganda) and by cultural traditions.

But, you may ask, if we cannot know reality, how can we assert that some images are distorted and others are not? Does this not leave us in a morass with no means of escape?

We can use an operational criterion to get away from this dilemma. *Some images are more dependable than others as guides to action.* The child goes through a tedious process of learning which sensory cues he can trust and which he must ignore. When the eyes focus on a near object, for example, distant objects are seen as double images; but one quickly learns that they are not really doubled. A stick in water appears bent; but by lifting it out or by running a finger along it, one finds that it is still straight.

For this process of sorting out images and establishing safe guides to action, we use the term "reality testing." Parents often must encourage a child to test reality by venturing upon some unfamiliar experience such as swimming. The water, which first appears threatening, is found to be a source of pleasure.

Reality testing is essential to survival. We "see" a great many things which do not exist. A coin seen from an angle looks like an ellipse, but it remains physically round. Colors change in dim light and under colored illumination. Adults say, "It looks like that, but it isn't, really."

The child tests reality by touch, by taste, by handling, by pushing, and by other manipulations. He learns to compensate for common illusions such as the bent stick in water, and he acquires some skill in detecting the real emotion behind expressions of friendship and affection. All of this depends upon reality testing, in the sense that the child can take some action and see what happens. For example, he learns to use yardsticks and other measuring devices to reduce perceptual error. Gradually, he comes to identify cues that tell him that the appearance is not quite in agreement with what he will feel or lift.

The same problem exists in relation to other nations and other social groups. The child may acquire certain images of the British, French, Russians, Japanese, socialists, pacifists, communists, Jews, and Negroes. How can he apply reality testing to these percepts? It is most difficult. In a typical middle-class community, he may have no personal contact with any of these as real persons. Especially with Russians and other "enemy" groups, he will have no opportunity to ascertain whether they really have the nasty characteristics legend attributes to them. And no adult in the child's vicinity is likely to admit to having a communist idea or anything remotely resembling one!

Reality testing in the realm of national stereotypes, then, is difficult for children. Even at the adult level it is not simple. The world today grows smaller, but European travel is still a luxury limited to a small proportion of Americans; and even fewer Europeans can afford to visit the USA. All too often the only visitors to America are officials, who are so completely blinded by their duties as agents of a government that they cannot see the "real" Americans. And vice versa — Americans overseas rarely have any friendly personal contacts with foreigners except in a commercial or governmental role.

Delusions persist, then, at the level of international affairs. Our images of Italy, of Turkey, and of Austria are formed of biased history texts and loaded newspaper stories. In the absence of reality testing, these erroneous views linger on and determine our behavior. Similarly the legend of the crude, materialistic, uneducated American goes unchallenged in much of the world.[5]

THE SELF-FULFILLING PROPHECY

HISTORY OF THE PAST FIVE YEARS

Russian image of the West, in the immediate postwar period, made rearmament inevitable. (Cartoon by David Low. Reprinted, by permission, from *The Daily Herald,* London.)

Specialists in international relations have not been ignorant of this decisive role of perception. The English scholar, Joseph Frankel, has called attention to the shaping of policies by established images, which may screen out new information: "Once a statesman has formed an image of an issue, this image acts as an organizing device for further information and as a filter through which this information must pass. Images, not detailed information, govern political behavior."[6] In many instances, the problem is such that it compels the foreigner to act in the expected fashion. We call this kind of error "the self-fulfilling prophecy."

THE SELF-FULFILLING PROPHECY

Consider the case of a man, drinking in a bar, who decides that someone else is trying to start a fight. By acting belligerently, he elicits aggressive behavior from the other and so confirms his own expectation.

School teachers are familiar with a different example of this. The teacher who approaches Johnny with the assumption that he is stupid and inept will communicate this view to the boy. Johnny then will be upset and anxious and will probably behave foolishly or clumsily. The teacher then is confirmed in her percept, which actually may be quite erroneous.

We observe this phenomenon often in labor-management relations. For example, in one company, the union was viewed as belligerent, untrustworthy, and malicious; and the actions of company representatives seemed to bring out these kinds of behavior in the union, even if the behavior had not been present before. Surprisingly, a change to a company executive who showed a readiness to trust the union and to assume honest intentions led to a drastic change in union tactics and far greater cooperation.[7]

Now let us ponder the case of the diplomat who is dealing with country X. His view is that the people of this country are untrustworthy and aggressive. By making his attitudes clear, he irritates them and they behave aggressively. They may decide that he will misinterpret certain facts, so they try to conceal them. The diplomat is thus confirmed in his picture of these people.

Some psychologists talk about "possibilistic" behavior — meaning that one may leap from a possibility to a subjective certainty. The paranoid psychotic has delusions that he is being persecuted by some group such as the Masons or the Knights of Columbus. He is taken to a psychiatrist, who tries to help him. But the thought occurs to the patient that *possibly* his physician is really a member of the persecuting group; and, almost instantly, he finds evidence to convince himself of

this. The evidence may be far too flimsy to convince a detached observer; but the paranoid individual, firm in his delusion of being
persecuted, needs only a hint, a glance, a gesture to prove his case.

We note this currently in the suspicions expressed with regard to
the moratorium on nuclear tests.[8] The Russians are, by American views,
quite likely to cheat and conduct clandestine tests. From this possibility,
many observers leap to the certainty that the Soviets have repeatedly
violated their own announced ban on testing. The evidence is ill-
defined; but to the person with such a picture of the Russians, no
evidence is really needed. And if enough of us adopt this posture, we
encourage them to behave in accord with our expectations.

It is difficult to know reality, especially with regard to people and
groups. The self-fulfilling prophecy makes it even harder to escape from
the prison of our own images and get a workable conception of the
world situation. Yet this is the task that faces the human race if we
are to deal rationally with our problems.

The thesis of this book, then, is fairly simple. First, policy decisions
which lead to international tension and war are made by human beings,
and these humans are guided by their images of our nation and of
other nations. They cannot have direct knowledge of either reality. Second, these images are often distorted, and an erroneous image may
induce actions which are self-destructive. Thus, wise selection of leaders
and wise decisions by leaders depend upon an understanding of the
ways in which the human mind seeks to comprehend reality. We must
apply the most rigorous, dispassionate, scientific methods available to
find out which images offer the safest guides to action.[8] And we must
then choose leaders who will follow such guiding principles.[9] It is a
complex task, but we should work at it as if our lives depended upon
our success — because they do.

2
Images and Wars

Wars for the most part, turn out to be somebody's errors; and it is worthwhile to explore the possibility that they occur because of errors in perception. It would be tempting to conclude that every war between nations is evidence of a failure of reason; but this is really a moral judgment, not a scientific observation. It will be more constructive to try to identify the errors in perception which played a decisive role in initiating the war; the assumption is that such errors, if identified, might also be corrected.

Human behavior is always directed toward the achievement of some kind of goal. In the case of nations, a war policy is adopted only because it is seen as leading to some goal desired by those who speak for the nation. But policy decisions must be guided by knowledge of the situation; and this knowledge, of course, takes the form of images of the situation, the other nations, the economic forces involved, and so on. Wars, it can be shown with the clarity of hindsight, often break out because someone was influenced by images which were not close to reality. Given this kind of image, however, the war policy may have been quite rational.

This is not to say that images cause wars. The problem "What causes war?" is extremely complex. The causes of World War I include various events in the history of England, Germany, Austria, Russia, and so on. The assassination of Archduke Ferdinand was unimportant; it was, at most, a trigger for explosives already planted. Similarly, the causes of World War II include the Versailles Treaty, the economic hardships of the German population, the American Neutrality Act, and a whole host of other circumstances; the German feud with Poland was only one component in a whole complex of causes. In a sense, all of history is the cause of what happens tomorrow.

It is not, therefore, a fruitful process to try to determine *the cause* of a specific war. At best, we can identify certain factors, which played important parts in the decision. From the point of view of the present analysis, what I want to demonstrate is that certain distorted perceptions must be understood if we are to have a clear picture of how wars have broken out in the past.

Historians have often written about the "paradox of unwanted war" — the fact that leaders of each nation involved in a controversy profess their devotion to peace while getting ready to destroy the enemy. Is this really a paradox? Is there anything exceptionally difficult to understand here? In the frame of reference here presented, the paradox disappears. War broke out because the leaders were guided by unrealistic images.

Consider the situation of Adolf Hitler in 1939. Loudly proclaiming his desire for peaceful settlement of the "Polish question," he pursued his plan for expansion to the east in order to acquire new territory and economic resources. Knowing that the British and French had knuckled under to his aggressive acts in the Rhineland, in Austria, and in Czechoslovakia, he saw them as spineless, comfort-seeking nations, who would not fight. This was a misperception which he undoubtedly regretted at a later time.

Hitler's faulty decision was based on his incorrect image of his opponents. But Chamberlain and Daladier were likewise at fault for their unrealistic image of Hitler. In 1938, when Neville Chamberlain flew to Berchtesgaden and returned to proclaim "peace in our time," it was commented that he never really saw Hitler at all, but only his own image of what a sensible German leader would be like. Knowing the terrible destructiveness of war, he could not imagine Hitler opening hostilities after all the concessions he had won. Unless we see our opponent clearly, we cannot make intelligent policy choices.

It was particularly surprising that the Allied leaders misunderstood Hitler so thoroughly, since he had rather carefully blueprinted his plans for conquest in *Mein Kampf*. (This does not mean that we naively accept whatever a leader writes in a book; but we ought, at least, to read it and see if he is executing the plans he has set forth in print!)

Another example that merits consideration is that of the Japanese leaders in 1941. Like Hitler, they constantly asserted that they did not want war; but they did want to drive out western influences and establish their "co-prosperity sphere," with emphasis on prosperity for the Japanese in East Asia. As they saw the situation, the USA was too deeply involved in aid to the western allies to fight a two-front war; further, they expected to get so firmly established in their Asiatic holdings that we would negotiate a peaceful settlement rather than tolerate the casualties and costs of driving them out. This erroneous view of their opposition led to widespread devastation of their homeland rather than to the economic gains they had anticipated.

The delusions were not all on the side of our adversaries. It seems clear that the Roosevelt administration grossly underestimated the drive of the Japanese towards domination of Asia. And someone apparently had very inaccurate ideas about the probable military tactics they would employ.

Many other examples could be listed; the North Koreans certainly misinterpreted our intentions in 1950, with results which they can hardly have enjoyed. Conversely, General MacArthur refused to accept the Chinese Communist warning that they would attack if he drove to the Yalu River; and his delusion guided the military action which led to decidedly unpleasant consequences for the US and the UN. The current phrase "war by miscalculation" refers to these possibilities of war occurring because individuals in key positions misperceive the behavior or intentions of the opposition.

The problem of unintentional destruction of civilization has been phrased eloquently by the Spanish philosopher Salvador de Madariaga:

> On September 26, 1687, a Venetian bomb, falling on a Turkish powder magazine, blew the Parthenon to pieces. Men had risen to that height where such beauty is conceived and brought forth. Men had fallen to that depth where such beauty is destroyed. But while the building of the Parthenon was thought out and willed, its destruction was neither willed nor thought out. It just happened.[1]

THE DEVIL THEORY OF WAR

In part, de Madariaga sought to dispel the "devil theory" — the notion that wars happen because of bad men. This theory, unfortunately, has been widely accepted, especially in the USA. It is irrational because it leads to action only against the immediate disturber of our peace and ignores long-term processes which make further discord probable.

The devil theory is furthered by wartime (and prewar) propaganda which focuses on a specific individual. In World War I, this focus (by the western powers) was on Kaiser Wilhelm II; hence, it is not especially surprising that Americans believed the problem had been definitely settled with his abdication and exile. This had the unfortunate consequence of fitting in with the isolationist trend which was developing in this country. We saw no need for the League of Nations, no threat to us in the German economic breakdown in 1928. Our response to Hitler's seizure of the Rhineland in 1936 was to put up the futile curtain of the Neutrality Act. This gesture did nothing to postpone World War II.

After World War I, another kind of devil theory was proposed: that wars occur because of evil, greedy men engaged in the business of manufacturing arms. These men, including Sir Basil Zaharoff, the Krupp family, the Du Ponts and others, were alleged to have encouraged international hostilities for the sake of private profit.[2] It can hardly be doubted that economic motives play their part in precipitating wars, but it is now certain that the denunciation of the "merchants of death" was grossly overdone. In Soviet Russia, for example, private profit cannot be a factor in influencing belligerency; yet the Russians have hardly played a pacifistic role in recent years.

Similarly, excitable pacifists have picked on military leaders as the "devils" leading us to war. It is likely, because of his social role, that the military leader is extremely sensitive to questions of threat from abroad; after all, he would be delinquent in his responsibility if he were not alert to just such problems. But it is equally probable that he is more aware than the average citizen of the horrors of war and, hence, is disposed to be cautious about belligerent moves. We know of some instances (Hitler and his General Staff in 1941, for example) in which the military attempted to restrain a warlike civilian. And in the western democracies, military leaders have not generally been in a position to make the crucial decisions leading to war.

Devil theories are attractive at least in part because they are simpler than those requiring consideration of complex economic, strategic, political, and psychological influences. The average man has had some experience thinking of people as good, bad, or indifferent; he has had little experience with the enormously complicated interactions which occur in international affairs. Most people — even diplomats — prefer a simplified to an intricate solution. But it will not aid the cause of international cooperation if we act on the basis of an unrealistic, oversimplified version of events.

SOME DELUSIONS ABOUT TREATIES

George F. Kennan, a distinguished American diplomat, has some harsh things to say about "the extraordinary American capacity for self-delusion," particularly with regard to faith in treaties as devices for maintaining peace. He speaks with special scorn of the Kellogg-Briand Pact, that extraordinary document negotiated by the American secretary of state in 1928. This treaty, signed by some sixty-two nations — including Germany, Italy, and Japan — solemnly avowed that the signatories renounced war as an instrument of national policy. As subsequent events proved, in Manchuria, in Ethiopia, and elsewhere, such a treaty was truly a "scrap of paper." Kennan writes:

> Prodigious efforts were expended on these fruitless discussions at Geneva . . . And at the very time this mountainous labor was in progress, Weimar Germany was disintegrating miserably into the illness of national socialism, and new political realities were being created which were soon to sweep all this labor from the scene of world history, as though it had never existed.[3]

The more absurd implications of the Kellogg-Briand Pact can readily be seen if we note that the USA, since it had not formally abrogated this treaty, became technically a treaty violator by declaring war on Japan in December 1941. Few will argue that this nation had an alternative. Idealistic treaties, which take no account of changing political, economic, and military conditions, provide only a paper curtain to hold back the flames of war.

The point Kennan wishes to stress, of course, is the need for a new way of looking at international affairs — to get away from devil theories and isolationist delusions. We must concern ourselves, he says, with the struggle for power:

> And when the rude facts of the power conflict did finally intrude themselves directly upon us, in the form of the enemies against whom we were forced to fight in the two world wars, we found it difficult to perceive the relation between them and the historical logic of our epoch, because we understood the latter so poorly. These enemies appeared to us in the aspect of monsters that had arisen from nowhere, as by some black magic. We deluded ourselves with the belief that if they could be in some way exorcized, like evil spirits, through the process of military defeat, then nothing would remain of them and our world would be restored to us again as though they had never

existed. It was hard for us to see that these enemies were
the reflection of deeper causes which could be only par-
tially alleviated, and might in some cases be actually
aggravated, by the miseries of war and the abrupt im-
balances of national power implicit in such things as total
victory and unconditional surrender.[4]

The unfortunate aspect of this stirring analysis is that it does not
tell us how to identify the "rude facts" of the power conflict. As was
noted earlier, all facts depend on observers; and observers often disagree. We have recently fought two wars against Germany; in both
instances, we were allied, at least part of the time, with Russia. Yet,
today, whom do we fear and whom do we treat as an ally? The "rude
facts" keep changing.

THE DELUSION OF MILITARY DETERRENCE

Herman Kahn, in his book *On Thermonuclear War,* speaks of a
doomsday machine which we might devise and bury deep in the
earth.[5] It could be so controlled that, if the Russians launched a nuclear attack on the USA, the earth would be utterly blasted and all
life would be wiped out. Obviously, this kind of deterrent would not
work, since the Russians would not believe we would use it. However,
deterrents may fail because they are misinterpreted.

In 1946, the Americans believed that their atom bomb was a
deterrent to any Russian efforts at imperialistic expansion. But the
Russians perceived our bomb as a threat, and they worked furiously
to equal and surpass it with the hydrogen bomb. Similarly, the Russians
perceived the intercontinental ballistic missile as a deterrent to attack
by the "warmongering capitalists," but we saw their missile superiority
as a threat and mobilized our efforts to overpass their potential in
this area.

History records many similar situations. The pre-1914 arms race
between Germany and Austria, on one side, and England and France,
on the other, certainly led to catastrophe. Neither side was deterred
by the artillery and trained manpower of the other. Similarly, Hitler's
impressive Wehrmacht did not deter the western powers from declaring
war on him in 1939; they had, in fact, responded two years earlier
by expanding their military establishments.

One need not conclude from this that response to a military threat
is futile; it may be essential to self-preservation. In view of Hitler's
declared intent, and his policy in the Ukraine, one can only assume
that the Russian population would have been exterminated had they

followed a Gandhian policy in 1941. But the more adaptive approach is to identify trends toward irreconcilable conflict before these trends become unmanageable.

DELUSIONS ABOUT DISARMAMENT

Part of our difficulty in thinking about problems of war and peace lies in our tendency to treat them as distinct, and indeed opposite, conditions. This is incorrect. Conflict between nations appears long before hot war breaks out. It may seem that we have a historically unique situation today with our chronic cold war occasionally bursting into flames, but there are many historical precedents. Consider the long feud between Britain and France, which culminated in the defeat of Napoleon at Waterloo. This had been going on for over a hundred years, flaring up in various parts of the world (as in the French and Indian War and the American Revolution) and marked by piracy and looting on both sides.

Actually, the famous dictum of Clausewitz, to the effect that "war is a continuation of politics by other means," carries with it the implication of all degrees of conflict from cold through tepid to hot war. And if we should define peace negatively by saying that peace is no more than war carried on without organized hostilities, we should be reasonably accurate. Peace in our present system of nation-states is characterized by conflict within a set of rules.

Occasionally, people from one or another nation break the rules in order to achieve some advantage. In the eighteenth century, such individuals might have been acting without government approval or, at least, without formal approval—for example, Clive's conquest of India, British pirating of Spanish ships in the Caribbean, American settlers breaking treaties to drive the Indians west. In the twentieth century, with the technology required to support even guerrilla warfare, government support is essential even if not openly admitted. Thus, we gave aid to the Boun Oum rebellion in Laos against the neutralist government, just as the Soviets lent aid to the Pathet Lao.

Even with rules and machinery for conflict settlement, the possibility of war will still be with us. There will always be a temptation to resort to violence. Disarmament agreements are palliatives at best. They resemble ice packs for a fever: They may make the patient feel better temporarily, but they don't get at the disease. There is no hope for a foolproof peace settlement short of destroying the human race. (We may, of course, manage this; at least we now have the technical competence to do the job.)

DELUSIONS OF GRANDEUR AND PERSECUTION

The race has a long history of conflict. If we stand back and look at this history in perspective rather than concentrating on recent events, we are impressed with the fact that group conflicts seem always to show two psychological characteristics: the belief that "my" group, the in-group, is noble and virtuous; and the belief that "they," the out-group, are bad and dangerous.

On the basis of a common syndrome in abnormal personalities, psychologists refer to these paired symptoms as delusions of grandeur and delusions of persecution. In an individual patient, they characteristically take the following form:

> I am a very great person (Jesus Christ) or a member of a very wealthy family (Rockefeller) or a famous scientist (Einstein) or distinguished in some other way. Obviously I am entitled to a great deal of homage, respect, and prestige. But I don't get it. Why does this happen? It must be because there is a conspiracy against me. There are bad people (the Masons or the Catholics or the communists or other members of my family) who are in league to cheat me of my proper status in society. They slander me, prevent me from getting jobs, try to poison me. Surely, I am completely justified in attacking them.

All too often, of course, the paranoid patient does attack someone — generally, a person who has no possible connection with his troubles; sometimes an individual who has been trying to help him. Under the influence of his delusional system, the patient is incapable of looking realistically at what is going on around him.

Social groups show a phenomenon which is astonishingly similar. In the first place, most groups, small or large, grossly overestimate their own virtues. Many families show this trend. Small towns, lodge groups, states, and nations exaggerate the good points of their membership. Secondly, most such groups find an out-group, which they endow with undesirable traits, and which fills the role of persecutor.

This is particularly obvious when conflict is involved. Take the case of union-management disputes. The workers, organized in a union, make no secret of their virtues, of their devotion to the welfare of the individual, of their nobility and strength. They see the employer, however, as greedy, selfish, willing to break the law and use violence to cheat the workers of their rightful due. Conversely, the officers of the corporation see themselves as the noble defenders of the free enterprise system — trying to do a good job for owners, workers, consumers; fighting against a bad group, which is ignorant, aggressive, violent, indefensibly demanding, and generally obnoxious.

An ingenious psychological experiment deserves mention here. Dr. Mason Haire, a California psychologist, presented a man's photograph to the members of a San Francisco employers' group. He asked each of them to judge the man's personality.[6] They were told that he was about 40, had two children, was a Mason, etc. However, half the group were also told that he was treasurer of a small local corporation; and the other half were told that he was treasurer of a local labor union. The first group described this man as responsible, intelligent, thoughtful — generally, a desirable person. The second half described him as ignorant, violent, aggressive, undependable — a very undesirable character. Now the photograph was identical for both groups; indeed, everything was exactly the same except for the identification with corporation or with union. We interpret these findings as indicating that the picture actually was neutral, but half of the group distorted the image to find evidence of responsibility, integrity, and intelligence, while the other half distorted in the opposite direction to see proof of ignorance, aggressiveness, and irresponsibility. (To keep the record straight, I should add that Haire tried the same experiment on a labor group and got exactly opposite distortions.)

How is this related to group conflict? The answer is clear. If you perceive the man on the other side of the bargaining table as untrustworthy and belligerent, you will act in such a way as to encourage him to show these traits (the self-fulfilling prophecy).

We need not labor this point. Wherever we find an instance of group conflict — between juvenile gangs, union and employer, religious groups, political parties, or nations, we find evidence for these parallel delusions of grandeur and persecution. Technically, this pattern is known as ethnocentrism — the tendency to take one's own group as the center of the universe. We are, however, concerned with only a limited range of conflicts, and so we shall talk about *nationalism* as the key problem. Nationalism will imply this attitude-complex, which minimally includes glorifying one's own nation and vilifying nations seen as opponents. (There may be other components of nationalism, but we shall not be concerned with them.)

THE SPECIAL CASE OF NAZI GERMANY

Nationalism shows certain tendencies toward distorted views of reality. It will be valuable to examine what happens when these are

DELUSIONS OF GRANDEUR

"Adolf's dream highway."

These fantasies of power through national action are
gratifying not only to leaders but also to
the average citizen. (Cartoon by Hungerford, in
The *Pittsburgh Post-Gazette.* Reprinted by permission.)

exaggerated to an abnormal degree. R. M. Brickner has published an interesting study of German history, literature, and politics based on the view that a psychiatric approach would be illuminating. Let me cite his main conclusions:

> First, that massive evidence . . . shows that the na-
> tional group we call Germany behaves and has long
> behaved startlingly like an individual involved in a
> dangerous mental trend. Although many individual
> Germans may not partake in this trend, the mass-actions
> of the German nation are and, for over a century, have
> been typical of what the psychiatrist finds in certain highly
> alarming types of individual behavior.
>
> Second, clinical experience can identify the specific
> condition that Germany's mental trend approaches. It is
> paranoia, as grim an ill as mind is heir to, most difficult
> to treat, the only mental condition that frightens the psy-
> chiatrist himself — because, unless checked, it may end in
> murder. Murder is the logical denouement of its special
> outlook on the world.[7]

Aside from Brickner's tendency to imply greater inner unity than any nation can possess, we must agree with this passage. German poli-cies and German utterances elicit in the observer an awareness of a dangerous pattern. Brickner breaks this pattern down (to show its parallel with paranoia) into four components, as follows:

1. *Megalomania:* The paranoid is possessed of delusions of grandeur; he can do no wrong; he has a high moral mission. Similarly, Germany under and before nazism manifested this pattern. Hitler was by no means the first leader to voice the claim to a German mission, to moral superiority. Even Ernst Haeckel, a world-famous biologist, is quoted as saying: "One single highly cultured German soldier of those who are, alas! falling in thousands, represents a higher intellectual and moral life value than hundreds of the uncivilized human beings whom England and France, Russia and Italy oppose to them."[8] This rhap-sody was delivered during World War I, but Brickner cites later examples equally bizarre.

It is entirely compatible with Brickner's thesis that Goebbels should shout " . . . the National Socialist is always right. Those who are not National Socialists can never be right. What right have they to criticize?"[8] (It must be noted that spokesmen for other ideologies, notably communism, claim this same infallibility.)

2. *The need to dominate:* Since the paranoid feels superior, he con-siders it quite right that he should be dominant. This kind of person

is constantly plotting how to get higher and higher. Yet he is not happy, even at the top; for his imagination reaches higher than anyone can achieve. Pursuing the parallel, Brickner cites evidence that Germany followed a policy of domination — demanding world rule for the German people, if not by the German nation. Thus, he quotes Hermann Oncken, a German historian, regarding the invasion of Belgium in World War I:

> The fate Belgium has brought upon herself is hard for individuals, but not too harsh for the Belgian state. For the historic destiny of the immortal great nations is so important that in case of necessity it must overrule the right-to-existence of states which cannot defend themselves.[9]

Thus, Germany was given justification for overwhelming any nation standing in the way of the great mission.

3. *Persecution complex:* The paranoid patient feels superior, has a high mission, seeks to dominate others. But he is not given the respect and submission which is properly his. Why? Obviously, it must be because he is being persecuted by some jealous or predatory group. Germany showed this same pattern, Brickner says, complaining before 1914 about persecution by the Triple Entente (England, France, and Russia) and before 1939 about persecution by the Jews, the communists, the western democracies, and anything else handy. Since Germany obviously could not have been defeated in World War I by fair means, the Nazi Party invented the myth of the stab in the back by the Jews within their nation. This is a typical device for combining the delusion of grandeur with the delusion of persecution. If Germany were divinely ordained to achieve these high goals and had failed to do so, it must have been because of persecutory alliances and treachery.

4. *Retrospective falsification:* The paranoid individual distorts events from his childhood memories to prove his points. Similarly, German historians and political leaders have sought to reinterpret German history to fit the delusional system. It was claimed, for example, that the Germans did not lose World War I and that Jews holding medals for courage in war had bought them from needy Aryan widows, etc. Brickner mentions a German woman who asserted that Einstein's emigration from Germany was no loss, since he was merely a rich, ignorant Jew, who had bought the theory of relativity from a poor Aryan scientist.

Brickner does a convincing job of showing at least the parallels between German official policy and the symptoms of the paranoid patient. But there is a question that he does not face: Was Germany unique? Or is the whole mythology of nationalism a pattern of paranoid symptoms?

Consider Soviet Russia. Certainly the communists believe that they have a historic mission to overthrow capitalism and bring utopia to the working class. They too feel justified in dominating others, by force if necessary. They boast of many scientific discoveries in advance of the West. They claim that the Allies attempted to overthrow bolshevism in 1919 (as if this would have been difficult had the triumphant western powers really adopted such a policy!). The Russians even falsify such events as the Quaker food relief policy, which saved hundreds of thousands of their people from starvation, into a concealed attempt to subvert the regime.

Consider France. De Gaulle especially feels that he has a mission—France has a mission—to restore her grandeur, to build a great military machine, to enter the nuclear club. The French have claimed, with some justice, a high status in culture and the arts. They certainly feel persecuted by Germany; and, not infrequently, they mention mistreatment by Britain and the USA.

Consider the United States. The newspapers are full of speeches about our unique place in history, about our grandeur and our extraordinary accomplishments. Delusions of persecution by the British, by the cosmopolitan Europeans, by the communists, by the Jews, and by other groups are common.

It is an alarming possibility that all nationalisms contain seeds of paranoid thinking. To build national loyalty and unity, the leaders exaggerate the virtue and grandeur of their country; to explain their failure to achieve proportionate world status, they fall back on the charge of persecution. This seems to be a chronic, perhaps an inherent, danger in nationalism.

THE VALUES OF NATIONALISM

A consideration of the insane extremes of nazism and of the destruction achieved by nationalistic wars might lead to the conclusion that nationalism is an unmitigated evil. This is not justified. To evaluate the virtues of nationalism, we must compare the present world situation with that which preceded it.

Greek civilization was built upon very small units, city-states whose populations were numbered in the thousands. The delusions of grandeur and of persecution were tied to these small units. Thus, the Athenians saw the Spartans as bad and dangerous and waged war on them (and vice versa) until both were exhausted and helpless against invaders. In the Middle Ages, the Italian city-states followed the same pattern:

Assisi and Perugia, twenty miles apart, fought many bloody battles over what we would now consider trifles. But in these cases, too, we find the same noble images of the in-group and the same horrible images of the out-group.

Nationalism, then, has served to *expand the area* within which in-group solidarity holds good. Instead of war between French Normandy and Brittany, peace and mutual cooperation developed. The same situation was gradually achieved in other areas now known as Germany, Italy, Great Britain. The constant friction of small-group wars was replaced by a relatively large area in which law and order prevailed over violence.

Some observers would respond to this with the French proverb: "The more things change, the more they remain the same." Such cynics suggest that while violence is now confined to fewer units (nations) as compared with the thousands of little self-sufficient cities and counties of medieval Europe, the total impact of national war is so destructive as to counterbalance the advantages of peace within the national boundary.

It is difficult to estimate the accuracy of this assertion, and it is futile in any event. Nations are with us. The question is, can we take the obvious next step and impose restrictions on violence by nations? Can we move to a larger social unit, which comprises a number of, if not all, the major nations now in existence? Such a social change would increase the area of peace, the area of lawful rule. It seems likely that development along this line is the only permanent escape route open to us.

Two lines of inquiry must be pursued if we are to evaluate the chances of expanding nationalism toward internationalism. One is obvious from our considerations of the delusions of national grandeur and national persecution. What is the emotional dynamic that makes these nationalistic attitudes so powerful? We need not limit ourselves to the extreme case of Nazi Germany, but it is useful to consider the German example in the same way that a medical researcher learns from abnormal processes much about normal functioning. The milder nationalisms of the USA and the other western powers have points of similarity to abnormal nationalism. It will be worthwhile to examine these.

Secondly, we need to inquire into the possibility of redirecting these energies into more cooperative patterns. Are we doomed to repeat the history of Athens and Sparta? If so, it is irrational to try to build institutions for maintaining peace. But there is no justification, at present, for such a conclusion. The very fact of progress from the tribe or clan to the city-state and finally to the nation indicates that the area of in-group solidarity can be expanded. Perhaps a world of law and order is not an idle dream after all.

Our aim, however, must be to learn something about the role of human emotions in producing the distorted images of nationalism. Since this attitude-complex seems really fundamental in preventing rational dispute settlement, we must learn its properties and look for ways of modifying it. This does not mean that we need to destroy nationalism. If Catholics and Protestants have learned to live peaceably together without abandoning their religious faiths, it should be possible for patriotic citizens of different nations to settle their disagreements without violence.

THE RATIONALITY OF CONFLICT

Most group conflicts turn out to be irrational in terms of history. Most strikes, for example, cost the workers more in lost wages than what they gain in the raises they win; and strikes usually cost the employer more, in terms of profits lost, than his expenses saved as a result of refusing to meet union demands. Most recent wars have led to consequences quite undesired by all parties to the dispute. In the sense of war being a means to an end, therefore, most wars and other group conflicts are irrational.

There is, however, a way of looking at wars, which makes them seem rational; and we must understand this. If our image of the Japanese in 1941 was correct, we were justified in going to war with them; and if our image of the nazis was correct, we were justified in warring with them. But conversely, if the nazi views of the Poles and the Russians were sound, they were justified in waging war; and if the Japanese view of the USA was correct, they too were justified. It is the same with Catholics and Protestants, the Christians and the Moslems, the unions and the employers, and so on.

Herman Melville, in *Moby Dick,* has Captain Ahab say: "All my means are sane; my motives and objects mad." The point is that, if one distorts sufficiently the nature of the external situation and the character of the opponent, even the madness of nuclear war may seem rational. It is not the building of missiles and H-bombs which is insane; if the enemy were really as black as he is believed to be, the military program would be sane.

The rationality of conflict and war thus makes sense primarily in terms of perception. From the viewpoint of intelligent assessment of gains and losses, war is usually irrational. But from the viewpoint of individuals gripped by delusions of in-group grandeur and out-group villainy, war is a reasonable and defensible action. This is the basic reason for concentrating our attention on distorted views of reality.[10]

3
Images
in the Cold War

National policies are guided by the images of one's own nation, of the opposing nation, of the United Nations, and of other factors that appear to be relevant to the problem. Our decisions with regard to a ban on nuclear testing relate chiefly to our image of the Soviet Union. Our policy in the Congo depends somewhat on our view of the UN and of the warring Congolese factions; but, here again, a determining factor is our anticipation that the USSR would intervene and impose a communist regime if given the opportunity.

Similarly, Russian policy in these conflict zones derives from firmly held views as to the attributes of the USA. To most of us, their image of our country is distorted to an unrecognizable degree. Curiously, neutral observers find a startling similarity in the images held by one nation of the other; indeed, the term "mirror images" has become widely used in recent years to suggest that perhaps one view is only a reflection of the other.

The discovery of this similarity in perceptions sets off divergent reactions in different observers. Some, like Senator Dodd of Connecticut, mistake the image for the reality and assume that persons reporting on mirror images are declaring that the USA and the USSR are identical.[1] Others raise questions about whether this discovery provides any guide to action — a more useful kind of response.

Before examining the problem of the origins of these mirror images, let us see how closely they are similar.

MIRROR IMAGES OF THE USA AND USSR

We can obtain American images of the Soviet Union by a variety of means: public opinion polls, interviews with citizens, speeches of national leaders, newspaper editorials, and so on. It is less easy to obtain Russian images of the USA; the Kremlin has never encouraged public opinion polling, and citizens being interviewed are cautious in expressing certain views. It is possible to get information from Radio Moscow, from Russian periodicals, and from official statements. I have most confidence, however, in the results of interviews with a large number of Europeans who had lived in the Soviet Union for many years and who returned voluntarily — not as defectors from communism. (Obviously, defectors provide a biased picture since the regime frustrated them enough to provoke escape. We should be more interested in an approximation of the opinions of the 200 million who have not tried to escape.)

Dr. Ralph K. White of the USIA has recently reported on the parallels in our image of the USSR and the Russian image of the USA.[2] The following list summarizes his observations. (Need I repeat that no assumption is made that either image closely agrees with reality?)

American Image of USSR	*Soviet Image of USA*
1. They (the rulers) are bad.	1. They (the rulers) are bad.
The men in the Kremlin are aggressive, power-seeking, brutal in suppressing Hungary, ruthless in dealing with their people.	The Wall Street bankers, politicians, and militarists want a war because they fear loss of wealth and power in a communist revolution.
They are infiltrating the western hemisphere to attack us.	They are surrounding us with military bases.
They engage in espionage and sabotage to wreck our country.	They send spies (in U-2 planes and otherwise) to destroy the workers' fatherland.
They are like the nazis — an aggressive expansionist dictatorship.	They are like the nazis — rearming the Germans against us.

They are trying to divide us — split NATO, stir class hatred.

They are trying to divide us — split off Yugoslavia and Poland, incite rebellion against our government.

2. They are imperialistic.
The communists want to dominate the world.

They rigidly control the satellite puppet governments.

2. They are imperialistic.
The capitalist nations dominate colonial areas, keep them in submission.
The Latin-American regimes (except Cuba) are puppets of the USA.

3. They exploit their own people.
They hold down consumer goods, keep standard of living low except for communist bureaucrats.

3. They exploit their own people.
All capitalists live in luxury by exploiting workers, who suffer insecurity, unemployment, etc.

4. They are against democracy.
Democratic forms are mere pretense; people can vote only for communist candidates.
Rulers control organs of propaganda, education, and communication.
They persecute anyone favoring western democracy.

4. They are against democracy.
Democratic forms are mere pretense; people can vote only for capitalist candidates.
Rulers control organs of propaganda, education, and communication.
They persecute anyone favoring communist ideas.

5. They distort the truth.
They pose as a friend of colonial peoples in order to enslave them.

5. They distort the truth.
They falsely accuse the USSR of desiring to impose ideology by force.

6. They are immoral, materialistic, atheistic.
They are preventing freedom of religion.

6. They are immoral, materialistic, selfishly individualistic.
They are only out for money.

7. They (the people) are good.
The Soviet people want peace.

7. They (the people) are good.
The American people want peace.

This is an abridgment of a much longer list tabulated by Dr. White. On many points, of course, he found that an attribute held by one side was not matched on the other side — that is, the "mirror" parallel is not perfect. For example, Americans have an image of Russia as inefficient — an image which is not reflected on the Russian side. Russians view America as an old, declining nation; no parallel to this is observed in American perceptions of the Soviet Union. On the whole, however, White seems to have proved his point that the two populations see highly similar attributes in their adversary nation.

The stress in the above tabulation is on delusions of persecution, i.e., on the threatening characteristics of the opponent. White's survey also includes an examination of the populations' image of their own nation, giving support to our theme of delusions of grandeur. Because these findings are so obvious, I shall only list a few of the attributes each group ascribes to itself: peaceful, friendly, truthful, sincere, trying to relax tension, fostering steps toward disarmament, respecting independence of other nations, opposing exploitation, helping the unfortunate, strengthening democracy. In other words, Americans perceive their own nation as virtuous; and Russians see their country as virtuous.

White is not the only psychologist who has commented on the mirror-image phenomenon. Bronfenbrenner,[3] who speaks fluent Russian, interviewed large numbers of Soviet citizens chosen at random in parks and restaurants (to avoid getting people who were looking for a foreigner to whom they could complain). He was amazed at the parallels between our criticisms of Russia and their criticisms of the USA. The points he makes are virtually identical with those cited in the White study.

It is of particular interest that each of these mirror images makes a sharp distinction between leaders and followers of the opposing nation. The leaders are bad; the average citizen is good. (White calls this the "blacktop" phenomenon.) This distinction is rational enough; we are certainly aware, within our own nation, of diversity of interests. The Republicans can attest to the fact that a Democratic president advocates many policies which they find unacceptable. Similarly, it is almost certain that the Russian premier and his Politburo have interests which diverge from those of many Russian citizens.

This distinction, unfortunately, tends to become meaningless in practice. The reason lies in the phenomenon of nationalism. We have a tradition that "politics stops at the water's edge." This is not quite lived up to in practice; but, as a rule, our nation tends to close ranks behind the government when there is a threat from abroad. Similarly, the communist regimes find it convenient to keep their citizens frightened by dangers from the bad, capitalistic West in order to reduce dissension and conflict within the nation.

Nationalism is therefore an important pawn in the Cold War. We of the West ignore it at our peril — be it Russian nationalism, Ghanaian nationalism, or Iranian nationalism. Every aspect of foreign policy needs to be examined with this fact in mind.

THE NATION-HERO AND THE NATION-VILLAIN

At this point, I want to shift from a consideration of the USA and and the USSR as specific instances and, instead, consider the general psychology of nationalism. What we have shown so far is that the people of one nation are likely to see only good attributes on their own side and only bad attributes on the opponent's side. While it could happen that one nation was all "white" and another all "black," this does not seem likely. It is more probable that we have here another example of selective perception. The individual accepts some facts and rejects others, thus building an overall picture that he finds congenial.

The nature of this picture was pointed out, in general terms, by John Foster Dulles in a book published in 1939 — long before he became Secretary of State. Dulles wrote:

> We have pointed to the essentially emotional nature of human beings, particularly in the mass. Upon this foundation is built that form of patriotism which personifies the nation as a living being endowed with heroic qualities, who lives bravely and dangerously in a world of inferior, and even villainous, other-nation personalities.
>
> The creation of this nation-hero personality meets a fundamental and natural human need. Most of us lead lives which are lacking in drama, excitement, and adventure. We seek, through imagination, that which is lacking in reality. We read romances and see plays or movies which portray some hero or heroine in dramatic action, with whose exploits we tend to identify ourselves. This normal human trait has been capitalized to an extraordinary degree in the dramatization of the 'nation-hero' and 'nation-villain.'[4]

Psychologists will agree with the basic features of the Dulles analysis. Most people do indulge in a great deal of *personalized* thinking: It is easier to think of Uncle Sam than of the complex of power blocs, pressure groups, lobbyists, officials, and politicians who somehow hammer out laws or executive decisions in Washington. In the same way, we think of France as De Gaulle (ignoring the interplay of blocs and interests there). In addition, most of us tend toward *polarized* thinking:

What is good is very, very good, and what is bad, is horrid. Whether
there is really a need for polarization into extreme stands on issues can
be debated. Still, the evidence is clear that, especially in times of tension, people tend to adopt such extreme positions. Thus Dulles' "nation-
hero" and "nation-villain" are the personifications of the polarized
delusions of national virtue and national persecution.

Such perceptual distortions are supported by selective perception,
selective learning, and selective forgetting. In an earlier passage, I described the experiment by Mason Haire on selective perception of
photographs. This process of selecting from the available evidence only
those bits that confirm one's prejudices and of rejecting anything that
doesn't fit is far more widespread than his simple investigation would
suggest. It applies to our selection of items from history, our view of
current events, our perception of foreign leaders, and so on.

Dulles tends to place the primary responsibility for nationalistic
distortions on those who write the nation's history books:

> In order to build up the desired personification, his-
> tory in each nation is written and taught in the manner
> of the dime novel. Emphasis is placed on dramatic epi-
> sodes — war and adventure — which stir the imagination
> and arouse admiration and hero worship. In order to
> secure a maximum of emotional excitement, one or more
> other nations are cast in the role of "villains." One's own
> hero, always in the right, is in constant peril from such
> other nations. In the face of intrigue and peril the per-
> sonified nation-hero comports himself with courage,
> forbearance, and wisdom. Never a bully, he sponsors the
> cause of righteousness and of the oppressed; never belli-
> cose, he has, nevertheless, a high sense of dignity and of
> personal honor which others affront at their peril. If he
> is forced to battle to defend his integrity or honor, to
> succor the oppressed, or to secure justice against wrong-
> doers, he conducts himself with bravery and honor. He
> usually emerges successfully from his hazardous adven-
> tures. If setbacks occur, which cannot be glossed over,
> they are portrayed as but temporary, like the incidents
> of a melodrama which, to sustain suspense, must admit
> of occasional failures that serve to spur on the hero to his
> final and more dramatic triumph.
>
> This background, built up by history as commonly
> taught, is kept up to date by the current utterances of
> political leaders, and by the press. Throughout it all runs

the theme of the nation as a living and heroic personality, always gloriously right but always menaced by the planning and plotting of other national personalities. And each of us is part of this hero.[5]

Dulles may have been unfair in singling out the professional historian for criticism in connection with this state of affairs. We should note, first, that all human beings seem to have a strong tendency toward forgetting any embarrassing, humiliating, or shameful experience. Thus a patriotic citizen, not wishing to recall unethical acts of his nation, may honestly forget them. Second, other professions than history show this trend toward exaggerating the defects of the opponent. Bronfenbrenner tells of speaking to an American newspaperman in Moscow and asking why he had not written despatches covering the enthusiasm of the Russian citizens for the nation's achievements, their commitment to helping with other national projects. "If I want to be sure that it will be printed back home," was the reply, "I have to write about what's wrong with the system, not its successes."

Even the reporting system within the State Department itself distorts the inputs of information. Many consuls and even ambassadors have learned that factual reporting of events can lead to demotion or dismissal; like the kings of Persia who used to kill a messenger bringing news of a military defeat, our government punishes those who tell unpleasant news. This was publicly exposed in connection with the collapse of the Chiang Kai-shek government in China: Those who had sent in despatches describing the corruption of the Kuomintang and the lack of popular support for Chiang were attacked as communist sympathizers or even charged with treason.

It is of course true, as Dulles implies, that every nation teaches a biased history of events. We never hear the Carthaginian side of the war with Rome nor the Moorish version of their rule in Spain. Even within the western framework, history in France and England differs quite astonishingly on the Hundred Years' War; and, as far as that goes, American textbook publishers have often put out two versions of history texts, one for distribution in the North and one for the South. The censoring of history is done in part by boards of education and local citizens, who howl with outrage at statements contradictory to their emotional convictions.

Since one can be sure that our newspapers, history texts, and diplomatic pouches are not unique, we should not be surprised that every government acts on the basis of distorted information. Perhaps we should rather feel grateful that occasionally a realistic picture is developed from this collection of misleading images.

ONE VIEW OF A LEADER

In this cartoon, the British represent Churchill as a kindly
"master builder." (Cartoon by Robinson, in
The London Star. Reprinted by permission.)

ANOTHER VIEW

This German cartoon depicts Churchill as a poisoner.
Observers in neutral nations and in the rebellious British
colonies had still other images of Sir Winston.
(The cartoon is reprinted, by permission, from
Kladderadatsch, Berlin.)

CONFORMITY PRESSURE AND IMAGE FORMATION

It is easy to see how this phenomenon of biased presentations facilitates the development of the images of opposing nations among citizens of the USA and of the USSR. If one is never exposed to conflicting information, one will necessarily accept the prevailing view — as when almost everyone believed the world to be flat in 1492.

However, the wholehearted belief in these images of other nations seems to depend even more upon the child's response to conformity pressures. He learns early in life that adults have more information, more knowledge of reality, than he does, and so he accepts their views on what constitutes a fact. If his parents, his teachers, and his friends agree on a certain point, he is not likely to stand up for a different view.

The potency of conformity pressures can best be illustrated by describing the "Asch phenomenon," a classical experiment devised by S. E. Asch. [6] Imagine a row of seven college students watching pictures projected on a screen. Three straight lines are shown, and each observer in turn is to state which seems longest. The first six, calmly and firmly, give an answer which is obviously incorrect. The seventh student is "on the spot." Shall he tell what he sees, or go along with the group? In a surprising number of instances he gives the same answer as the first six, who are actually confederates of the experimenter. Even more interesting is the fact that some of those who yielded to group pressure said they actually began to doubt their own vision, especially when the differences on the screen were small.

When the same experiment was repeated using statements of opinion, the percentage agreeing with the faked majority jumped from about 35 percent to 80 percent. Apparently, it is easier to get a person to change his position and agree with a controversial statement—for example, "All communists should be put in jail"—than to overcome the tendency to trust his senses on such matters as the length of a line. Further, retests weeks later indicated that the group-supported changes in opinions were still held, whereas the change in visual perception was very shortly corrected. [7]

This experiment is important as we consider particularly our images of foreign nations. One gets virtually all of his information about other nations from books and from other persons. Few people visit foreign nations to see for themselves. Thus, the real stimulus is ambiguous, and it is easy to accept the majority opinion as factual. If "everybody says so," it must be true. Since dissenting opinions are rarely heard (who listens to Radio Moscow?), the illusion is built up that we know exactly what the Russians are like.

WHAT IS THE NATION REALLY?

Dulles gives us a useful approach to the question of how we get our images of our own nation and of others. But he implies a highly fallacious notion as to the "real" nation behind the image. This is the notion that the nation is a living organism, an entity which has unity embracing all of its citizens. Because this false idea tends to creep in and deflect much of our thinking about international affairs, it requires at least brief analysis.

The first point to remember is that a nation does not exist apart from its citizens. Carthage is no longer a nation, though her soil still fronts the Mediterranean Sea. Further, the existence of a nation depends on the attitudes of its citizens. England, Scotland, and Wales now make up a reasonably coherent nation, whereas 400 or 500 years ago they were frequently at war. The citizens of Great Britain have accepted the idea of a single central government. Occasionally one doubts whether Texas has quite been integrated into the USA; but, on the whole, it seems that our nation exists as a unity.

Without citizen acceptance, the decision makers of a national government would find themselves without power. In times of rebellion or in cases of incomplete integration, the policies of a central government may be ignored. Quebec often presents problems of this kind in Canada. A nation does not exist as a unit until the citizens see it as a unit of which they are a part.

Observers of the communist world disagree on the extent to which these nations are units. Some would like to believe that the Russians are seething with discontent, ready to overthrow the government at any sign of hope. The record of support for the Russian leadership during World War II casts serious doubt on this view. The probabilities are somewhat greater that the satellites are disunited, but for the present it appears that we are in no position to exploit the situation if it does exist.

The role of a nation in world affairs also depends somewhat on how it is perceived by the citizens (more properly, the leaders) of other nations. We get an impressive illustration of this from the behavior of the "neutrals," as at the Belgrade conference in 1961, when these leaders criticized the USA for previous atomic testing but were afraid to denounce the Russian test series. In a nutshell, these men perceived the USA as nonthreatening, so that their criticism was safe; the USSR, on the other hand, was perceived as punitive and dangerous, hence unsafe to scold. We could argue that this state of affairs is flattering to us, but many Americans were annoyed at the double standard of morality so exemplified.

To return to the problem of unity: A nation obviously is not a
living organism. Within the body, decisions are normally made and
acted upon without conflict. If I decide to walk up the street, there
is no internal argument as to which muscle will do the work; internal
coordination is effective. This is not true within the nation in a wide
variety of cases. (I must also concede that the individual may have
serious conflicts about which decision to make; he may prefer to sit at
home instead of walking. But normally, there is no conflict after the
decision has been made.)

In our perception of our own nation, and of others, there is an
erroneous tendency to imply unity more than is justified. A newspaper
headline, for example, speaks of "the policy of France" regarding
NATO. Actually, France is highly in conflict about NATO, irrespective
of the decisions imposed by De Gaulle. There remains a strong core of
support for NATO, and our policies cannot wisely ignore this division
of opinion. The spurious appearance of unity is provided as De Gaulle's
decision is carried out, but the concealed opposition must not be
neglected in thinking about other nations, whether our allies or
our opponents.

The Group Mind as an Irrational Factor

Social scientists who were impressed with the degree of national
unity concocted the theory of the "group mind" to explain it. According to this view, the nation, while not exactly a single organism,
developed some mysterious kind of spiritual unity, which had a decisive
effect on the behavior of its citizens. This view can briefly be illustrated
by a quotation from Gustave LeBon, an influential French psychologist,
writing about the onset of World War I:

> The individual mind has only an ephemeral existence,
> but the mind of the race is permanent and not subject to
> disintegration. The race-mind, or, in other words, the
> national mind, is not made in a day, but is the product
> of a lengthy past . . .
>
> As we have seen very clearly during the present war,
> the ancestral mind has the power of making men who be-
> long to the same country think and act alike upon great
> occasions. If all Frenchmen of military age have unrepin-
> ingly forsaken their situations and individual interests and
> are exposing their lives from day to day, it is because their
> selfish individual impulses have suddenly become subject
> to the mind of the race.[8]

Perhaps we are more cynical today, but probably we are more realistic. At any rate, few modern readers will believe that "all Frenchmen of military age" went into service "unrepiningly." Anyone who had contact with the armed services in World War II or during the Korean episode knows that soldiers often complained bitterly about about their situation; some deserted; most were patriotic; but only a few were enthusiastic.

The fallacy of the LeBon analysis, however, is best demonstrated by the failure of his predictions. Stressing, as he did, the overriding power of the national mind, he could write, "in Russia even the anarchists and revolutionaries are now transformed into loyal supporters of the Throne."[9] Yet we know that at the very moment he wrote this, Lenin and Trotsky were plotting the overthrow of the czar; and less than two years after his book was published, the Bolshevik revolution was an accomplished fact.

Unfortunately, many scholars still lapse into the group-mind fallacy. A single recent example will suffice. In a chapter of a book with the hopeful title *If Men Want Peace,* we find this poetic but meaningless statement: "The modern highly emotional over-self-conscious nation suffers from deep-seated doubt and attempts, by propaganda and symbolism, to conceal its own inner disharmony and disquietude."[10] A moment's reflection should convince anyone that a nation cannot experience doubts, nor can it be self-conscious. The men who lead the nation, on the other hand, can have anxieties about the conflicting groups within the nation and may doubt that the nation as an organized unit will survive. This latter kind of thinking about the nation is not only more realistic; it is also more practical. When we speak of the nation as having feelings, desires, and doubts, we locate psychological processes where they cannot be reached to induce change. To speak of the leaders as having such experiences is to keep the key processes within individual persons; we then know how to appeal, persuade, argue for a change of policy. Thinking in terms of the "national mind" leads only into a blind alley; one cannot discuss issues with a national mind.

The Nation as a Complex Structure

In contrast to the view of the nation as a unit having a mind of its own, modern scholars see the nation as a stratified complexity with conflicting inner groups. These groups, while they may cooperate when a national policy has been decided upon, often argue bitterly as to what this policy should be.

Any American can readily comprehend this as it applies to his own country. Isolationist sentiments are stronger in the Midwest than in New England. Businessmen have different views about foreign aid programs, depending on how the programs meet foreign competition. Most of us understand that when Senator Fulbright makes a speech on foreign policy, it may not reflect public opinion or even administration opinion. But Europeans often fail to grasp these important internal distinctions about us.

Nations do, of course, have some internal unity. This unity is largely a matter of perception and emotion. Citizens of a nation tend to perceive certain symbols and historical events as evidence of unity, and they feel that the nation must be a unit even if it in fact is not. The patriotic Republican and the patriotic Democrat — as each speaks for different regional and economic interest groups — may agree completely on their desire that the USA be a closely unified nation and then diverge sharply on what this nation should stand for. Neither group is unpatriotic; they have common emotions and common expectancies as to national cooperation, virtue, and unity against the outside. A foreign observer, then, may assume that this means a pervasive unity, when, in actuality, we have many internal differences of opinion. Further, such differences often affect our foreign policy.

It would be a great mistake for us to adopt an image of India as being critical of the USA just because Krishna Menon made a sharp speech in the UN. Similarly, we should not view West Germany as united in a pro-western stance simply because the Adenauer government was able to maintain this policy. Yet, it is clear that both our citizens and our leaders often make the mistake of assuming national unity in a given area where it does not exist.

How is this important? In the first place, government tactics in a specific crisis may not reflect overall policy but rather the need to pacify some pressure group. In early 1962, the Frondizi government of Argentina was forced to strengthen its anti-Castro stand by military pressure. (Many Americans who would object to our military officers taking part in politics cheered the Argentine development.) When possible, British policy is molded to avoid giving the opposition party good election issues. An American administration must tread cautiously on regional and other vested interests. It even appears that the Russian premier must modify his foreign tactics from time to time in accordance with internal group pressures.

In the second place, national governments do not remain the same. Krushchev's Russia was not Stalin's Russia, though we may have seen it as only a slight improvement. Britain under a Labour government is not the same as Britain under the Tories. Power relations shift, and the group which dominates today may be out tomorrow. The distinctive feature of a democracy is that the changeover is blood-less. But national unity over time is, at least in part, a fiction; as the rulers change, so the guidelines for policy shift. This is easily overlooked because the major changes are in domestic policies; foreign affairs tend to be handled more uniformly. (Thus, the shift from Eisenhower to Kennedy was more distinctive in domestic than in foreign policy.)

One great value of public opinion polling lies in its ability to re-mind us that the nation is not a true unity. When we read that 76 percent of Canadians favor an international police force, we automat-ically note that this is not unanimity. When these data are broken down by regions (Quebec differs sharply on this issue), we are even more forcefully notified that Canadian opinion is complex, not a simple unified view.

A particularly valuable study, in this regard, has been done by Lloyd A. Free and is reported in his book, *Six Allies and a Neutral*.[11] In this investigation, Free actually interviewed members of the parliaments of Britain, France, Italy, Japan, West Germany, and India and con-gressmen in the USA. His findings dramatically underscore this internal division in governments, as in the case of French policy on NATO. Such observations should remind us constantly that we must not think of France as a unit. Its unity could perhaps best be described as that of a can of squirming earthworms; they are held together only by an external boundary.

I am concerned here to point out the importance of such facts for the making of government policy. Newspapers often criticize France for failing to take a firm stand alongside (or inside) NATO. But our State Department must continually keep in mind that there is no agreed French position on NATO. There are competing internal pressures. If we ignore these internal divisions (as we apparently did in Laos), we do so at our peril.

It is important for us to think of the totalitarian states as split by internal differences. These disputes may be minor compared to the great divergence between the communists and the democracies, but they offer anchoring points for our policies. To picture all of Russia as a mono-lithic unity is to be deceived by Russian propaganda. And similarly, we must never believe that the communist world is tightly unified. The communist nations have a little — not a great deal — more consistency among themselves than the western nations. But there are, and will continue to be, opportunities to encourage these little differences to grow. Such opportunities will be lost if we assume a tight, integrated, communist unity.

National Goals and National Interest

In light of this discussion, what can we say about such concepts as "national goals" and "the national interest"? It is clear that they are not simple. The *nation* does not choose its own goals; the *nation* does not decide what is in its own interest. Only human beings can make such decisions.

A national goal exists first in the mind of some person. We might, to take a noncontroversial example, say that free public education was a national goal. But this was not adopted automatically. Some groups favored and some opposed this policy. Eventually it was accepted by virtually all American citizens, and the only dissent is over details such as federal versus local financing.

Other possible national goals are far more debatable. Some Americans would like one of our national goals to be that of restoring Chiang Kai-shek's government to mainland China. It should be obvious that the nation does not reach a decision on this issue; various pressure groups agitate for one or another approach; and government officials balance these pressures and adopt a policy that comes nearest to satisfying everyone — or, at least, the most potent groups.

Such goals are advocated as being "in the national interest." But it is hard to define the national interest, just as it is difficult to define the public interest in labor-management disputes. The unions always assert that the public interest is in higher purchasing power for the great mass of workers; management always takes the stand that the public interest calls for lower prices on desirable goods. Here it is clear that the public interest may include both of these; and decisions, if made intelligently, would seek to optimize the benefits to the entire population. Unfortunately, in most such disputes the settlement is based on economic pressure, not on intelligence.

Similarly, in deciding whether a given policy abroad is in the national interest, the government is likely to be influenced by the loudest voices and the strongest political pressures. In a Congress where farmers are grossly overrepresented, a program of subsidies for farm exports gets powerful support regardless of what this does to our allies. It is therefore essential, when a policy is said to be in the national interest, that we ask: "From whose point of view? In the interest of what portions of the nation?" Farmers, labor unionists, exporters, importers, manufacturers, and shippers differ widely in their views of the national interest. Such differences occur in every nation. I stress them only because we cannot think rationally about foreign policy if we continue to hold the image of a unified nation.

Leadership and the National Image

The habit of personifying nations, or of concocting the nation-hero and nation-villain images, may go back to the days of the absolute monarchy in Europe. Louis XIV could say with considerable truth, *"L'etat, c'est moi!"* He *was* the state; his decisions, once made, could be opposed only by open rebellion. The image abroad of France was profoundly influenced by the personality of the current ruler, and this was true also of Britain and of other unified European nations.

Our present-day image of the USSR is profoundly influenced by the personality of Josef Stalin, whose paranoid personality exaggerated the usual nationalistic delusions of grandeur and of persecution. Stalin was devoted to the national interest of the Soviet Union *as he saw it*. He believed tight central control, rapid industrialization, and insulation from foreign contacts to be essential to his country's welfare. Those who opposed his views were ruthlessly liquidated (it has been reliably estimated that over 300,000 Russians were shot in his purges, entirely aside from the millions of peasants who were starved in the collectivization program). Such a ruthless leader naturally projects to the outside world a *national* image of brutality, of ruthlessness, of complete unconcern for the welfare of others inside or outside the national boundary.

The leader in a democratic country may not decide on national policies with such complete disregard of human values. But, within limits, he has substantial power. The President of the United States has access to public opinion influences — the newspapers, radio, and television, by which he can mobilize support for a program. He also has political rewards and punishments (appointments, tariff concessions, government contracts) which can be utilized to line up political support. Since the president has tremendous prestige by virtue of his office, he can get many of his ideas accepted. The example of Woodrow Wilson, however, must remind us that a leader sometimes cannot commit his nation, when powerful groups within the population oppose him. The leader does not alone make national policy, but he can dramatize and communicate it to other countries. The kind of image that others have of us (and that we have of other nations) is thus affected considerably by leadership.

It is important to emphasize that the leader is human. A president gets hungry and must eat, catches cold and sneezes, and receives information, which may be inadequate. Sometimes he may misunderstand what he receives, and sometimes he may make erroneous decisions. The same is true of the Russian premier and of every other national leader.

Our consideration of the problems of perceptual distortion, delusion, and irrational decision making is therefore relevant both to the average citizen and to the leadership. If — as in Nazi Germany and Fascist Italy — a minority group with a rabidly nationalistic policy gets control of the government, they may shape policies in ways that are disastrous. As I have already noted, national catastrophe results when a leader fails to assess correctly the potency of the opposition he is building up abroad by his aggressive policies. Delusions of persecution cause him to exaggerate the need for aggression; delusions of grandeur lead him to overestimate the power of his nation to overcome obstacles.

In our relations with our allies and with the communist world, we must beware of both of these tendencies. There are real threats abroad, which must be considered. But there is also a significant possibility that we exaggerate the threat and make matters worse by ill-conceived policies in relation to it. Specifically, we must recognize that we are not omnipotent and that we have no monopoly on national virtues. We must be chary of our tendency toward self-delusion and of the notion that we know reality whereas other countries lack our wisdom. In these respects, we need constantly to be aware of the problems of national images and to avoid the extremes of the nation-hero and the nation-villain in our thinking.

4

The Dynamics of National Loyalty

The preceding chapters have identified some instances in which our ways of looking at reality have influenced the history of nations. The evidence indicates that men exaggerate the virtues and grandeur of their own group — the nation — and seek its aggrandizement, more or less without regard to the damage done to other human beings in the process. The aggressive attacks on others are facilitated by delusions of national persecution, i.e., images of other nations as bad, aggressive, expansionistic, and untrustworthy.

NATIONALISM — THE CRUCIAL ISSUE

In the present context of nation-states, the crucial psychological factor is nationalism: the complex, illustrated in the previous chapters, of desires for national power, of feelings of national virtue, and of perceptions of national enemies. Men follow a belligerent leader because he promises the aggrandizement of the beloved nation; they rebel against a leader who is perceived as weak — as selling out the nation to a bad enemy. Leaders themselves, of course, are likely to be obsessed with the need to be tough and to strive aggressively for the nation's interests. If a particular official lacks this dynamic, he is likely to learn that advocacy of a soft line of cooperation and compromise is a speedy way to oblivion in most nations today.

Perhaps it should be noted that this emphasis on nationalism is contemporary. In the past, the emphasis would have been on loyalty to a tribe and on action to further the tribe's interests. And even today, a major problem in some areas is that tribalism is still the dominant emotional complex among the people and that nationalism has not become sufficiently established to provide a basis for a unified government. The repeated uprisings in the new African nations are due in large measure to the lack of nationalistic feelings among their inhabitants.

From the example of occasional African anarchy it would seem to follow that nationalism cannot be considered a bad aspect of modern civilization. Nationalistic feelings constitute the psychological cement that holds a nation together. National patriotism induces people to undergo discomfort and disruption of routines (as when young men are drafted); and it enables leaders to override regional and local interests in favor of the national welfare (we need not, at this moment, try to guess what the national welfare is). One need only look at India and other nations where nationalistic emotions are quite weak to realize the implications. Lacking nationalism, people riot to obtain special advantages for their linguistic, regional, or communal group; they are unwilling to subordinate these motives to the general good. Nationalism, in short, can serve to expand the area within which peaceful cooperation is the norm of behavior.

On the other hand, as noted earlier, nationalism is a major source of misunderstandings and tensions between nations, which have the means of mutual destruction. In a 1938 survey of outstanding American social scientists, it was found that an overwhelming majority considered nationalistic policies, particularly in the economic sphere, to be the major danger of war at that time.[1] History shows that in a short time the aggressive nationalism of Germany, Italy, and Japan, with their efforts to seize empires and control trade areas, set off World War II. We must thus recognize that nationalism has both positive and negative aspects and is, in any event, a major feature of our world today.

Human Motives and Nationalism

The dynamics of history derive from human motives. This is not to say that victories of the Roman Empire occurred because thousands of different soldiers wanted these accomplishments, or that the present power status of the USA is to be ascribed solely to the vigor of its early inhabitants. Manifestly, there are such factors as resources, technology, organization, and leadership which must be taken into account. But a leader will get no followers if he cannot appeal to human desires and emotions.

Political speeches about God, home, and country are effective because they appeal to the powerful emotions and desires of the listeners. We therefore find ourselves faced with two questions: Why do politicians make such speeches? And, why do the citizens respond so enthusiastically? The second is really the basic question, since we can assume that the politician would appeal to regional (white supremacy) or tribal (ethnic) loyalties if he did not anticipate winning votes by nationalistic tactics.

In brief, people born into such advanced, systematically organized nations as those of the western world today develop feelings of love for their country, idealization of its policies, belief in its virtue, and desires for its aggrandizement because they are taught to do so. It should surprise no one that patriotic societies watch the teachings in the schools closely and pounce on anything seeming to favor internationalism. In the communist nations, similar chauvinism is observed. The schools in every nation play the role of indoctrinating young people with patriotic fervor.

Nationalism can also serve as a substitute gratification for many motives that are frustrated in daily life. The young man who daydreams of wealth and power becomes the middle-aged factory worker or minor clerk. If he cannot achieve his own personal goals, he can gain some gratification from the wealth and power of his nation. Adolf Hitler once shouted that it was better to be a street-sweeper in the Third Reich than to be wealthy anywhere else. Such sentiments can be very soothing to those condemned to dull, poorly paid work.

Parents and Nationalism

Before there were nationalistic schools, there were parents who indoctrinated their children with this same fervor. A graphic illustration comes from the autobiography of the Greek novelist Nikos Kazantzakis. He quotes a letter from his father to him, when he was a young boy and his father was in the army: "I'm doing my duty, fighting the Turks. You fight too; stand your ground and don't let those Catholics put ideas into your head. They're dogs, just like the Turks. You're from Crete, don't forget. Your mind isn't your own, it belongs to Crete. Sharpen it as much as you can, so that one day you can use it to help liberate Crete. . . . Do not disgrace me!"[2]

Note how this kind of message tried to sharpen the lines of group differences, to increase the boy's sense of belonging to one community

PROTECT THE MOTHERLAND

"The greater the need, the stronger the Fuehrer"

In 1940, the German Nazis represented themselves as
protecting the good mother (Germany) against
the onslaughts of Jews, communists, the West, and other
enemies. The words on the banner mean "Loyalty, Order, Honor."

and his belief in the bad features of other groups. There is also a strong appeal to family pride, an indirect suggestion that affection for the father should become transformed into love for Crete. Sigmund Freud and other psychoanalytic writers had earlier proposed that nationalism constitutes a transfer of love and affection from parents to nation. They noted, for example, that such phrases as "fatherland" and "mother country" are found in virtually every language known to man.

This theory has received at least some support from statistical studies. Students at an eastern college for men were found to differ in nationalistic sentiments in the same ways that their attitudes toward their fathers differed. Those who felt very close to their fathers and seemed to identify with them agreed with strongly nationalistic statements on an attitude survey. Men who reported neutral or cool feelings for their fathers were relatively more inclined to endorse internationalistic opinions. In the first group, obedience to national leaders was approved; in the second, doubts and suspicions of national leaders were frequently expressed. [3]

This view of the nation and of the national leader as a parent-substitute is supported by numerous observations after the deaths of Presidents Roosevelt and Kennedy. The literature, particularly on the latter, is extensive. Large numbers of respondents, in speaking of their grief after the assassination, used the comparison of losing a father.

Similar observations were made in England at the time of the death of King George VI (of course, in a monarchy it is quite deliberate policy to represent the king as the "father of his people"). From USIA interviews of Russian emigres, we learn of comparable reactions to the death of Stalin. A Russian wife, interviewed outside Russia, said, "I loved Stalin almost as my own father. I cried when he passed away. Only now do I realize what harm he had done." [4] The last sentence refers not to what she heard in the West but to the Khrushchev denunciation in 1956.

MOTIVES, IMAGES, AND NATIONAL POLICY

Images guide human behavior. But images would not be important if they were not related to human motives. Hitler's misperception of Anglo-French determination in 1939 would have been trivial if it had not been so closely tied to his desire to expand Germany's territory and strategic power. Russians may have sizable inaccuracies in their image of Bolivia, but there are no issues (in the immediate future) which are likely to result in basing important decisions upon this image.

THE NATION AS A MOTHER-FIGURE

The Able Doctor, or America Swallowing the Bitter Draught

Even before the American colonies united, propagandists were appealing to nationalistic feelings by representing the "mother country" as being assaulted by the despicable British. (From an engraving by Paul Revere after a caricature in London Magazine, April, 1774.)

On the other hand, inaccuracies in the Russian image of the USA are related to goals strongly desired by the Soviet leadership, and they may lead to serious errors in action. This could, of course, also happen in our decisions regarding our Russian policy.

Some years ago a magazine article was headlined, "What does Khrushchev *really* want in Berlin?" The question reminds us that superficial motives, those frankly admitted, may not be the underlying decisive influences. A man's behavior may be guided by impulses of which he is not conscious. We also recognize that a person may prefer to conceal his intentions for tactical reasons.

There is a further important point here. The author was not interested in what Nikita Khrushchev wanted in his individual life. He presumably enjoyed good food, comfort, and other pleasures. But American concern was with the motives which influenced Russian policy and with Khrushchev in his roles as head of the USSR and high priest of the communist movement. It will be essential for us to distinguish between personal and national goals.

Let me emphasize once more that there is no group mind, no national soul, and that imputing motives to nations is a lot of nonsense. "The Russian bear's craving for warm water" is a poetic but meaningless phrase. Individual Russians want an ice-free seaport for a variety of perfectly valid reasons. Others want such a port only because their leaders tell them it is in the national interest. On many issues of national significance there will be divisions within Russia, just as there are within the USA. Our Midwest is isolationist to a degree much greater than other regions. Clearly, we do not explain this by imputing to the Midwest a soul that dislikes crowds; rather, we make some progress by looking at the economic and political advantages to be derived by certain groups of individuals in accordance with that policy.

The topic of human motivation has filled a number of books. I shall only sketch here a brief outline of some needs and desires which energize human behavior and which play important roles in guiding national policy.

The Desire for Autonomy

Aside from the simple biological needs such as hunger, thirst, and pain, the human infant shows in the very first days of life evidence of a dynamic pattern which we may call the desire for autonomy. Its earliest manifestation is annoyance at having freedom of movement restricted. If his arm or leg is held tightly, the baby will thrash, kick, and scream. While he may come to tolerate such interferences with his freedom, as in cultures where infants are wrapped tightly in swaddling clothes, there is no reason to assume that this motive ever disappears.

We can see evidences of the same kind of motivation in the young child when his play is interrupted. Adolescents are characterized, around the world, by rebellion against adult restraints. And adults show vigorous action when any cherished pattern is blocked, even if there is no particular goal being sought.

A need for autonomy seems naturally to develop out of the need for survival. Primitive man resists efforts to restrain his movements. In Africa today nomadic herdsmen precipitate hostilities by refusing to recognize arbitrary national boundaries that would shut them off from vital water and grass (for example, on the border between Ethiopia and Somalia). But modern society demands that the individual accept many restraints on his behavior. Consider such a simple activity as noise making, which healthy young animals normally enjoy. On a farm such noises disturb few if any other humans. But in a large city they constitute interferences with the activities of others. Complex civilization, in other words, compels all of us to abandon some autonomy.

The craving for freedom from external controls does not thereby cease to exist. It takes other forms. Melville Dalton, in his interesting book *Men Who Manage*,[5] gives shrewd observations of factory managers seeking autonomy from central office control within their departments. Labor unions represent an effort by workers to achieve some freedom from managerial control. City mayors protest against control by state legislatures, and state governments issue blasts against dictatorship from Washington.

The manifestation of autonomy with which we are most concerned, of course, is the insistence of nations upon freedom from external interference. Under the doctrine of sovereignty — of which more later — national leaders refuse to accept an international police force, an international legal code, and a world court. Now, if nations were isolated from one another as families were in our early colonial days, this might have little importance. But nations must interact daily, and what each nation does affects the autonomy of others.

Robert S. Lynd was fond of a little aphorism: " 'Each for himself, and God for all of us,' said the elephant as he danced among the chickens." Autonomy and self-determination are fine — for the elephant. But his unrestrained freedom presents a major threat to the chickens.

We Americans must come to recognize that our nation now has somewhat the status of the elephant in the chicken pen; almost any action, or even inaction, has striking repercussions on the welfare of many smaller countries. Whether the elephant dances or merely sits down, he is likely to crush a neighbor. Like it or not, we have the responsibility of considering the impact of our policies across the world. The only way in which we can escape that responsibility is by going

back to a smaller, weaker, poorer America. Few of us would be pleased
by such a prospect.

The alternative is to select among the varied courses of action
open to us — and the variety is really substantial — with careful regard
to the consequences of our policy in other nations. Most important of
all, we must consider *how our actions will be perceived* by our friends and
neighbors. We may feel convinced that a given procedure, such as
selling wheat at cut prices to countries with food shortages, is in the
best interests of everyone. But it is essential that we give more than a
passing glance to the effect of that action on such wheat exporters as
Canada and Australia. They, too, may wish to help the underprivileged;
but they are also concerned about loss of markets and the damage to
their farm populations.

Does this amount to giving up some of our sovereignty? In a sense,
it does. We cannot ruthlessly adopt a course of action and say it is
not the business of anyone else. Traditionally, sovereignty meant exactly
that: complete egocentrism, complete indifference to the rights of any
nation except our own. This kind of sovereignty never did exist in
practice; the most absolute of monarchs still found it necessary to balance the costs of possible wars against the advantages of unhampered
policy decisions. In the modern world, sovereignty is limited in
many ways.

Americans have cherished the dream of a nation subject to no
higher restraints. Forty years ago we rejected the League of Nations;
today we insist upon veto power in the UN Security Council; and we
still refuse to accept the rule of law through the World Court. These
manifestations of autonomy represent major threats to our survival; we
must somehow come to terms with them if our more fundamental need
to escape suffering, injury, and death is to be met.

The Desire for Power

Closely allied to the desire for autonomy is the desire for power.
If one wants to be really certain he will not be interfered with, he
almost has to achieve a status in which he has power over others and
can block any of their actions that threaten him. Our earliest conceptions of power derive from the parent-child relationship; the child is
constantly being pushed around by people bigger than he is, and many
adults describe their power strivings in such terms. The industrial
executive, for example, often sees his employees as likeable but irre-
sponsible offspring who must be supervised wisely and chastised when
they get out of line. A career in military service appeals to some individuals because of the power exercised over those in lower echelons.
The gratifications to a Hitler, a Stalin, or a Khrushchev in attaining

the top position in a power-concentrated nation must be tremendous.

The admixture of power motivation in nationalistic thinking is usually obvious. National rivalries are struggles for power. The Russians fear us because we have the power to destroy them, and we return the compliment. But each side struggles to achieve more power, forgetting that when one has enough force to kill an opponent, one can't kill him five or ten times. Any gain that is felt to result from the development of such monstrous military force is strictly irrational.

Power motivation tends to intrude in a wide range of international affairs. Control over such a strategic raw material as uranium may represent freedom from outside interference, but it is also a weapon in the power struggle. Trade also becomes a weapon. We scold the Russians for using their economic power against Finland; we use our economic power against Cuba. The admission of new members to the UN is evaluated in terms of its bearing on the power struggle.

When Lord Acton wrote "Power tends to corrupt; absolute power corrupts absolutely," he was referring to the satisfaction experienced by leaders who find it possible, in carrying out their social role, to exercise power over large numbers of their fellow men. The anticipation of power is undoubtedly a dynamic influence attracting men to compete for leadership roles. When Oscar Wilde transformed the aphorism into "All power is wonderful, and absolute power is absolutely wonderful," he may have had the average citizen in mind. To have been a citizen of Rome at the height of empire must have been very gratifying. Human beings can enjoy vicariously the power of their nation; thus, they support leaders who — however erroneously — promise a steady increase in national power.

The Desire for Prestige

A somewhat attenuated form of the power motive appears in the craving for prestige. The child enjoys the attention of his parents or of his peers. He wants others to look up to him. Teen-agers go in for clothing fads, and juvenile gangs develop distinctive uniforms, idioms, and ways of acting. These are designed to attract attention.

Nationalists demand prestige symbols for their country. Fifty years ago the battleship was the prestige symbol par excellence; many small nations spent far more than they could afford to have at least one powerful ship. Colonies have also been prestige symbols, although the economic motivation has usually been more significant. A fairly pure instance, however, was Indonesia's demand for West Irian, the western tip of New Guinea, from the Dutch. The area offered no economic benefits for Indonesia; the people are racially dissimilar; there was no strategic gain involved. Prestige was the issue.

More and more, the prestige symbols are becoming those of modern industrialism. When the Egyptians demanded a steel mill despite the obvious lack of raw materials to supply it, they were expressing prestige motivation. France cannot hope to achieve nuclear capabilities comparable to those of the USA or the USSR, but membership in the nuclear club is a prestige item. Today, the A-bomb has taken the place of the crown jewels for many a nation.

This kind of prestige competition is, we must add, socially preferable to naked power struggles. The Egyptian steel mill may eventually add something to the standard of living in that nation, even though at first it is a severe drain on the economy. And it is better that the USA and the USSR should compete to be the first on the moon than that they measure their military power by a nuclear war.

Altruism

The psychological importance of altruistic motivations has received little attention from recent social observers. It would seem that we live in a dog-eat-dog jungle, where each man's hand is raised against his brother. And some of the evidence does point that way.

There are, however, encouraging facts to support the view that altruistic needs have considerable dynamic power. In husband-wife and parent-child relationships especially, we see strong motives to be helpful, to give up personal pleasure in order to provide gratifications for the other. Indeed, we suspect that the human race could not have survived without some built-in altruism; the helplessness of the pregnant female and of the newborn infant would indicate the neccessity of some such motivation.

Evidence for altruistic motivation is not lacking if we look for it in adult life. Industrialists, for example, find it surprising that workers, when put on an incentive pay plan, do not show marked increases in productivity. Exploration indicates that the reason is fairly obvious. In any work-group, there are some more efficient and some less efficient workers. On a typical job, the range of differences is usually such that the best worker can turn out twice the production of the poorest. These efficient individuals see that if they turn out more, the weaker ones will lose their jobs. To protect their fellows, they actually reduce their take-home pay. Group solidarity and helpfulness explain the refusal of the efficient workers to increase production under these pay plans. (Further proof of this interpretation is given by the success of group incentives and of guarantees that no worker will lose his job if production goes up.)

Altruism, unfortunately, has generally been excluded from the image of the nation. As Charles Beard has pointed out in his book *The*

Idea of National Interest,[6] both leaders and citizens have viewed the nation as bound to concern itself only with selfish issues. This position has been held in every modern nation; both the USA and the USSR defend their programs of foreign aid as being in their selfish national interest. Indeed, they may be. But there ought to be room, in the image of our own nation at least, for straightforward altruism, helpfulness, cooperation — not because we hope to benefit, but because we want to reduce suffering abroad.

There is an important difference between doing good for others to win allies and doing good because the welfare of the world is one's own welfare. Assistance which is offered to buy loyalty (or votes in the UN) will provoke resentment even as it is being accepted. A nation that sells its vote today may sell it elsewhere tomorrow. This approach to international assistance is wrong.

There is an alternative view: that one cannot be complete and fully adjusted in the world until the world is freed from its conflicts and suffering. "No man is an island." We are all members of the human race, and its suffering diminishes each of us.

While this viewpoint smacks of the poetic or the idealistic, it is fully compatible with the scientific conception of man's mind, which has been developed in earlier pages. Strictly speaking, I cannot behave toward the American government, but only toward my *image* of the government; I have no contact with a "real" United Nations, but only with my image of the United Nations; I cannot prove that the human race has any specified set of attributes, but only that I *see* humanity as having certain attributes.

This view has important implications for behavior. If I realize that I am not reacting to a "real" Russia but only to my image of Russia, I have the opportunity to stop and consider that changing Russia is, in part, a matter of changing myself. This is even more impressively true in my reacting to *my* American government and *my* United Nations with which I have more common elements than with Russia. We seek the welfare of our country as an extension of ourselves, and we seek the welfare of the human race for the same reason. Anyone who attempts to destroy part of humanity is destroying part of himself.

Morality

There is little if any indication that man is born with any motive toward moral or ethical behavior. He is, obviously, endowed with the capacity for developing moral standards. Most psychologists, however, believe that the desire to behave in accord with a moral code is learned in the home during early childhood.

The Freudian term for this development is "superego," which refers to a facet of personality that imposes restrictions on ego or purely selfish motives. Thus, if there is an innate trend toward altruism, this will fit in with and reinforce the superego. For the most part, it appears that the child learns to inhibit selfish grasping for immediate satisfactions because of punishment and because of the fear that he may lose the love of his parents. (Punishment often sets off rebellion, whereas the judicious use of parental love builds a strong conscience or superego.)[7]

The problem of moral codes is relevant to international policy in two important respects. First, the nation is assumed to be above the moral limits imposed on individuals. The nation may steal or murder and be praised for it. Individuals are forbidden such acts.[8]

Second, the individual acting in his capacity as an agent of the nation may feel that moral restrictions do not apply. "Our country, right or wrong" is an axiom all too often observed. It is remarkably easy to find excuses for seizure of territory from others in the name of the nation. The customary superego controls over individual actions are not seen as applying to national policy.

Wherever possible, though, spokesmen for nations try to establish the high-minded, virtuous, moral stance of their country. Thus, aggression may be described as "liberating this area from oppressors," and saber rattling is "warning the evildoers that a righteous fate awaits them."

These manifestations suggest that most of us are motivated to have our nation act in an ethical way. This is a hopeful trend. But it will be necessary to arrive at some agreement as to what constitutes an ethical code for nations before this motivation can be very effective. Nationalism, in any event, will interfere seriously with enforcement of national morality, because nationalists express their drives for power and autonomy by insisting on national sovereignty. Until ethical values are placed above national welfare, progress will be limited.

The Will to Survive

Desires for power, autonomy, prestige, and altruism are all important in shaping human decisions. But it must not be thought that these are the most potent drives to human action. The most potent drives are the biological impulses, which we may collectively label "the will to survive." The potency of this need is readily demonstrated when we consider the irrationality of people when panic breaks out in a burning theater: All evidence of civilization goes up in smoke. The strongest civilized taboos break under threats to survival. Hunger and pain have tremendous coercive potency; the success of the Chinese brainwashing in Korea depended upon judicious use of these powerful physical motives to break down the defenses of captives.

It is not mere cynicism to assert that, generally speaking, the more civilized motives such as altruism, prestige, friendship, and patriotism can be ripped away by the naked physical drives. The evidence is pretty clear. In Nazi Germany, for example, friendship, faith in liberal causes, and other idealistic motives gave way to the sheer will to survive torture and destruction. Most Germans showed no concern about the Jews who were being exterminated; they were afraid to protest unjustified arrests and arbitrary executions. In Russia under Stalin, even relatives of a man who was seized by the secret police were afraid to inquire as to his whereabouts. The apparatus of violence, mobilized by the state, can be used to threaten the individual with pain and dissolution if he opposes official policy. Under these circumstances, dissent, for the most part, disappears.

INDIVIDUAL MOTIVES AND GROUP GOALS

The will to survive is an individual matter; no nation can have such a motive, nor indeed any motive. But individuals may desire that their nation survive, and under stress conditions they may be willing to die on behalf of group survival. How do the motives of individuals relate to group goals?

First, the individual may identify with his nation; he may feel that national destruction is equivalent to his own death. Many patriots are willing to die in order to preserve their nation — note, for example, Nathan Hale's reputed regret that he had only one life to lose for his country. Others suffer a feeling of deep loss for years: The refugees from the Baltic states, swallowed up by Russia in 1940, are illustrations.

Second, the individual may obtain economic and ego gratifications by way of national policy. The nazis drove out Polish and Ukranian populations and seized their properties for "good Germans." The European nations, which acquired vast empires in the nineteenth century, confiscated land and other sources of wealth for their leaders. Nationalistic policies have been economically beneficial to many businessmen and political leaders throughout recent history.

Third, the person who has achieved little in the way of wealth or power may receive substitute gratifications from the security, grandeur, and prestige of his country. While little is known about the exact mechanisms which make this possible, it is certainly an important psychological element in national unity, hence in national power.

The person who achieves a leadership role is quite likely to feel closely identified with the nation. He may thus perceive the attainment of desirable national goals as beneficial to him in a personal way. Nikita Khrushchev may have been motivated primarily by a desire for personal power, but he was able to think of this in terms of strengthening the nation (food production, better distribution of benefits). He expected that such measures would increase his chances of retaining his privileged and satisfying position.

This is another aspect of the fact that people behave differently in official roles, as compared with their behavior as private citizens. The nation exists only as an object of perception; but if the leader seeks to strengthen the nation, he follows policies which may not in any immediate sense be selfishly beneficial.

The "motives" guiding the nation, then, are not simply the personal motives of the leader. Even in the case of Adolf Hitler, whose raw hostility and drive toward power were closely related to his decisions on German policy, the national goals were formulated in terms of seizure of land, extermination of native populations, and resettlement of Germans. In the long run, of course, the greater glory of Germany and the glory of Hitler were seen as identical.

The motives of the leaders of a nation may similarly be quite remote from those of the rank-and-file citizen. Leaders may be looking forward ten or twenty years to aggrandizement and world influence. while the average man is looking forward to better housing next year. Edward Crankshaw[9] (*Cracks in the Kremlin Wall*) has pointed out that after World War II, the Russian people overwhelmingly wanted food, clothing, and housing. But the Stalin regime compelled them to rebuild heavy industry. The national goal, in this instance, would have been rejected by an enormous majority of the population if they were allowed to vote. The average American likewise does not determine national goals, although there is probably much greater harmony between the goals perceived by leaders as appropriate and those perceived by the citizens as acceptable. When President Kennedy called upon citizens to sacrifice for the national welfare, businessmen wanted labor unions to do the sacrificing, while the unionists cheerfully offered to let profits be reduced in the national interest. But members of each group wanted to continue seeking their personal gratifications with little regard to national goals. In no nation do we find unity of motivation between citizenry and government, except perhaps in time of war; and even then there are likely to be dissident groups who see a different policy as desirable.

In predicting the policies of other nations, consequently, we must evaluate the situation as it is perceived by political leaders, military men, industrial executives, labor union officials, and perhaps other special groups — as well as the citizenry. And we must take into consideration the ways in which the selfish motives of these groups may influence their perceptions of national policies.

How, then, are individual motives relevant to national policy decisions? The answer is that individuals perceive certain national goals as desirable according to the manner that these goals fit into personal motivations. C. E. Wilson stated this epigrammatically in his famous *faux pas,* "What's good for General Motors is good for the country." Wilson was wrong only in the sense that the relation between individual desire and endorsement of national policy is considerably more subtle and complex than he suggested it to be.

THE QUESTION OF UNCONSCIOUS MOTIVES

We must also consider the phenomenon of unconscious motivation. The foregoing discussion seems to carry with it the notion that the individual is conscious of his motives and that he may deliberately select national power as a means of satisfying his own power drive. Both assumptions would be subject to serious restrictions.

It is easy to find an individual who is quite unaware of his most intense motivation. Strivings for prestige and power, particularly, may meet social disapproval; and, therefore, the person may learn to say that he is acting only to help others, when in fact he is acting to enlarge his personal power or his power as an officer of a group. (This charge is often leveled by union and management spokesmen against one another.)

Furthermore, the selection of group channels to satisfy individual motives is not deliberate. We have little firm knowledge of just how this choice is made. Certainly some aggressive, power-seeking businessmen find it easy to become power-seeking government officials, and some labor union leaders shift to business careers with no apparent change in motivation. The best guess at present is that the individual will strive to satisfy his motives in whatever way is available; if the only path is to become leader of a gang, this is what he accepts. But he is selectively sensitive to information about other ways of satisfying his desires; and so he may be attracted to a different social role, which offers more of what he desires.

So much for leaders; what about followers? The best interpretation available runs like this: Each individual has some of this craving for power, for prestige, for autonomy, and so on. But in his daily life he achieves very little of such goals. The newspapers, the schools, and other media of communication offer him an opportunity to get some feeling of power through the nation's power. It is proposed, therefore, that nationalism be thought of as a means of obtaining satisfactions out of reach to most individuals, but without any awareness by the average man that this process is going on.

Some authors have developed rather imaginative accounts of how nationalism, war, racial discrimination, and religious persecution grow out of conflicts between the child and his parents. For example, Hopkins[10] proposed that the unresolved Oedipus complex (rivalry and hostility of the child toward the parent of the same sex) provided the dynamic basis for militarism and pacifism. Unfortunately, it is most difficult to obtain research data to support or to reject such hypotheses.

It is compatible with the view of human nature already developed that unconscious motives may influence behavior. I have stressed the notion that each person behaves toward reality *as he sees it*. Thus, a young man who has a deep, unrecognized hostility to his father may perceive foreign leaders as father-images who are blocking and threatening him; hence, he must mobilize national power to knock them out of his way — if necessary, to destroy them. For our present purposes, it is not really important to decide just what role sexual strivings, id-superego conflicts, and other theoretical concepts play in this process. It is, on the other hand, necessary to relate this discussion of human motivation to earlier comments on the image of the nation and images of other nations.

Wishful Thinking

Let me first note that motives may induce us to see affairs in such a way as to foster the illusion of wish fulfillment. We notice this in dreams, where desires are often gratified in a somewhat blatant fashion, and in daydreams, where one may fantasy a situation which provides satisfaction for all kinds of pressing motives.

Wishful thinking is especially relevant to the concept of delusions of grandeur. Young children early show signs of flights of fantasy in which they acquire wealth, fame, and power. The culture encourages this with fairy tales, legends, and historical accounts of national heroes. Adults generally come to realize that by personal effort alone one simply does not achieve this high status, and they usually come to be content with friends, a pleasant home, and modest achievement in some sport such as bowling. But if a man's unsatisfied desires persist, it is easy to understand that overestimating the power and status of the nation (of which he is a part) may be gratifying.

Wishful thinking may also contribute to our all-too-frequent mis-understandings of foreign nations. Consider the case of the Soviet Union, our chief rival on the world scene. It would be nice if the Soviet regime were plagued with inefficiency, with rebellious subjects, with discontented satellites. One is prone, therefore, to pick up bits of information which point to such conclusions and to exaggerate them to create a very pleasing picture — just as industrial executives regularly exaggerate the hostility felt by union members toward their leaders. We are deluding ourselves if we expect the USSR to fall apart because of these internal problems.

Delusions of national virtue are likewise supported by this human tendency.[11]All of us would prefer to think of our nation as having stood always for virtue, morality, and justice. Thus, Americans like to forget about the way we have treated the Indians, the Mexicans, and the Negroes. It is easy to find many evidences of national virtue — our general adherence to religious tolerance, our progress on race relations, our freeing of the Philippines, our making grants of food to hungry peoples abroad — in which we take justifiable pride. But if we build this up to an exaggerated degree, it becomes a delusion. This is a hazard we face, especially if the schools collaborate by ignoring the less attractive aspects of our history.

Repression and Dissociation

The more complex forms of perceptual distortion arise not out of a single motivational need, as is the case with wishful thinking, but out of conflicts between motives. A businessman may experience a conflict between his desire for money and his desire to maintain ethical standards. A husband may find himself in a conflict between his sex drive and his idea of morality. It is impossible to gratify one motive without denying the other. In such situations we observe the most intricate (and intriguing) distortions of perceived reality. Voltaire once quipped that "language is the art of concealing thought"; what he did not add is that thought often functions as a device for concealing our inner emotions.

One widespread method for getting out of a conflict situation is to refuse to see part of it. This may constitute complete denial of the facts, complete blindness to them, or diminishment of them so that they are seen as unimportant. For example, the man tempted by an extramarital affair may say to himself, "This is just a whim; I'll indulge it this once and then drop it." He tries to make his violation of the moral code seem trivial. The businessman may prefer to set up a barrier between his economic transactions and his ethics: He says,

"Religion and business don't mix." Another familiar formulation of this is "All's fair in love and war."

If all is fair in war, then the individual may be called upon to engage in many activities which are contrary to his altruistic motives, as well as to his moral and ethical codes. It should not be surprising, given this situation, that we find ample evidence of repression in international affairs. Most Germans denied any knowledge of the nazi concentration camps and gas chambers. The Russians often denied the existence of the slave labor camps before finally admitting that they had been closed. Some people were undoubtedly telling the truth when they made such assertions; they had closed their eyes to evidence which they wanted not to see.

Repression operates particularly with respect to the dreadful consequences of our military policy. Most people simply refuse to listen to discussions which mention 50,000,000 to 100,000,000 American dead in a nuclear exchange with Russia. The pain elicited by even symbolic awareness of such an event is so great that the individual denies its reality. Such blindness makes intelligent planning for the future far more difficult.

George Orwell, in his brilliant novel *1984*, used the term "doublethink" to identify a process by which an individual could simultaneously believe two completely contradictory statements. Thus, the communist could believe that Hungary was a "people's democracy" and at the same time believe it necessary to keep Russian troops there to suppress rebellion. Thus, the American believes that the West is an alliance of free democracies, although he knows full well that Formosa and South Korea are far from democratic — not to mention the Franco dictatorship in Spain. "Doublethink" depends on the phenomenon of dissociation. The individual simply refuses to see that there is any connection between one event and another.

DESIRE AND DECISION: A SUMMARY

The argument so far can be recapitulated very briefly. The decisions which lead to war are made by human beings; and these decisions, being human, are prone to error. Decisions are made on the basis of facts *as seen by the decision maker.* But one can never know reality directly, and so decisions are based on images — pictures which are intended to represent reality. While the individual is himself convinced that these are real, other observers may find that they are distorted in significant respects as compared to a more objectively determined set of facts.

A major source of distortion comes from the leader's inner motives. Because he craves security, power, or economic gain, and because he sees the possibility of attaining these through national policies, he unconsciously accepts misleading views of major issues. He exaggerates the virtue of his own nation and the vices of opposing countries. While we cannot eliminate these personal motives, we may make progress by increasing our awareness of their dangers.

Decisions are also based on social roles. The diplomat may personally dislike violence, but he feels compelled, by his conception of duty to the nation, to press policies which clearly are provocative of war. The military officer knows that civilians will be killed, and he deplores this; but his sense of duty causes him to order a bombing raid just the same. We must therefore recognize two sets of motives influencing national policy decisions: the quest for prestige and power of national leaders, and the perceived demands of the office — of the social role.

5
The Dynamics
of National Hostility

The preceding pages have outlined a psychological basis for understanding the positive aspects of nationalism: the pride, loyalty, and self-sacrifice, which have played so conspicuous a role in western history since about 1500. But there is also a negative side to this picture. People are astonishingly willing to sacrifice *somebody else* to the glory of their nation. Usually they rationalize this behavior by seeing the opposition as bad, vicious, subhuman, aggressive, power seeking, and treacherous. Can we achieve any more useful insights into this psychological mechanism?

Writers for hundreds of years have ascribed wars between tribes, cities, and nations to man's instinct of pugnacity, his impulse to fight. It is implicit in such explanations that this innate impulse must be transferred from face-to-face relations (fighting one's neighbors) to distant group interactions (fighting another tribe or an opposing nation). Since this is substantially what seems to happen in the case of national love, loyalty, and patriotism, there is nothing essentially objectionable in such a view.

It is also obvious that political leaders do not hesitate to appeal to emotions of anger, fear, and hostility in their efforts to

PUBLIC OPINION RARELY ENDORSES WAR

National leaders (even Adolf Hitler) have found it
politically advisable to proclaim an aversion to war and to
insist that war is forced upon the nation by enemy action.
(Cartoon by Herblock. Reprinted by permission of NEA
Service, Inc.)

achieve and keep leadership positions. Aristotle and Machiavelli advised kings to stir up a foreign war when the people were rebellious at home. The principle involved is that anger displaced onto a foreign foe will not be available to energize an attack on the king. Some German businessmen in 1929 financed Adolf Hitler because they felt that he would channel revolutionary impulses, which might otherwise destroy their privileged position, into hatred of communism and the western world.

These tactics do not necessarily prove the instinct theory correct. Many psychologists believe that aggression arises within the individual only as a result of frustration and not simply, as in the welling up of hunger, because of normal bodily processes. The majority of professional psychologists, at least in the USA, clearly reject the instinct theory.[1] The general preference is for a theory which starts with positive motivation (hunger, sex, power, security) and explains aggression as a dynamic response when one of these motives is blocked. After all, no man grows to maturity without encountering many frustrations, and the anger so generated can apparently be deflected onto persons or situations not involved in the original frustration.

HOSTILITY AND GROUP FORMATION

Whether it derives from an instinct or from an experience of frustration, hostility can provide a focus for group formation. Nikos Kazantzakis, whose autobiography has already been quoted, tells of forming a club of adolescent boys:

> [We] founded a new 'Friendly Society.' We held sessions in secret, took and received oaths . . . gave our lives a goal: to make uncompromising war on falsehood, servitude, and injustice . . . we did what we could to remain faithful to our vows. We never told lies, we beat up all the Turkish children we happened to meet in outlying lanes, and we replaced our collars and ties with undershirts striped white and blue, the colors of the Greek flag.[2]

A curious mixture of the highest idealism and brutal aggression toward the helpless is clearly illustrated here. This mixture has long been characteristic of nationalism, just as it characterizes communism and other militant ideologies. The young Greeks in Crete saw nothing wrong with beating up an isolated Turkish lad, who had done them no injury and whose only crime was that of being Turkish.

Joining together to fight a common enemy is, of course, characteristic of national policies; the USA and the USSR managed to
cooperate, in an uneasy way, to fight nazism. But this did not result
in true group formation, i.e., there was no development of a feeling
of common membership in a larger unity. It is probable that groups
formed only around a common enemy never achieve this more durable
unity. Nationalism may be accelerated by hostility to a colonial power
or to an external threat, but lasting solidarity probably must always
depend on the desires for security, wealth, and power.

HOSTILITY AND INTERNATIONAL AFFAIRS

It still is necessary for us to consider whether the hostility of the
average citizen, or of the national leader, is a decisive factor in international conflict. Clearly, the same considerations hold as in the case
of patriotism. Leaders are selected because they appeal successfully to
hostile feelings of voters; leaders generally represent the population, so
their reactions may be expected to resemble those of the man in the
street. Most important, hostile feelings lead to distortions of perception
and to misinterpretation of the acts of foreign nations. For example, in
1955 the Russians signed an Austrian peace treaty and withdrew their
troops from that little country. Optimists said this proved the Russians
were cooperative; pessimists said the Russians were angling for bigger
game, that this was giving up a "Danubian sprat to catch a fatter
German mackerel." Ten years later, it appeared that the pessimists
had been wrong; but, in the meantime, policies based on their
interpretation had interfered with possible cooperative developments.

Obviously, the feelings of the average citizen do not directly determine the course of national policy. American men in 1961 felt no
hostility toward the Viet Cong or North Viet Nam; yet they were sent
to Asia, first to advise on fighting, later to fight. It is doubtful that
the Russians who were sent to Cuba about that time felt any fondness
for Castro, although they may have been effectively indoctrinated with
anti-American attitudes. Policy decisions such as these may be influenced by the hostilities of leaders, but they are slightly, if at all,
affected by public opinion.

Where the citizens' emotions can be effective is in the execution
of policy. A decision to continue, to escalate, or to withdraw from an
action such as that in Korea will be based to some extent on the
effectiveness of displacing public hostility onto the enemy. If the pre-
ponderant emotional tone becomes one of anxiety about casualties or
of hostility toward national leaders wishing to pursue the action, a
change in policy is quite likely.

Dehumanization

One of the characteristic perceptual distortions resulting from anger and hatred is the dehumanization of the opponent. This simply means that we see the enemy as inhuman, perhaps subhuman; he is bestial, uncivilized, and consequently is not covered by our code of ethics regarding proper treatment of human beings. This happens in face-to-face conflicts, as between husband and wife; it is also easily noticed in international controversies, especially in war, when the accusation of subhuman behavior is readily turned on the enemy. This theme was particularly common in anti-Japanese propaganda during World War II; it is interesting to observe that American publicists now find the Japanese among the more civilized peoples of Asia.

Dehumanization affects policy decisions because it is easier to order harsh measures against a group perceived as outside the pale of humanity. Our superego inhibits cruelty to other human beings; but, by setting the opponent outside this category, anything is permissible. This was true of the nazis in their torture of Jews in concentration camps; it has often been true in the treatment of other minority groups.

Projection

A related phenomenon is called projection. This refers to our tendency to project our own bad traits onto others in exaggerated form. Thus, if you feel aggressive, you will be inclined to exaggerate the belligerence of other people. The drunk in the tavern who accuses others of trying to start a fight is actually reflecting the release by alcohol of his own concealed aggression. Some men with a very strong sex drive see others around them as engaging in all kinds of sexual misbehavior. People who become self-appointed censors of books and movies also often fall in this category.

The hazards of projection in international relations must be obvious. If a national leader is himself frustrated and full of hostility, he inevitably magnifies the hostility of those leaders of other nations with whom he deals. Projection includes the misinterpretation of all kinds of minute details. A new highway proposed by nation X is seen as primarily military in character. A new research program is seen as a search for new weapons. Proposals for disarmament are interpreted as plans to render us helpless.

We are constantly trying to infer the intentions of other nations. An act usually is not so significant in itself as in what it may predict about the future. But the future is inherently ambiguous; thus, these emotional distortions can operate with great ease.

Does an awareness of the frequency of projective misinterpretation help us in evaluating foreign affairs? Certainly. Consider, for example, our belief that the Russians are about to attack us. Visitors to the USSR find apparently quite sincere fears that we are about to attack the Soviet Union. We can, I think, be quite certain that their view of our intentions is wrong. We might then be wise to explore the possibility that our estimate of their intentions is likewise in error.

Displacement

The phenomena of hostility are important in international affairs because of the extent to which hostilities within a group can be displaced onto out-groups. Each of us encounters frustrations and wants to attack someone near at hand: parent, spouse, business competitor, or perhaps just a person driving an automobile in a reckless fashion. For the most part, these feelings are not expressed directly, but the tension builds up and apparently can be displaced either onto other nearby helpless objects or onto distant, and thus non-threatening, groups.

Hostile feelings may be displaced under a variety of conditions. The child loves his parents and so does not wish to feel hostile to them. He finds it more comfortable to hate some person or animal outside the family.[3] The adult hates his boss but fears the punishment which would follow any expression of such an attitude. Thus, he inhibits the expression of his immediate feelings but is psychologically "set" to react with hostility to someone else.

A man may be frustrated but not know the source. For instance, it has been shown that lynchings of Negroes in the South, over the past 90 years, fluctuated with the price of cotton.[4] No one will assert that Negroes influenced cotton prices. But the farmer, annoyed about his economic difficulties, was "set" to be angry with someone, and the Negro was unable to fight back — hence, was a suitable scapegoat for these aggressive impulses.

Do these comments seem remote from any consideration of national policy? Consider the following observations of James Reston, an experienced journalist, regarding conditions in Washington just after the Cuban rebels attacked Castro at the Bay of Pigs in April 1961:

> This city is in a psychological spin over Cuba. It is full of men who want to "do something" — anything to avenge the bloody nose in Cuba. Also, even in today's meeting of the National Security Council with the president, there were officials who, in their anger and

frustration, were flirting with military moves which would transform the fiasco in Cuba into a disaster in Laos. [5]

How can we avenge ourselves against Castro by taking strong measures in Laos? The idea is irrational on its face. But hostility is often irrational, and the displacement of anger from one object to another is quite common. (This is one reason why some experts oppose tactics intended to heighten frictions *within* the communist bloc; the resulting hostility could easily be deflected onto the West.)

Contemporary ideas about displacement, therefore, run as follows: If one is blocked from achieving some desired goal, the first tendency is to attack the blocking agent. If this agent is too powerful, or is unavailable (how can a cotton farmer attack a commodity exchange?), he is disposed to hate something and to attack a convenient scapegoat. Therefore, citizens within a nation may find it convenient to displace their hostilities onto foreigners and to express attitudes favoring attack and destruction. This need not imply knowledge of the "real" attributes of the foreign nation; several studies suggest that it is easier to hate some group about which we know virtually nothing than a group with which we are well-acquainted.

How do these generalizations apply to relations between USA and USSR in the so-called Cold War? There are at least three possibilities that must be taken into account:

1. Kremlin leadership might fall into the hands of an aggressive, paranoid individual, as it came under the dominance of Josef Stalin. If such a leader achieved dominance in the USSR, we could do little other than keep our guard up and try to avoid provocative actions.

2. The Russian leaders might find themselves in a potentially revolutionary situation because of mass frustration. In this case, they may prefer to encourage displacement of this hostility onto foreigners for fear that it become focused on the national government.

3. A more likely possibility is that the Kremlin group, though not physically frustrated, might find themselves blocked in their search for greater power through the spread of world communism. If the leaders of the Russian Communist party feel personally involved in the expansion of communism — and it is almost unquestionable that they do — we may expect that they will feel quite hostile toward the USA as a major block to their ambitions.

Hostility toward America and the West may then serve two purposes in the Soviet Union. It may faithfully reflect the attitudes of the governing clique; and it may serve as a safety valve for popular feel-

AN ENEMY IS USEFUL IN DOMESTIC POLITICS

"UNITED WE STAND!"

Conservatives in the 1939-1941 period freely accused
President Roosevelt of muzzling his critics by
appealing for national unity in the face of a foreign
danger which they considered grossly exaggerated.
(Cartoon by Carlisle, in *The Portland
Press-Herald.* Reprinted by permission.)

ings that might otherwise threaten Communist party control of the government. In the absence of more precise evidence, we must maintain both of these as possible influences.

What about the hostility of Americans toward the USSR? Here we have a more complex situation, if only because the alternatives cited above are much less useful in the USA. Since our citizens have a far higher standard of living and more personal freedom, we cannot give much credence to the notion that the American government is trying to displace internal aggression. And, likewise, our national leaders are not crusading for a world revolution; hence, the Russians are not a blockage to such a goal. However, here are some factors which *do* elicit American hostility toward the USSR:

1. Most important, many Americans perceive the Russian government as a physical threat, a danger to survival. This is the most powerful of all motives. A threat in this area leads correspondingly to intense hostility.

2. Communism as an ideology threatens the property and comfort of the well-to-do. But, compared to most of the world, even the American worker is rather well off, and he may readily feel threatened by a communist ideology.

3. Communism has been imposed by force on many nations of Central Europe, and the USA has many citizens from these areas. While these individuals are loyal Americans, they may still feel patriotism for their homeland and may resent the imposition by the Red Army of an alien government. Their attitudes may easily be communicated to other Americans. It is likely that other sources of aggression contribute to the hostility directed against Russia, but these seem to account for most of the observed feeling.

HOSTILITY AND FEAR

The foregoing considerations lead us to an important but often ignored point: Hostility grows out of fear. The Russians fear our power and hate us as a consequence. We fear their political system and the revolutionary economic ideology of communism, and we thus oppose vigorously any development which might favor the Soviet bloc.

How much of this is based on fear of loss of power, prestige, or confort, and how much on fear of physical pain and death? It seems probable that both are inextricably mingled in the Cold War. The men in the Kremlin, we may assume, are hostile because they fear loss of power or threat to their expanding ideology. Some capitalists may fear and hate communism because, under such a system, they would lose wealth and power. But the Russian people, like the Americans, fear the death and destruction of nuclear war. If they are persuaded that we are the potential source of such a catastrophe, they will hate us; and our people respond in the same way. The will to survive is still our most powerful motive, and threats in this area will evoke the most potent hostility.

This approach shows that hostility, in itself, is *not* the key problem. Hostility is a symptom. Fire does not cause a conflagration; it is a visible sign that something else has gone wrong. Similarly, aggressive attitudes indicate the operation of some other, more fundamental, process. To quote George Kennan: " . . . armaments were a symptom rather than a cause, primarily the reflection of international differences, and only secondarily the source of them."[6] An English psychologist, E. Graham Howe, put the issue more dramatically: "If there are mad dogs in Europe today, it is not enough to cry for guns and chains. *Who bit the dog, and why is he so mad?*"

Fear of being blocked or harmed in some way is a major stimulus to violent action. This suggests that — while we may want to get chains and protect ourselves from the mad dog — we must explore the frustrations and fears which arouse his ire. In many cases, we may discover that the hostility is easy to understand. We are not surprised when nine million Algerians become angry on finding themselves dominated by fewer than one million Frenchmen. And we can even understand the destructiveness of the French minority in Algeria under the pressures of fear — fear of retaliation, fear of expropriation. My point is that we cannot deal with hostility alone; we can approach it intelligently only if we take account of the underlying causes.

HOSTILITY AND DETERRENCE

If fear leads to hostility, then any hostile steps taken by one nation must be expected to raise the tension level in another. Our measures to improve our military stance frighten the Russians; their parallel steps frighten us. Each group thus tends to hate the other more intensely. The strategy of deterrence, in itself, thus tends to lead toward arms races and heightened danger of war.[7]

But there is another respect in which the psychology of aggression must be related to a strategy of deterrence. Are national leaders finding it necessary to incite hostility toward the opponent nation in order to make deterrence credible?

Consider the situation facing the American leadership. Our strategy vis-a-vis the communist bloc is one of deterrence. We have great nuclear power and versatile means of delivery. A key question then becomes: Do the Russians believe that we would use this power? Specifically, do they believe that we would engage in a nuclear exchange with frightful casualties to protect West Berlin? Greece? London?

Since our strategy must appear *credible,* we must somehow communicate to the Russians that we really would strike in such circumstances. National policy, therefore, must envision the possibility of deliberately evoking hostility toward the Russians to support the *credibility* of our deterrent threat. If we had spoken only good of the Russians, they might disregard our assertion of a readiness to demolish them with a retaliatory force. Such a view of the situation would lead our planners, even though they had quite calmly decided on the tactic, to emit statements and encourage fulminations from military and nonmilitary spokesmen reflecting intense hostility toward at least Russian leaders. Conversely, the Russians might well decide that they, too, would have to growl ferociously in order to make their deterrent more believable.

So far, so good. We may view the propaganda charges and rocket rattling as imitations of two strange dogs, snarling at each other until a convenient excuse arises for separating without combat. Such a view is somewhat encouraging. But is there a concealed danger here? What of the possibility that our aggressive noises are interpreted as evidence that we are about to launch a preemptive strike, a preventive war? In that case, credibility has been carried too far; the opponent did not simply receive the message — he magnified it. If this happens, he too is tempted to launch an attack in the hope of beating us to the draw.

Such an analysis of the situation is admittedly speculative. Neither the Pentagon nor the Kremlin is likely to confess to having inflated the amount of local hostility toward the enemy nation. Nor are they likely to endorse officially any leanings toward a "first-strike" or preemptive war policy. Yet the latter possibility has been discussed by highly placed individuals on both sides of the Iron Curtain. The opportunities for miscalculation are alarming.

Open expression of hostility also increases the chance of a "war of misadventure," as illustrated by the film *Dr. Strangelove.* Specifically, let us consider the case of a junior officer, who has been thoroughly indoctrinated with hostile feelings toward our opponents. In a crucial situation he finds himself in charge of a nuclear missile unit and confronted with what seems to him clear evidence of an impending attack. Is he not unduly prone to push the button which sets off destruction? It is extremely unlikely that we (or the Russians) would wait to ascertain that this missile was discharged by error.

TENSION AND OVERLOAD

The possibility that individuals might become so dominated by hostility as to behave in a truly irrational way is most important. Intense danger can produce the phenomenon of "blind panic," which is characterized by complete loss of rational judgment. Hatred can produce the same results. The individual may become so obsessed with his desire to attack the enemy that he forgets the goal he originally sought. The behavior of baboons shows a similar phenomenon: Two males occasionally fight over a female and, in their anger, may tear her to bits as they lash out blindly at anything within reach. The parallel here might encourage Charles Darwin, but it does not warm the heart of the seeker after international peace.

The similarity of all strong emotions in interfering with reason has often been noted. Marcus Aurelius warned against the power of the emotions to induce irrational behavior. Strong emotion in social affairs, as in the case of intense prejudice and hostility toward other nations, may prevent us from assessing rationally the backlash upon ourselves of national policies.

All such emotions have in common the production of tension. I refer here primarily to "tension" as a subjective phenomenon — an experience. Its importance can be illustrated by a remark like "Let's bomb the Russians and get it over with!" The continuing state of tension builds up to a point at which it seems intolerable; even a nuclear war may appear to be the lesser evil.

Each of us has a tension threshold, a certain level of tension which can be tolerated. This may not be a constant; perhaps it varies with fatigue and other factors. But, in general, we know that children lose control with relatively low tension loadings whereas adults can endure more. And those adults whom we consider to be exceptionally mature are characterized especially by their ability to continue to function rationally under high tension loads.

The symptoms of a tension "overload" are merely the extremes of the phenomena already described. The individual loses his ability to discriminate among cues. He may blindly repeat actions which have already been found to be futile; he may lash out in blind rage at innocent bystanders; he may go into panic and fail to see perfectly obvious escape routes from his danger situation.[8]

The nonsurvival value of such loss of realistic evaluation of situations is obvious. What must be stressed here is that we must be on guard against those persons, especially if they seek leadership roles, whose tension threshold appears to be low. Such individuals, losing their capacity for rational evaluation of alternatives, may opt for all-out nuclear war simply because they can no longer bear the strain of the Cold War.

Overload is a very real phenomenon. We see it in juvenile delinquents, who are unable to tolerate the frustrations of socialized living and thus fly into senseless violence. We see it in the manic patient, who throws dishes and furniture or attacks his physician and his nurse. But its most dangerous form is that which might occur in someone responsible for great military forces. The damage that could be initiated by such a person in a high position in the USA or in the Soviet Union is unimaginable.[9]

The present situation is one in which leaders on both sides apparently indulge in occasional rocket rattling to convince the other side that "we mean business." We may sympathize with an argument that this is necessary to keep the Russians from underestimating our determination to resist unwarranted pressure, but we must recognize the serious danger of overload in terms of public response. While only about 1 percent of Americans are at present sufficiently tense to suggest that we start the war and "get it over with," this number could increase. The results, in terms of pressure upon government, would be alarming.

A basic psychological law is that aggression induces counter-aggression. If we express a high level of hostility, this will elicit more hostility among the Russians. At a certain point, the fear that we may strike first can induce them to begin the preventive war. It is this possibility which must be kept in mind at all times by leaders on both sides.

Our chief hope, perhaps, lies in the strength of the will to survive. True, a person obsessed by hatred may die willingly, if he can take his enemy with him; but such a person is quite rare. Probabilities favor the expectation that the public can be persuaded to accept a relaxation of tension; most people would sigh with relief and abandon their hatreds — or at least limit them to verbalization. Where there is no immediate environmental support for hostility, it will extinguish and disappear.

6
Emotion
and Ideology

The proposition developed so far is that international conflicts are often exacerbated by perceptual distortions based on the attitudinal complex called nationalism. There are, however, other strong belief systems that may produce comparable effects on political, economic, and military decisions relevant to international relations.

Of these the most important current factor is the communist ideology. Faith in communism, of course, gets inextricably intertwined with nationalism in those nations where the movement controls the government. But in other nations, communistic fervor, dedication, and fanaticism — plus, in some instances, anti-communist fervor, dedication, and fanaticism — complicate the scene as viewed by both leaders and followers. It is thus worthwhile to explore the motivational, emotional, and cognitive components which form the psychological basis of communist thinking.

Note has already been taken of the intensity with which individual motives and emotions may become focused on the expansion and strengthening of the nation. History reminds us that other social movements, such as religious crusades, have shown the same capacity to mobilize human energy. The struggle for democracy against the divine right of kings and other dictatorial regimes is another example of individual dynamics affecting the fate of political institutions.

Communism has many of the attributes of an evangelical religion. The devoted communist puts his faith above his loyalty to his nation — as do many deeply religious people. The communist is firmly convinced that he has The Truth, and he is intolerant of deviation or error. He has great faith in his leaders when they are speaking on matters of communist doctrine. He is willing to make amazing sacrifices to advance the movement, and he is completely oblivious of the harm he does others in the process.

Our thinking about communism is likely to be seriously distorted because of the conflict, on nationalistic grounds, between the USA and the USSR. I should like, therefore, to make a brief detour and examine the characteristics of a fanatical religion in which few Americans have any emotional involvement and which can therefore be treated with reasonable objectivity. This is the Mohammedan religion, Islam — particularly in the form it took about one thousand years ago.

ISLAM AS A PROTOTYPE

While Moslems speak of the House of Islam (to refer to the Mohammedan nations) as opposed to the House of War, their faith actually spread by violent coercion. Fanning out from the Arabian peninsula, they swept across North Africa, making converts by the simple procedure of chopping off the heads of those refusing to join.

This approach was justified by the familiar view that "error has no rights." If, as they believed, the Mohammedan faith was the one true religion, then it was obviously justifiable for them to convert unbelievers by force. As they saw it, they were actually doing the heathens a good turn by forcing them to abandon evil ways. There are many people who still subscribe to this philosophy; a devoted communist will assert that his dogma is good for the workers even if they have to be bludgeoned into accepting it.

Islam paralleled the communist movement in still another way. The movement was simultaneously religious and political. Monnerot writes:

> The Egyptian Fatimids, and later the Persian Safavids, were the animators and propagators . . . of an active and organising legend, an historical myth, calculated to make fanatics and obtain their total devotion, designed to create in neighboring states an underworld of ruthless gangsters.[1]

This "underworld" was utilized for the seizure of political power, just as the communist movement is utilized today.

The role of Stalin or of Khrushchev as the head of both a state and a religion is likewise paralleled in the Islamic tradition. This situation, writes Monnerot, "allowed the head of a state to operate beyond his own frontiers in the capacity of 'commander of the faithful' (*Amir-al-muminin*); and in this way a *caliph* was able to count upon docile instruments, or captive souls, wherever there were men who recognised his authority."[2] Through this mechanism, the Islamic states expanded by subverting established governments, just as today the Communist party seeks to overthrow noncommunist governments for the greater welfare of both the movement and the Soviet Union.

Mohammedanism as a religious doctrine has many desirable features. When Mohammed was founding his church, he preached against polytheism, against the oppression of the poor, against dishonesty in trade. It is not surprising that he and his followers were persecuted by those whose vested interests would be injured by his new doctrine. During the period of rapid expansion of the movement (632-713 A.D.), however, the Mohammedans "converted" the infidels by fire and sword. Their policies during this period provided elements of realism for the hostile attitudes of Christian Europeans toward them; this fear of Moslem persecution eventually gave rise to the Crusades and to countless deaths and miseries.

The combination of internal subversion and external military pressure is startlingly similar to the technique of communism. Its effectiveness depends upon the similarity in their ways of looking at situations. "We are right, virtuous; the enemy is wicked; we are therefore justified in using every means to achieve his downfall."

RELIGIOUS WAR IN EUROPE

While Islam is particularly instructive in its parallels to communism, we can find delusions of grandeur and of persecution in other religious wars. When Catholics fought Protestants in Europe in the 17th century, each group attributed all virtue to themselves and identified the opposition with Satan. The Catholics held that they represented the true church and that all others were agents of the devil. The Protestants asserted that they had cut away the cancerous Papacy, an instrument of Satan, and had gone back to the true Christian theology. As we know, they killed each other with great enthusiasm, aided by these parallel delusions.

Today we are generally able to coexist, Catholic with Protestant, each tolerant of the other's virtue, neither insisting that the other must be rooted out as an agent of hell. But during the Thirty Years' War, 1618-1648, in central Europe (mainly Germany and the Low Countries), it is estimated that two thirds of the population was killed, either directly or by famine and disease and five sixths of the villages were destroyed. In that case, as today, other issues besides ideology were involved, but the religious difference was unquestionably an important one.

A somewhat similar instance may be cited in the case of the Albigenses, a dissident group within the Roman Catholic Church. This group, centered largely in southern France, was attacked by military forces of the Papacy in 1209 and was virtually exterminated by 1229. Several hundred thousand persons were killed in this religious feud.

How did it happen that Moslems came to live in harmony with Christians and Protestants with Catholics after these bloody events? It became possible as the struggles for power became muted or eliminated. The Mohammedans abandoned their dream of conquering Europe; the Protestants abandoned their efforts to eliminate the Papacy; and governments of England, Germany, France, and the Netherlands ceased to function as power centers, beneficial to one religion and hostile to another.

The history of western Europe indicates that people who have vilified and attacked one another have also learned eventually to live together in peace. This has become feasible as religion has been divorced from control of the state and from questions of wealth and property. It must be remembered that, during the religious wars, estates were confiscated and granted to those who adhered to the momentarily dominant church — just as in Spain, during the Inquisition, lands were seized from heretics and added to the properties of the faithful. (This was even true in New England during the persecution of the ''witches'' of Salem. Confiscated land was added to the estates of church elders.)

The role of the aristocracy, especially the royal house, was crucial in the shift to coexistence. When the king of England decided that a unified, peaceful nation contributed to his power and prestige and that these advantages outweighed his religious involvement, he put an end to persecutions and expropriations. And in the USA, the diversity of religions made tolerance a necessity of survival when New England had to make common cause with the other colonies against Britain. The recognition of other values as more important than expansion and power of a church thus seems to be the key to peaceful coexistence.

There are obviously situations in the world today in which conflict persists at least partly because of continued linkages between religious values, property ownership, and political power. One such situation is in South Vietnam, where the large landholders, preponderantly Catholic, appear to control the Saigon government; others are in Latin-American countries, where the same linkage appears to be common. The decisive issues appear to be economic and political, but religious ideology is certainly a complicating influence.

A clear separation of religious issues from ownership and power — as when political parties appeal to members of all religious denominations — favors peaceful settlement of ideological disputes. But can this generalization help us with the communist versus anti-communist dispute, in which property rights and political power appear to be fundamental to the ideology? In later pages I shall propose an answer to this question in terms of separating ideological from nationalistic energies. The solution assumes that conflicts will be less intense when these powerful motives are not united in support of a single policy. Clarification of this solution will be easier after the psychological basis of the communist movement has been explored.

REALITY AS SEEN BY COMMUNISTS

It is not enough to say that the communist acts like a religious fanatic. This merely condemns without clarifying. What we must ask is: What do the facts look like to the typical communist? What motives impel him to act as he does? Answers to these questions will help us to understand the world conflict today.

Scientific psychology finds no basis for assuming that communists are different by heredity from democrats — no reason for treating them as inherently bad or aggressive or untrustworthy. The images described in an earlier chapter must be taken as subjective, not objective, evidence. If the leaders of the western nations were indeed as malicious as the communist believes, then his suspicion, evasion, and hostility would be quite sensible; and the reverse also follows. But the evidence is subjective and must be viewed with caution.

The differences in perception which provide a continuing foundation for the Cold War go considerably beyond what has already been described. The communist typically has a whole set of images and values which must be taken into account in seeking to comprehend his policies and behavior.

Exploitation

The communist image of the western world begins with the classical description by Karl Marx of industrialism in Great Britain in the first half of the nineteenth century. It was a cruel time, with little children of six years working in the mines and in the textile mills.

Great fortunes were amassed by the owners of these properties, and the communist view holds firmly that nothing has changed in capitalist economies.

There is a joke, alleged to be popular in various Iron Curtain countries, about the difference between capitalism and communism. "Capitalism is a system of society in which man exploits man. Under communism, the reverse is true." While there is clearly some truth in this irony, we shall not make progress in international discussions by talking to the communists about how thousands of peasants died when their grain was seized by the government to pay for foreign machinery. There was bitter exploitation of labor in the West years ago, and there will always be exploitation of some segment of society as any nation tries to become industrialized. We shall advance in our discussions with the communists when they learn what we have done in ending exploitation. If Russian trade unionists visited the West, they would see factory parking lots jammed with workers' cars; they would become aware of the falsity of much of their own propaganda.

Brotherhood

The communist ideal places a high value on the brotherhood of man. In theory, the communist system will put an end to human inequalities, and all men will be brothers because they will not be divided by economic class interests. Few westerners would cavil at such an ideal society. It would seem wiser, instead of attacking communism indiscriminately, to note that we too believe in brotherhood and that we are competing with the communist states to achieve even more rapidly equal treatment for all.

In objective terms, neither East nor West is close to the ideal of equality in rights and opportunities. Higher education, for example, is far more readily available to children of professionals, factory managers, and government officials than to the general population of either society. The distribution of power and influence is manifestly unequal in both.

In proportion to their resources, the communist nations have probably done more to provide equal health care, protection for the aged, and maternity care than some western states. But differences in these areas, too, are diminishing as welfare legislation is widened in scope.

Materialism

It may seem ironic, in a social system allegedly founded upon the

Karl Marx philosophy of dialectical materialism, that leading communist spokesmen hail the dominance of spiritual or idealistic values over
the material. Yet this is quite common. The West is often attacked for
excessive concern with material possessions, with physical comforts, and
with luxuries. The Russian government newspaper, *Izvestia,* is quoted
thus: "In our society material things do not dominate man. Man is
above material things . . ."[3]

It is unlikely that any but a small group of saints and martyrs
can ever be really "above material things." Psychological analyses of
human motivation suggest that the average person in every society is
powerfully influenced by material rewards such as food, clothing, and
shelter. On the other hand, it must be noted that in many harsh areas
of the world, such as Korea and Vietnam, the advocates of a communist policy have shown a degree of dedication, a willingness to undergo
physical discomfort on behalf of their ideals, considerably in excess of
the dedication shown by groups affiliated with the West. We may not
glorify the Chinese Communist soldiers who marched barefoot through
the snow of North Korea, but we can respect their dedication and
their willingness to endure hardships in their quest for victory.

Perhaps this is the most important psychological problem in the
Cold War. One hundred and fifty years ago, belief in democracy had
a dynamic value which led many American crusaders to organize revolutions in European monarchies. Today, we seem to have lost the zeal,
the faith in our ideals, which inspired such willingness to sacrifice physical security on behalf of the democratic ideal. If — as some people
interpret history — those social movements that can dynamize individuals to dedicated self-sacrifice are the movements that inherit the
earth, then perhaps communism is on the way in and democracy is
on the way out. Many people believe that unless we can rekindle faith
in and enthusiasm for our way of life, our future looks bleak.

A desire for material comforts, however, is built into human nature;
it is not tied to western ideology. The communists, particularly in Russia, are now disturbed by the materialistic cravings of their citizens.
Izvestia is quoted in 1966 as scolding "bourgeois communists" for becoming excessively concerned with selfish comforts. (Americans were
amused, because one of the symptoms of this concern was identified
as demanding "an asphalt paved path to one's own privy!")[4]

The argument that the Russians, as they become more prosperous,
will show less ideological intensity and more concern with creature
comforts is based on just this tendency. While it seems to be a
safe bet, we would be unwise to rest too much of our defense on
this expectation.

COMMUNIST INDOCTRINATION

The communists have an advantage, in training new cadres and in their propaganda campaigns generally, of adopting a uniform position within which relatively little deviation is permitted. The new convert can thus find it rather easy to ascertain what attitudes will meet with approval, what actions will earn rewards, what values are held in high esteem. Perceptual distortions are there in plenty, but these operate in the direction of creating an overly simple picture of "blacks" and "whites" — something like our TV westerns — in which it is easy to tell the good guys from the bad guys.

It would be a mistake to overestimate the psychological advantage of the communists in this area. Let me repeat that there is no group mind, no crowd spirit which can exercise mystical control over the individual. The Communist party instills loyalty and dedication in much the same way that nationalism is instilled in children.

A nation induces a uniform way of seeing facts by education, by national heroes, by legends, by organized activity. The Communist party does the same: The recruit undergoes intensive indoctrination in party policies, including Marxist theory as most recently revised. He learns to revere the proper heroes, he learns myths of capitalist brutality and exploitation, he marches with his fellows on picket lines and in demonstrations. This is not brainwashing, as that term should be understood. It is only a highly efficient form of what every other modern nation practices in a less orderly manner.

It must be noted that the typical communist, at least in the USA, will not be an average citizen. He is likely to be a person with a strong need for dependence, a need to lean on a leader or an organization. He finds security in the dogma of the party, just as some people find security in the dogma of religion. He wants a substitute father, but the usual symbol (the leader of the nation) is for some reason unacceptable to him. He is thus susceptible to the cult of personality, which is apparently an inevitable feature of all communist organizations.

Obviously many nationalists fit the same pattern. Members of the John Birch Society, the Ku Klux Klan, and similar groups have the same personality needs as the communist. They crave an outlet for hostility; they want a feeling of power through group membership; they want clear-cut, black-and-white pictures of reality; they want to give unquestioning loyalty to some leader or group. They are, however, selectively sensitive to the appeals of the nation rather than to the appeals of an ideology; and their hostilities are directed against any group seen as threatening the nation, while the communist is hostile to enemies of his party.

The absence of any crowd mind which controls party members is well illustrated by the frequency with which individuals break away and denounce party rigidity. It is also illustrated by the drastic loss of membership by the communists in 1939, when the Nazi-Soviet Pact was announced, or by the similar loss of members, especially in Italy, when Khrushchev revealed officially the brutalities of Stalin.

A striking example of individual disenchantment is given by Ignazio Silone from his own personal experience. Silone and Palmiro Togliatti went to Moscow in May 1927 for a meeting of the Executive Committee of the Communist International. Ernst Thaelmann, a German communist leader, read a violent condemnation of a document that Leon Trotsky had addressed to the Politburo of the Russian party. Silone asked to see the Trotsky document and was strongly denounced for refusing to accept the Politburo stand without question. It was not, he was told, a question of whether Trotsky's remarks were true; this was a power struggle and Trotsky's group had to be crushed. Silone refused to vote for the condemnation and soon decided to leave the communist movement.[5]

Our knowledge of human tendencies for conformity leads us to suspect that men of Silone's fortitude are rare; most of us give in to social pressure, whether from a Stalin or from a McCarthy, and endorse the stand we consider "safe."

It may thus happen that an apparent source of communist strength carries the seeds of dissolution. Strong-minded national leaders of Communist parties do not take well to dictation from Moscow. The Tito heresy was only the first. China has rejected Russian leadership; Poland and others are also breaking away from the monolithic organization. This may well mean that the western disadvantage, in terms of disunity and diversity of leadership, will diminish as divisive trends continue within the Soviet bloc.

COMMUNIST LEADERSHIP

It was suggested above that the communist movement has a strong appeal to those who need the security of a rigid organization and a sharply defined doctrine. This does not mean that ambitious power seekers will be scared away. Men who see little chance of attaining power within an established elite will be tempted by the chance that a communist revolution could bring them to power.

A common source of error in American evaluation of communist behavior has been our failure to recognize the powerful motive to get or keep the leadership role in the world communist movement. Because the American Communist party is minuscule and powerless, we have tended to assume that no party member would be really concerned about status in the communist movement. Yet this motivation is very strong. The bitterness of the Stalin-Trotsky feud, which eventuated in Trotsky's murder, is one example. Another is the development between Moscow and Peking of a hostility which was grossly underestimated in the USA for years because Americans ignored this intense desire of individual communists to play a leadership role in the world communist movement.

Struggles over leadership seem to be correlated with fanaticism in a group. Within the old, established Christian denominations, in which ideological enthusiasm is only moderate, conflicts over the controlling offices are relatively mild. The small, evangelical sects, by contrast, often erupt in intense struggles over leadership roles; and losers in this power struggle often break away to form new, even smaller organizations. European political leaders show a similar desire to dominate a small group, as opposed to sharing power in a large organization. Finally, as evidence for this generalization, we may note the intensity of the schisms and factionalism in the world communist movement thirty years ago, when the fervor of party members was on the whole higher than today.

The west should feel encouraged either by a diminution of communist fanaticism or by fission in the communist movement as national communist parties seek autonomy. Social violence is fostered if strong motives, such as nationalism and ideological fervor, reinforce one another. A plurality of power centers within the communist world will, therefore, reduce the dangers of a world war based on ideological issues.

Efforts to separate the nationalistic and ideological components of the existing east-west conflict call for some reexamination of our ideas about the use of military force to resolve disputes. In a confrontation with Russia we can, in extremity, resort to missiles and H-bombs. But such military tactics are futile against an ideology. To quote Stringfellow Barr, commenting on Secretary Dulles and his futile efforts to use military methods where they could not function: "We did not roll back communism—except in sonorous speeches . . . We built a *cordon sanitaire* of CENTO, METO, and SEATO and were amazed to find that ideas flitted over them and agents filtered through them."[6]

It is not likely that dedicated communists will be deterred by our technological superiority and military power. Our history teaches us that repressive measures of the British in 1775 merely fanned the flames of revolt. If people believe in communist ideology, they are not likely to give up their beliefs under military threat; and if they did, they would be like the thousands of heathens converted by the sword to Christianity — they would give only lip service to the imposed ideals.

DEMOCRATIC IDEOLOGY AS A RESOURCE

Policy decisions in American resistance to communist expansion have ignored the principle that the best way to oppose a religion is with a better religion. Ideas cannot be stopped by bullets, nor by radar and Nike-Zeus missile defenses. An important resource in this conflict is our own heritage of a democratic ideology.

History teaches us that oppressive rule by European monarchs generated a democratic revolution, and that this revolutionary belief was capable of mobilizing the same human fervor, the same intense dedication, which communists often manifest today. The ideals of 1776 were considered exportable; indeed, in the early years of the USA, the American embassy in almost every European capital was seen as a hot-bed of subversion. Robert Palmer notes that "In Ireland and in the Dutch provinces, they (the sympathizers with the Americans) formed militia companies, wore uniforms, attended drills, and built up an actual revolutionary pressure."[7] It is worth noting that the Bolsheviks, in repudiating foreign property rights after the 1917 revolution, could have pointed to an American precedent: Much British-owned property was seized without compensation during and immediately after our revolution. Thus there are psychological similarities in the manifestations of these two ideologies.

This parallel does not imply that communism and the democratic ideology are the same; in some respects they are opposites. The important point is this: Discontented, oppressed people in various parts of the world are looking for a solution to their troubles. Communism offers a dramatic instance of a successful revolution. If we offer them no alternative, leaders of frustrated groups will tend to adopt the communist ideology and to imitate communist tactics. As will be noted later (Chapter 10), the emerging nations show this tendency to an alarming extent. And we cannot deal with the problem by sending military equipment to shore up regimes like that we fought in 1776. Not only are such policy decisions contrary to our own cherished ideology; they are also doomed to failure. The only way to deal with this phenomenon is to seek the causes of discontent and remove them. If we revive our own American ideals and preach them in the under-developed areas of the world, we may find that we have a far more effective weapon against the communist religion than any military alliance.

We cannot, of course, stop with mere preaching. Our actions at home must be in harmony with these ideals. We cannot indulge our anti-Negro prejudice, for example, if we wish to win wholehearted co-operation from the colored two thirds of the human race. Nor can we

inspire enthusiasm for our economic system if we again allow great
factories and millions of workers to stand idle. Our domestic policies
are in a very real sense a part of the Cold War.

IDEOLOGY AND NATIONALISM: A CONCLUSION

The democratic ideology is not now so distinctively American as
it was in 1783. One can advocate individual freedom without being
stigmatized as an American propagandist. Similarly, there seems reason
to hope that communism and Russian nationalism are becoming separate loyalties. This is a hopeful sign for world peace. The dynamic
power of an evangelical ideology and a potent nationalism is very great.
Acting independently, they are perceptibly less threatening.

We of the West must strive, in every way possible, to accelerate
this separation of communism and Russian nationalism, so that the two
can be dealt with independently.[8] Just as peace between England and
Spain became feasible after the religious issue was separated from the
power question, so peace in the modern world may be a practically
attainable goal after the "religious" issue of communism versus capitalism is separated from questions of national power. As long as these
competing ideologies are identified with the power and welfare of specific
nations, violence is almost inevitable. When it becomes possible to deal
with communist nations without regard to political ideology, we
shall make significant progress toward a stable mode of international
existence.

The possibility of a split between these two powerful dynamic forces
was demonstrated in 1948 when Yugoslavia broke away from Soviet
domination. The split was primarily a reflection of Yugoslav nationalism, but the Stalinist policy of milking the satellites economically was
also a factor. Trade was arranged in such fashion that most of the
benefits accrued to Russia, while the satellites remained agricultural.
(It is interesting to note that the recent five-year plans of the satellites
have provided for diversified industrialization in all of them, at times
to the point of inefficiency; this change is probably intended by communist planners to minimize the likelihood of further Titoist rebellions.)

In exploring tactics in the world struggle, therefore, we must not
make the mistake of assuming that communism is nothing more than
Russian nationalism. Communism is a religion, a faith, with the same
tremendous power to release and activate human energies that such
movements have possessed in the past. Further, every communist dreams
of his own personal power and of material comforts; and these dreams
reinforce his dedication to the strengthening of the party. Unless the

democratic West can find some comparable source of human dedication, it may be that communism will prove to be indeed "the wave of the future."

7
Economic Influences on Thinking

Emotional states such as hostility, fear, a desire for power, or other strong motives may distort human thinking. But these are by no means the only factors which need to be considered. Images of foreign nations may also be affected by such day-to-day influences as a man's occupation, his income, his church affiliation, and his friends.

My concern is with the question: Do these factors produce any kind of systematic bias in opinions and judgments? It is important to inquire, for example, whether decisions on foreign policy are affected by a man's economic background. Will nationalistic delusions of grandeur and of persecution be related, in any dependable fashion, to economic influences?

The importance of economic factors in the causation of war has been discussed at length by historians and philosophers. Some have asserted that all wars are simply property feuds, or looting expeditions. Such a view would assign a primary and uncomplicated function to economic issues. Other experts have held that international wars are ways of displacing hostility from economic hardships and frustrations at home.

A more sophisticated view suggests that

a man's economic stake in society may, perhaps unconsciously, determine his thinking about foreign policy. He may endorse aggressive, nationalistic policies without consciously realizing that he is furthering his own economic welfare. (And, as in the case of the Krupps and Thyssens in Germany, he may in the long run damage his economic empire.)

THE DELUSION OF ECONOMIC ADVANTAGE

The simplest case of economic motivation for war is that of primitive war for slaves, for loot, for hunting grounds or fertile soil. This has become more complex in recent years with wars for territorial expansion or control of markets. In these cases, economic issues have played a fairly important part in the official explanations of the cause of a given war. About the accuracy of such explanations under primitive conditions, there can hardly be any doubt. The Babylonian king who marched the Jews into slavery or the Arab who captured Negroes to be shipped to the New World had no problem explaining his military project. It was purely economic in motivation. The seizure of India by Britain, of Angola by Portugal, and of the Congo by Belgium likewise had frankly economic as well as prestige motivation.

There is ample evidence that certain individuals within the conquering nation profited mightily by these imperial ventures. But did the nation as a whole benefit from imperialism? Sir Norman Angell, in a dramatic book called *The Great Illusion,*[1] tried to show, even before World War I, that the economic gain from conquest was illusory. Kenneth Boulding, a respected economist, comments that "There seems to be a good deal of casual evidence that Norman Angell was right and that, from an economic point of view, war is a great illusion; but nobody has tried to explain why the illusion has so powerful a hold on the minds of men."[2]

Actually, many writers have speculated on why war has such an appeal for men. Some of their conclusions have been examined in earlier pages of this book. The crucial point, they argue, is found in the phenomenon of nationalism. "If I cannot be wealthy myself, there is some gratification in being a part of a wealthy, powerful nation." Further, nationalism fosters the delusion that imperialistic conquest is for good ends. The Briton (immortalized by Rudyard Kipling) who was out to civilize the "lesser breeds without the law" has been replaced by the communist who holds that "communism is in their best interests, and we'll give it to them if we have to shoot them all in the process."

There are, of course, other major aspects to economic nationalism. Tariffs and trade restrictions are rationalized on the theory that I ought to put the welfare of my close neighbor above the welfare of some not-quite-human fellow five thousand miles away. And national defense arguments are especially effective in building support for trade restrictions: "We shall need the horseshoe industry if a war comes, so we must keep out all alien horseshoes."

In the long run, the explanation for the powerful hold that nationalism has on the minds of men must be found in the motives and perceptions of the citizens themselves. Once this attitude has been firmly implanted (as it is in most little children of the civilized world), policies calculated to help "us" and harm "them" are readily accepted. The nationalist, moreover, is selectively blind to evidence which opposes his views. Thus, even though tariffs and protectionists do economic harm at home and stir up hostility abroad, the nationalist refuses to face up to these facts.

The Devil Theory: Armament Makers

Perhaps the simplest version of the economic factors causing war is that which became popular in the 1930s. One popular book, *Merchants of Death,*[3] suggested that owners of munitions factories coldly and callously stirred up hostility between nations for the sake of profitable sales. This theory was not without some factual support. George Seldes, in his *Iron, Blood and Profits,*[4] recounts incidents such as the following:

> A false item was planted in a French newspaper announcing plans for a new, large order for machine guns. The German newspapers seized upon this and demanded to know what their government was doing to counter the French menace. The German government bought more machine guns, and then the French actually increased their own orders. [pp. 57-59]
>
> Zaharoff, a Greek armaments builder, presented his nation with a submarine. Then he sold two to Turkey. The Greek government then felt impelled to buy two more, and so on. The British navy supplied missions to both the Greek and Turkish navies and encouraged them to buy British military equipment; loans were made with the proviso that the money must be spent in Great Britain. [pp. 33-35]
>
> Japanese armaments firms were supplying more than 30 percent of China's munitions purchases in 1930, only a few years before the Japanese army attempted to take over the Asiatic giant. Wars among the Chinese warlords were encouraged by salesmen for European firms. [pp. 110-111]

That these instances are not fabrications and are fairly typical of dealings at the time is attested by the hearings of the Nye Committee of the U.S. Senate and by a special commission of the League of Nations. Men want money, power, and profit; they are prepared to bribe government officials to get orders and to hire newspaper writers who will exaggerate "threatening" incidents in order to increase defense purchases.

It would be nice to dismiss these tales as evidence of the bad old days. Many people feel that capitalists have reformed and that wars are no longer started for financial gain. Some doubt is cast on this optimistic view by a *New York Times* account of the career of Juan March. According to the *Times* obituary, Señor March financed the Franco revolution—including chartering the plane which took General Franco to Morocco, where he organized the army that attacked the legally elected government.

> After the war Señor March was amply rewarded. The national tobacco monopoly was returned to him (he had held it under Alfonso) . . . He arranged barter deals with Hitler and Mussolini . . . In 1950, by a legal ruse in a provincial court, Señor March gained control of a foreign-owned public utilities empire worth $250,000,000 . . . while the United States, Belgium, and Canadian governments protested in vain.[5]

Among other events in his career were these: In 1923, he was arrested on charges of selling guns to the Arabs in Morocco (who were rebelling against Spain!). During World War I, he profited by selling to both the English and the Germans.

Much of our knowledge of the role of economic self-seeking by business men, especially those in the arms field, came from the Russian Revolution of 1917 and the German Revolution of 1918, both of which made available the secret documents of the czar and the kaiser. Another major source of information is the Nye Committee investigation of 1934, which had subpoena powers. Currently lacking such studies, we may be grossly underinformed with regard to the role of the armament industry in troubles in Cuba, Laos, Viet Nam, Korea, and elsewhere. It has been freely asserted that members of the Kuomintang sold American military goods (supplied in order to aid the Chiang government) to the communist rebels in 1947 and 1948. This probably did not cause, but it may have hastened, the triumph of the communists in 1949. Perhaps evidence of a similar sort is concealed in various chancelleries around the world; the archeologists who explore the ruins of this hemisphere after World War III may find even more spectacular evidence of profit-seeking activities, which increased the probability of war.

In all realism, however, we must note that much of the contemporary high-pressure selling of munitions has been done at the insistence of governments. The U.S. Department of Defense has openly encouraged defense contractors to make sales to smaller nations embroiled in bitter quarrels with their neighbors; in some instances, we have genially sold equipment to both sides. Over $4 billion worth of such materials, often financed by loans or grants from our foreign aid program, were shipped abroad in the period 1962-65. While these sales were rationalized as strengthening the security of the USA, they often diminished the security of other nations; e.g., Argentina bought 50 jet fighter-bombers from Douglas, whereupon Chile asked for arms to defend against anticipated Argentine aggression. As noted elsewhere, our aid to Pakistan contributed materially to the brief war with India in 1965.

We cannot, therefore, picture the arms salesman as a "devil." He sees himself as a patriotic agent of our defense program and accepts no responsibility for the carnage his products facilitate. It will not even help a great deal to curtail his activities unless we simultaneously work on reductions of the frustrations, conflicts, jealousies, and suspicions which cause the weapons to be used.

The Devil Theory: Imperialism

Another considerably oversimplified view of the economic cause of war places the blame with the need of capitalism for expanding markets. Lenin,[6] of course, is the most famous exponent of this theory, but he is by no means alone in endorsing it.

We may judge from statements of American businessmen that the capitalist system does indeed function smoothly only when it is steadily expanding. The argument about the "growth rate" — now intensified because the communist bloc sometimes appears to be growing faster than we are — makes it clear that our system develops serious problems when opportunity for expansion is missing.

Imperialism refers to the notion that the businessman will expand even if this means grabbing off territory by military means, bribing subservient local governments, etc. India was first invaded not in the name of the British government but rather for the British East India Company. Similarly, in North America, the Hudson Bay Company fought wars and drove the Indian population out of territory they desired. In the USA, private companies sold large blocks of western land to settlers, who then demanded military protection against the Indians who had become hostile because of being dispossessed. More recently, we can point to the annexation of Alsace-Lorraine by Germany after 1871 and by France in 1919. The mineral and industrial wealth in these provinces made them an attractive prize.

While national strategic considerations may be important in the drive to seize such territories, it would be unwise to overlook the very substantial profits which will be reaped by industrialist friends of the winning government leaders. The potency of such economic motives reminds us that we cannot plan for an international order that freezes the status quo. We must provide some legal means for the peaceful growth of dynamic expanding economies.

It would be misleading to imply that capitalists have always operated to heighten national hostilities and encourage violence. In some instances, business interests have perceived international hostility as a disruptive factor interfering with profitable ventures at home. In such circumstances, the weight of the business group is thrown against aggressive adventures. A conspicuous example in American history is that of the Spanish-American War, for which business as a whole showed a profound lack of enthusiasm. Foster R. Dulles notes that Hearst and other newspapermen played up "atrocities" in Cuba and shouted for aggressive action against Spain:

> In spite of all such agitation the conservative business interests in the country steadfastly resisted any idea of intervention. They remained fearful of its possible effects on the national economy, and they still saw no advantage in the possibilities of overseas expansion that war with Spain might open up. Commercial and banking journals almost without exception declared that war would endanger the newly established currency stabilization, interrupt commerce, and injure all business. Support for this position by the moneyed class created what often seemed to be a sharp division of opinion along social lines. One contemporary letter writer stated that he had not met a single man in "the aristocratic upper crust" who felt that there was any justified cause for hostilities with Spain, but when one went "below that crust . . . the wish for war is almost universal."[7]

The greater belligerence of the poorer groups in the population may perhaps have been a function of the depression of 1896 and the corresponding insecurity felt by many farmers and manual workers. We do not have enough evidence to be certain on this point, but it is at least clear that the capitalists did not support this particular belligerent adventure.

Profit seeking, at least in an individual sense, is not an essential element in imperialism. History reminds us that the Russians seized Lithuania, Latvia, and Estonia in 1939, as well as part of Poland. In 1940 they annexed a segment of Finland. In 1945 the Red Army installed communist regimes, subservient to Moscow, in Poland, Rumania, Hungary, and Bulgaria. Czechoslovakia got the same treatment in 1948. The economic resources of these satellite nations were exploited for the benefit of the Soviet Union until about 1953, when rebellious uprisings impelled an easing of pressure. Many economists hold that military power is being used to keep terms of trade favorable to the USSR, but statistics on trade within the communist area are so restricted and distorted that it is difficult to validate or to disprove this assertion.

The communists probably sought expansion on the basis of their quasi-religious belief in their mission to bring a new world to birth and without consideration of economic gain to Russians. It is, however, also quite possible that communist leaders were aware of the potential economic advantages to Russian citizens gained from exploiting the Baltic states and the satellites in eastern Europe. Thus, ideological fanaticism and economic gain reinforced one another as dynamic impulses. The communist, of course, would not see any harm accruing to the workers and peasants in the conquered territories. It would be only the "fascist" landlords and capitalists whose wealth would be siphoned off into Russia.

ECONOMIC NATIONALISM AND INTERNATIONAL FRICTIONS

Not all efforts to gain national economic benefits involve seizure of territory. Tariffs, quotas, exchange restrictions, and a variety of related devices have developed as ways of achieving the same aim without direct conquest. These tactics, however, stir up hostility, raise the tension level, and so must be assumed to contribute to the causes of war.

The important role of tariffs and similar measures in causing wars can be attested by a survey of experts conducted in 1938. A committee of psychologists, set up by the Society for the Psychological Study of Social Issues,[8] polled several hundred American social scientists on policies which would help reduce international tensions and wars. Virtually unanimous support was given to proposals that tariffs and economic discrimination between nations be abolished. These proposals were more favored than any others in a list of fifty-nine.

The reason for this unanimity is not hard to locate. The citizen of a nation is likely to take a short-run view of his own welfare and to ignore the harm done to citizens of other countries by tariffs, quotas, export subsidies, and other forms of economic warfare. The experts, looking at the problem in a larger perspective, saw that every such action provokes a reaction: Aggression breeds counteraggression; discrimination fosters counterdiscrimination.

Economic hardship induces hostility. Hostility is likely to lead to impulsive, ill-considered countermeasures. If these produce hostility abroad, a vicious cycle gets under way. Trade wars have, in the past, been preludes to military conflicts. We must be aware of these possibilities in deciding about economic policy.

Further, a policy is perceived differently if it is a national rather than private decision. If American businessmen oppose Japanese textile imports, this produces some friction; but if the American government bars such imports, the Japanese hostility is focused on the entire nation. Conversely, we feel more indignant if the Japanese government takes action to bar American products from entering Japan — although it is obvious that, if we do not buy from them, they cannot purchase our products.

A major tenet of nationalism is that we take care of our own citizens regardless of the hardships inflicted on others. Unfortunately, a short-sighted interpretation of this can lead to much greater hardships for ourselves in the long run. We must learn to take into consideration the welfare of other human beings, not only because we value people as such but also because our own long-run welfare is at stake. The world has grown too small for us to ignore the impact of our policies abroad.

The fallacy of economic nationalism can be sketched briefly as follows: Bananas can be grown in New Hampshire, but only in very expensive greenhouses with elaborate equipment to provide the temperature and humidity conditions this plant requires. The Americans engaged in banana culture in New Hampshire obviously cannot sell in competition with Guatemalan growers, who do not need this elaborate installation. It is thus necessary to put a tariff of $1 per pound on bananas imported from abroad in order to protect this essential American industry. After all, if Guatemala goes communist, we might be cut off from our normal source of supply.

The example is fanciful; the logic, however, is utilized by all economic nationalists. Despite the obvious waste of resources and labor in production by inefficient means, the nationalist demands protection of "our workers" (he usually means our industrialists) and is indifferent to the damage done to our suppliers as well as to the high cost to our consumers. He exaggerates the role of his industry in relation to national security. He relies on an appeal to patriotism and concern for his fellows in order to rally support for what is, in most instances, a quite irrational policy.[9]

These are the ways in which economic factors truly play a significant role in foreign relations. Only a fool would suggest that the patriotic businessman is plotting to have men killed for his personal profit. He is certainly not engaged in such a cold-blooded process. However, the businessman is human. Like others, he will distort information he receives. He will exaggerate the threat to his nation if the supply of a certain commodity is controlled by foreigners. He will also magnify the injury to his workers and his stockholders if he fails because of foreign competition. Because he sees "us" as good and the foreigner as bad, he can readily rationalize the notion that legislation should protect the good against the bad. He refuses to be aware of the harm done to "us" as consumers by raising prices above the normal import level, and he also blocks out any awareness of the injury done to our suppliers abroad by his tactics. Thus, with a clear conscience, he can advocate a policy which realistically will engender friction and hostility between nations.

The desire of the businessman to have a private and profitable preserve, protected from competition, is not restricted to the USA. Japan's conquest of Manchuria and China was calculated to provide Japanese manufacturers with exactly this kind of protection. In October 1938, during the diplomatic skirmishing with Japan which preceded Pearl Harbor, our Department of State published a note expressing strong protest against the "discriminatory exchange control . . . monopoly . . . and censorship" which were operating to handicap American enterprise in those areas. And in the negotiations in late 1941, Secretary of State Cordell Hull told the Japanese envoys that " . . . if the Japanese could not do anything now on those three points — getting troops out of China, *commercial policy,* and the Tripartite Agreement — he could only leave to Japan what Japan could do."[10] And in the four principles that Hull submitted to Ambassador Nomura on Nov. 25, 1941, "equality of commercial opportunity and treatment" ranked as a major principle.

American manufacturers have often complained of unfair Japanese competition because of low Japanese hourly wages. The manufacturers in Japan complain about low American costs of production because of high mechanization. The nationalist who wants a protected market does not care whether his argument is logical; it need only appeal to national patriotism and offer him a profitable advantage.

Does economic nationalism increase international hostility? The answer is self-evident. In recent years our newspapers and magazines have been filled with articles describing American resentment of foreign trade restrictions or recounting foreign annoyance at our tariffs and arbitrary customs valuations. West German chicken growers complain about our shipments of chickens; American steel makers complain about imports of German steel pipe.

Do trade restrictions provoke hostile retaliation? Here we can be somewhat more precise. In 1930 the U.S. Congress passed the infamous Smoot-Hawley Tariff Act (signed by President Hoover over the protests of one thousand American economists.) The tariff was raised on hundreds of articles normally imported — to "protect American workers." The result was a volley of restrictions on our exports. To cite a single case: Our imports from Canada dropped approximately $250 million (1929 to 1931); our exports to Canada dropped approximately $500 million in the same two year period.[11] Thus we damaged perhaps twice as many American jobs in this interchange as we protected.

Many other figures could be cited of the same sort, but this is not a book on economics. My point is only that, in past attempts to protect "our" people at the expense of "their" people, we have not only aroused hostility toward the USA but also hurt our businessmen and employees more than we aided them.

While economists have in recent years said little about economic sources of friction between the western nations, these factors are still important. In 1958, when the Eisenhower administration became alarmed about inflation and took such steps as raising interest rates and limiting overseas travel by dependents of military personnel, some of our European allies were hurt rather sharply. The British complained of deflationary effects on their economy, as did the French. Similarly, opposition to Japanese imports among the American pottery and textile industries has elicited some hostility among the Japanese. Even our Canadian neighbors frequently make unpleasant remarks about our "economic imperialism."

Can these kinds of economic frictions lead to war between nations now members of the western alliance? Not at present, for two obvious reasons. The first is the overwhelming power of the USA. Even when the Common Market is fully functional, it will lack the military potential to match American strength. The second is the general fear of Russia and Communist China, which will keep the western powers in the same bed, even if unhappy about the relationship. But, as tensions have obviously developed between Russia and China, so it is obvious that tensions exist and could be exacerbated in the western world. The exact issues in the Sino-Soviet rift may be primarily ideological, economic, or strategic; we are not kept well informed by our opponents. But the main issues in the West are economic, and a relaxation of tension vis-à-vis the East may well allow these to flare up in at least open expressions of resentment and hostility.

A fundamental aspect of this problem is, of course, the notion of sovereignty. Each nation acts in its own interest and disregards the welfare of enemy and ally alike. Such actions are guaranteed to provoke anger, if not retaliation.

As Premier Clemenceau said to President Wilson forty years ago, America wants peace but is unwilling to pay the price. We want *both* our high standard of living and the loyalty of our allies. But the latter will be difficult to maintain if the former is protected at their expense.

Economic frictions among allies are, of course, affected profoundly by the ever-present Cold War. Thus, the Japanese textile industry becomes a source of international tension as import restrictions in Europe and America force the Japanese to consider a more amicable approach to Communist China. Western leaders, appalled by the strategic implications of such a shift, attempt to devise compromise solutions to the problem of markets. In such an instance, the underlying dynamic is economic, but its effect is mediated by strategic considerations of military alliances rather than by simple profit-and-loss figures. The West will find itself faced with the necessity of imposing some economic hardship upon its own entrepreneurs and workers for the greater benefit of military security in the Far East.

Similarly, our concern with establishing intimate relations with the new European giant, the Common Market, is not based simply on profit-making calculations. American industry could compete in other parts of the world with Common Market firms. But possible frictions with our European allies over such competition might weaken the strategic bonds of NATO; we run the risk of rendering ourselves less secure vis-à-vis the communist nations.

We might say, then, that contemporary theory as to the economic factors in international tension is a kind of economic-psychological mixture. It grants that capitalist nations seek favorable trade outlets, that entrepreneurs are looking for profit opportunities. But it also recognizes the emotional implications of competition, especially when this gets involved in national policy (tariffs, quotas, etc.). And it is the damage to our system of military alliances which is the immediate dynamic agent producing change in economic policy.

Finally, it is important that we relate our sketch of economic influences on thinking to the displacement of hostility. When economic conditions are bad, people become frustrated and aggressive. If they blame the king for their hardships, they may decide to revolt. It was for this reason that the wily old German chancellor, Bismarck, stated that his expansionist foreign policy was "a lightning rod for the Social-

Democratic danger." His wars with Denmark, Austria, and France aimed both at territorial expansion and at diverting revolutionary hostilities away from the ruling class in Prussia.

It is probably not irrelevant that the Japanese invasion of Manchuria in 1931 followed closely upon the collapse of the world silk market, with consequent unemployment and dangerous unrest in Japanese cities. Historians have noted many other such coincidences of incipient revolution and aggressive foreign policy. The most notable instance in recent years is undoubtedly the rise of nazism. Hitler was laughed at by the Germans during the brief prosperity of the Weimar Republic; but, after 1929, his nationalistic belligerence attracted a wide and active following.

The communist world may have similar problems. The strife within the satellites in 1953 and 1956 seems to have been associated with a tough line toward the West. Red China overran Tibet at a time when peasant unrest was rapidly increasing because of decreased food supplies.

I suggested earlier that, as the communist nations became prosperous, there would be an inevitable tendency toward comfortable relaxation, with a decline in evangelistic fervor for spreading communism. This is based upon the implicit assumption that communist expansionist ventures are often utilized by the men in the Kremlin to divert hostilities which might otherwise threaten their power position.

ECONOMICS AND DELUSION: A SUMMARY

While the term "economics" identifies "the dismal science" to college students, it signifies everyday bread-and-butter relationships for adults. Like the man who suddenly learned that he had been speaking prose all of his life, many of us discover at a late date that while earning a living we were also engaged in economic activity.

As regards the precarious balance of nonviolence, which we today call peace, economic factors play at least three roles:

1. Economic advantage or threat may influence us to accept delusory ideas about ourselves or about other nations.

2. Economic motives impel some of us, deliberately or otherwise, to foster and spread such delusory notions, especially the delusion of persecution by foreigners. This includes use of such propaganda by leaders who wish to deflect hostility deriving from economic hardships at home onto enemies abroad.

3. Measures of economic nationalism — tariffs, quotas, trade licensing, embargoes, and similar devices — are hostile devices, appropriately called economic warfare. They resemble, and may promptly be followed by, overt military action.

In all of these instances I have emphasized the probability that the individual is not consciously acting to maximize his economic advantage. The makers of the Polaris missile would not deliberately stir up fears of Russia to increase their profits. But the mind is subtly biased to exaggerate one kind of information and to ignore other kinds. Just as no one expects the tobacco industry to accept the evidence about lung cancer, so we cannot expect the armament industry to view the Russians as peace-loving and harmless. On the contrary, these industrialists are selectively sensitive to every bit of information showing the Russians to be evil, aggressive, and dangerous. The Russians, I note, cooperate well in this process.

We must also note that labor union leaders and members are economically motivated toward nationalism. Unionists regularly testify in favor of tariffs and quotas to protect their jobs from "unfair competition." Just as the union official seeks gains for his members regardless of the cost to consumers in higher prices, so he will support protectionist policies that are harmful abroad when he believes that such policies will help him and his members. It is interesting also to note that unions in the defense industries seem to be much more concerned about the Russian menace than are unions in consumer-goods areas.

The psychologist would not accuse either employers or employees of cynically seeking larger incomes at the risk of their countrymen's lives. But it can be pointed out that anyone having an economic stake in a certain industry will see world events in such a way as to favor that industry. When we consider the large percentages of the work force in the USA and in the USSR who are engaged in production of war equipment, it is obvious that warnings to fear the enemy will fall upon receptive ears. This makes the task of seeking rational solutions to international disputes even more difficult.

The picture is not completely gloomy. As many observers have pointed out, a few economic influences are loaded in the other direction — toward international cooperation, and hence toward peaceful settlement of disputes. The importer of raw materials, or even of manufactured goods, will not wish to see his supplies cut off and so will perceive issues in a manner favorable to international cooperation. Persons with investments in troubled areas may foresee the destruction caused by war and hence oppose a decision to use violence. But, in general, the cooperation between economic interests and nationalism operates to favor forceful (i.e., warlike) solutions to problems.

8
Social Role
and Policy Decisions

The human mind is a frail instrument, and thinking is far too easily distorted by such factors as the opportunity for economic gain. But this is only one of many kinds of influences which may lead to faulty perceptions and biased judgments.

With respect to international affairs, there is one further category that needs special examination. This is the influence of a definite social role upon an individual's mode of thinking. I refer specifically to the consequences of taking on a certain responsibility, a task, in the area of international relations. Just as the officer of a corporation takes on certain obligations for the welfare of his firm, so a governmental official assumes obligations for the welfare of his nation. Each instance involves effects upon the thought processes, but I shall comment only on the influence of roles in government.

THE CONCEPT OF SOCIAL ROLE

We can, of course, easily think of a social role as separate from the person executing the role—even though the role would not exist if no one filled it. A role is composed chiefly of a set of socially prescribed behaviors. The role of President of the United States tends to remain constant, although different presidents have modified the pattern in varying degrees. The role of admiral is fairly sharply defined by organization tables and assignment of duties. When a new man takes on such a task, he knows reasonably well what is expected of him and how the role has been handled in the past. The role of a department head is defined by an organization chart, and a job description—and expectations of superiors and co-workers.

It should be clear, then, that the role is really defined more by the people surrounding it than by the incumbent. If an army major decided that his role included denouncing the president as incompetent or traitorous, he would be removed from his position. A corporation president who decided that his primary role was to make employees happy, regardless of profits, would be fired by his board of directors. In some instances, the general population, or a substantial part of it, determines role content: A congressman may win reelection despite a jail sentence if the voters approve of his behavior.

My interest, however, is not so much in the constraints imposed upon the individual by people around him. I wish rather to demonstrate the extent to which his role modifies his thinking; so that after functioning in a role, he sees events differently, weights evidence differently, and arrives at different conclusions as compared with his prior behavior. I have, for other purposes, already introduced the illustration of John Foster Dulles, who has been described as excessively rigid in his policies as secretary of state although he had, in an earlier book, advocated a flexible approach to problems of diplomacy. Is there anything in the concept of role to help us understand this change in his actions and attitudes?

THE PRINCIPLE OF AGENCY

Every governmental official must accept the *principle of agency*—the rule that he cannot act on his own impulses but must be guided by his responsibility to the government. This rule is not limited to bureaucrats, of course: An industrial employee who refuses to obey orders is fired, and a soldier in like circumstances is court-martialed. The principle of agency says that one's ethical standards and personal values may not influence an official's decision; he must decide on the basis of the obligation he owes to his organization.

The necessity of such regulations may seem obvious. Few will argue that the secretary of the treasury should feel free to contribute our national funds to persons, however needy, who are not legally entitled to receive them. He may give away his personal fortune but not the funds for which he is responsible to the nation. Similarly, our secretary of defense might feel that it would be perfectly safe to provide nuclear weapons to Italy; but under present legislation he is forbidden to do so. He must make decisions in light of these pressures.

This, however, is only the top of the iceberg—the 10 percent which is readily visible. The principle of agency has a more subtle and far-reaching effect upon the process of judgment. When a man first takes on a job, he is conscious of the distinction between his personal desires and the rules he must follow. As a consequence of repeated behavior within this framework, he becomes accustomed to disregarding some considerations while paying close attention to others. He knows well the kinds of evidence he must use as a guide to action in his role as agent. Soon he fails to see conflicting evidence at all. The learning process operates to make him selectively sensitive to facts bearing on his social role while he becomes blind to contradictory material. At this point, he is often unconscious of any conflict between his personal values and the policy lines of his government or bureau or military unit.

Dehumanized Perceptions

The principle of agency has its psychological corollary in the principle of dehumanized perceiving. If an agency requires a man to do something which his moral training forbids, he can resolve the conflict by seeing the victim as subhuman. Thus German bureaucrats, required by their positions to implement persecution of the Jews, found it convenient to believe nazi propaganda and see the Jew as some kind of animal not entitled to humane treatment. In a sense, the bureaucrat also dehumanizes himself. He denies that he, as a total individual, is acting; it is only his social role which is involved.

The trial of Adolf Eichmann served to bring into focus the problem of agency. Eichmann pleaded (we know not with how much sincerity) that he was but a cog in a machine, that he had no freedom of action, that his personal conscience was not involved.[1] Without attempting to exonerate Eichmann, let us consider what other implications arise here. Col. Clyde Eatherly, a pilot involved in the bombing of Hiroshima, has been hospitalized for a mental breakdown because of the tremendous guilt he says he felt over killing so many people.[2] Should he have refused the order to do so? Should Eichmann have refused to obey Hitler?

Consider the circumstance of a guerrilla warfare situation in Viet Nam. We have been burning villages which are used by the communist guerrillas, and pushing the peasants into new, fortified towns. Can we leave such decisions to the tender consciences of individual officers, or

Our emotions often lead us to underestimate the power
of other nations and exaggerate our superiority.
For example, this cartoon represented American thinking
early in 1940. (Cartoon by Seibel, in
The *Richmond Times-Dispatch*. Reprinted by permission
of Fred O. Seibel.)

do we indoctrinate them with the requirement that they must obey orders no matter what suffering is inflicted on the Vietnamese families involved?

And let us now move this decision back to the diplomatic level. We are told that Sir Edward Grey, British foreign secretary in 1914, wept at the necessity of declaring war on Germany. But he took the essential steps none the less. Each diplomat may—and probably does—sincerely regret the necessity for war. But as he sees his obligation to his nation, this is unavoidable.

The principle of agency, the view that "I am not personally responsible; I am acting only as an agent of a larger and more powerful group," lies at the root of this problem. To some, it is inconceivable that we should allow individual conscience to operate in realms of military and diplomatic decision; the fact that Col. Eatherly was horrified by the thought of killing 100,000 civilians is irrelevant. To others, the only hope of achieving a more humanitarian world lies in just this breakthrough: In requiring that each individual, from Eichmann to Eatherly, assert his right and his power to refuse those demands of his national leaders which are contrary to higher ethical values.

The individual who takes such a stand must, of course, be prepared for punishment. The punishment, for either Eichmann or Eatherly, would have been death. The nazis had no qualms about liquidating dissenters, and Eatherly was under military discipline in a global war. Not many human beings have the courage to put their necks on the block in the service of their ethical principles.

Sovereignty and Autonomy

The doctrine of unlimited national sovereignty is also relevant to the problems just cited. If the nation possesses the absolute right to adopt a course of action in its own interest, with no obligation to consider the welfare of other nations, then the destructive implications of agency are underscored.[3] The chief executive of a nation then has an obligation to advance the welfare of his country with completely ruthless disregard for others.

Realistically, of course, no national leader (Hitler possibly excepted) acts in this fashion. We recognize a *de facto* limitation on sovereignty, even if we deny any limitation in principle. The limitation is shown by the coalition of powers which organized against Hitler. Any ruthless pursuit of national aggrandizement such as his must have the same consequences.

The facts suggest that it would be helpful to propose a revision of the doctrine of sovereignty. This revision would accept the realistic situation that no nation, not even the USA with its incredible concentration of industrial and military power, is free to decide on policy with complete disregard of other nations. It would also concede that, since the nation is not above constraints, the diplomat is justified in according ethical values an important place in his guide lines for making decisions about policy. He should consider effects on other nations, not merely on his own country.

The issue can perhaps be clarified by commenting on the question of foreign aid. An economist, J. S. Berliner, has noted that the USSR provided aid to underdeveloped nations only when such aid is in the Russian interest; he speaks of the Russians as pursuing "something other than purely philanthropic purposes."[4] But this is also true of the American aid program. The president and the Congress have repeatedly asserted that our mutual security funds are appropriated because this is "in the best interest of the United States."

The use of such phrases in congressional speeches and in public testimony by the secretary of defense provides ready ammunition for communist propagandists. They point out to the new nations of Asia and Africa that the USA is not really interested in helping them; Uncle Sam is only out for his own advantage. Foreign aid is thus a concealed form of exploitation.

It would be far more constructive for the USA to take a firm stand in favor of human welfare and to stop propping up the delusion of a sovereignty which no longer exists. In the long run, our welfare is inextricably tied to that of the peoples of South America, Africa, and Asia. Congress should assert that our aid program is not dictated solely by our selfish interest (as it probably is not, in the short run) but by our concern for human welfare. The role of the diplomat would thus be made more complicated but perhaps less frustrating in that he would not be compelled to ignore ethical issues when these conflict with a traditional definition of his role as an agent of a sovereign nation.

Regional Loyalties and National Policy

A less pressing but still important aspect of the principle of agency derives from fractionated or regional responsibilities. The average member of the Congress will state quite frankly that he feels obligated most of the time to vote for the interest of his region and not solely for the welfare of the entire nation.[5] Usually, he will expand on this by asserting the identity of the two—what's good for cotton is good for the country; but his policy decisions are guided by his role as agent for his constituents.

This fractionation within the legislative body is responsible for one curious phenomenon of American politics; namely, that only the president speaks for the entire nation. Being charged with protecting and advancing the welfare of *all* the people, he is obligated to be alert to issues which are ignored by the regionally minded congressman. He is also faced repeatedly with the need to resist moves that are to the selfish advantage of one region but damaging to the whole. In practice, he engineers various kinds of compromises in which regions get some selfish advantage—but balanced and whittled down in such fashion that the national injury is minimized. Farm subsidies and tariff policy are obvious examples of this process.

Bureaucratic Loyalties

Similar to regional loyalty is the devotion of a government official to the welfare and expansion of his agency. He will support policy proposals which will increase his budget, get him closer to positions of power, or provide more prestige. While selfish gain is not hard to find in such policies, the individual often is conscious only of his wish to strengthen the fine, noble, virtuous department in which he serves.

Unfortunately, this delusion of departmental virtue tends to evoke its polar opposite, the delusion that other competing departments are bad. Thus, intense rivalries proliferate between State and Defense, between Labor and Commerce, between Agriculture and Interior. (We shall comment later on competition between military services.) Loyalty causes bureaucrats to conceal evidence which would indicate the failure or error of their agency. At the same time, they allow journalists access to data which point to wrongdoing in a competing department. I quote from a report of a subcommittee of the House of Representatives, which had investigated a particularly unpleasant example of this kind:

> We cannot condone the type of interdepartmental rivalry which was evidenced in the steady stream of ''leaks'' originating in the State Department, undoubtedly intended to preclude any other disposition of this proposed undertaking. This type of contention between agencies of our government can hardly serve to advance the interests of our foreign policy or of our national security.[6]

The extent to which these rivalries may influence major aspects of foreign policy has already been illustrated by the contradictory information fed to President Kennedy in the Bay of Pigs affair. A second illustration of the bizarre consequences has been provided by Norman Cousins, editor of the *Saturday Review:*

> Another example of misapplied authority occurred in
> Laos in 1960, when the popularly elected government of
> Souvanna Phouma was overthrown in a military coup . . .
> This writer does not know which agency of the U.S.
> government facilitated the coup, directly or indirectly, but
> he does know that there was a strong difference of opinion
> inside the U.S. government on the matter, and that for
> several months after the coup the United States was in the
> incredible position of paying the salaries of the armed
> forces both of the government and the insurgents.[7]

We are, I think, justified in assuming that the individuals involved
in such tactics are deeply convinced that their actions are patriotic and
essential to our national welfare. In fact, however, the action furthers
the expansion and potency of an agency within the government, while
preventing effective coordination and damaging the nation.

AGENCY: THE ROLE OF THE MILITARY OFFICER

The psychological effect of taking on a specified social role can also
be illustrated by considering the military officer. Just as the diplomat
is instructed to focus his attention on certain classes of events which may
affect his nation, so is the military man required to attend selectively.
Mainly, he looks for threats to our physical security; but this may
rapidly expand, as when he attempts to assess all developments within
this frame of reference. For example, a Russian general will not accept
American statements that a new cargo plane is just for civilian traffic;
he analyzes its possible use for transporting military equipment. The
effect of these role requirements is also illustrated by the traditional
conservatism of military men: Labor unions may tie up military production; hence, unions are to be distrusted and hobbled if possible.

To say these things is not to criticize the soldier. History certainly
indicates that one nation has often invaded another. The development
of the military role in all countries indicates that it has, in the past,
been useful for survival. (But it may now be obsolete, just as the role
of the king's astrologer has become obsolete. I shall comment on this
possibility later.)

The process of military training has two major effects upon thinking.
First, it sensitizes the individual so that he interprets all incoming
evidence as a probable threat. If the Germans are building a new highway, this may indicate a military plan for invasion of France. If the
Russians reduce the size of their army, this may mean that they now
have enough ICBM installations to pull a sneak attack on us.

Second, the training for violence inevitably disposes the military man to think in terms of forceful solutions. He has little confidence in negotiations, in peaceful settlements, in compromises. The only definitive solution is the one imposed by force. This is, of course, in the Clausewitz tradition. It does not, however, facilitate international cooperation.

The Narrowed Frame of Reference

Every social role involves narrowing the frame of reference for interpreting events. For the military man, it means focusing on military protection of his homeland without regard to incidental outcomes of his policy.

A regrettable example is that of our military aid to Pakistan. To shore up this nation against Communist China, the USA sent nearly $2 billion in armaments during the years 1955-65. This was done despite warnings from our ambassadors in New Delhi that the arms would be used against India—as actually happened in September 1965. No less an expert observer than John Kenneth Galbraith, the former Ambassador to India, testified that "The arms we supplied... caused the war between India and Pakistan... If we had not supplied arms, Pakistan would not have sought a military solution (to the Kashmir dispute)."[8] One can quibble with his use of the word "cause"; the causes included religious hostilities, economic interests in Kashmir, memories of the bloody riots at partition in 1948, and so on. But he is correct, apparently, in inferring that the armed clash would not have occurred if the Pakistani forces had not been well-equipped. (It should be noted that communist military leaders also make errors in supplying munitions; the anti-communist uprising in Indonesia in 1965 used Russian and Chinese weapons.) At any rate, it seems reasonable to conclude that focusing attention solely upon military protection of one's nation may have consequences of a deplorable type.

Institutionalized Hostility

The tendency of military men to make belligerent statements is notorious, although we have little information about the felt level of hostility involved. It may be that it is simply part of the social role to issue such warlike pronouncements, just as a politician naturally swings into a patriotic speech at the slightest provocation. On the other hand, we certainly must assume that the recipients of the speech overseas will interpret it as evidence of hostility and of danger to their country.

Consider the following fairly recent examples: General Nathan Twining was quoted as saying that if it weren't for the politicians he would settle the war in one afternoon by bombing Soviet Russia; and General Orvil A. Anderson was cited to the effect that he would be happy to carry out that bombing—"just give me the order to do it."[9]

When Americans read speeches by Zhukov, Malinovsky, and other Russian military leaders about obliterating us, we interpret them as evidence of their hostility. Further, we perceive them as threats of a *first strike,* not a retaliatory strike.

Have we any right to assume that the Russians are different? Is it not reasonable that they interpret speeches such as those by Twining and Anderson as also referring to a *first strike?* And—since it seems that our civilian government does not have much control over our military spokesmen—would it not be sensible of them to think that the military might act without governmental approval?

As I have noted above, a certain amount of hostility must presumably be communicated to the opponent so he will believe in our warning of a second strike. But if this hostility appears to him to be intolerably high, he must expect us to make a first strike. Under these circumstances, our hopes for a military détente, in which neither side attacks the other, begin to diminish. If the opponent is firmly convinced that he is about to be attacked with completely devastating force, he must, in duty to his people, attack us first.[10]

Why should 200 million human beings die in this kind of controversy? Because nobody is looking at the problem of the welfare and protection of the human race. The American military man has an obligation to protect and defend Americans only. The Russian leader is obligated to protect and defend Russians only. Given the delicate balance of terror now existing, it would be very easy for these 200 millions to die because rival nationalisms marshalled overwhelming power and could not control it intelligently.

I have referred earlier to the possibility that our propaganda depicting the Russians as villains might trigger some pathologically aggressive military officer into starting a war of misadventure. In this connection, it is interesting to consider the case of a false alert in November 1961, when SAC bombers were ordered to the runways (although they did not take off). A journalist reporting on the incident has this to say:

> For four minutes the alert was on. During that time [General] Power *did not notify President Kennedy of the situation* . . . We have learned from a well-informed source that in private briefings for important visiting firemen at his SAC headquarters Power has sounded off with political views that are dangerous for a man in his spot. He evidently subscribes to the opinion held in some Air Force quarters that coexistence is impossible."[11]

The journalist may or may not be correct in his evaluation of General Power. One point, however, is clear: It does not take a madman to foul up the controls and set off a "war by misadventure." All we need is an individual who is so sure of his judgments that he does not notify the president until the time remaining is too short for careful evaluation of the situation. In such a case, the president almost inevitably would be forced to approve an attack on the USSR.

Polarized Thinking

The tendency of the military man toward polarized thinking and the inability to see alternatives may be illustrated by the following remark ascribed to General Douglas MacArthur by Trumbull Higgins: "War's very object is victory, not prolonged indecision. In war, indeed, there can be no substitute for victory."[12]

No doubt MacArthur is correct in the sense of traditional ideas about the object of war. As Clausewitz said, the object of war is to impose one's will on the opponent; and this requires victory. Where the MacArthur statement is inadequate is in failing to recognize that victory is sometimes Pyrrhic. Today we could perhaps be victorious over the Russians but at the cost of suicide ourselves. In this case, prolonged indecision is a highly desirable substitute for victory.

There may be other substitutes for victory. An obvious one is a negotiated peace. According to many experts, the German military would have overthrown Hitler in 1944 if we had not been fixated on our slogan of "unconditional surrender." It is noteworthy that MacArthur deviated from the "unconditional surrender" formula for Japan and conceded points such as the retention of the emperor. And certainly, our settlement of the War of 1812 was not on a basis of victory; indeed, we were lucky to make any gains at all. Many other wars have ended in ambiguous settlements. Sometimes new disturbances led to reopening of the war, but in other instances a permanent basis for peaceful relations resulted.

The thinking of the traditional diplomat differs sharply from the military pattern on this point. A good diplomat always tries to leave his own way of retreat open from an exposed position, and most of the time he tries to avoid getting his opponent into a spot from which there is not escape but war. Many treaties incorporate face-saving devices by which the side which is retreating is allowed a minor gain to keep up the appearance of bargaining among equals. The demand for total victory mobilizes total opposition. For this reason the losses, even for the winner, are likely to get out of hand. Readiness to accept a compromise settlement, then, is a mark not only of emotional maturity but of intelligent bargaining. Unfortunately, the military man is trained to avoid compromise, to seek total victory, to impose his will upon the enemy.

The perennial controversy over whether high-ranking military officers should have unrestricted freedom to make public speeches about our foreign policy must be viewed in light of these factors. The traditional American position of civilian dominance over the military was based upon the fear that the professional soldier would be biased by primarily military considerations. This fear is not based upon doubt as to the patriotism of the soldier. It is based, rather, upon his tendency to see forceful solutions as the obvious and indeed the only techniques for dealing with international conflicts.[13] An appropriate analogy might be the conflict-of-interest statutes which forbid the secretary of defense to hold stock in industries which might benefit from munitions contracts. The fear is that the secretary, quite unconsciously, might favor his own firm. Similarly the military man is likely to distort situations in such a fashion as to exaggerate the importance of the armed services generally, while denying the relevance of potential solutions of a nonmilitary character.

Inter-service Rivalries

Just as the bureaucrat tends to magnify the importance of State, Defense, Agriculture, or whatever department he serves, so the military man exaggerates the contributions of his arm of service. The rivalries between army, navy, air force, and marines play an important part in thinking about defense policy. And the relative success of each chief of staff in influencing the president undoubtedly affects major national decisions.

The continued feuding over control of missiles and the space program illustrates this problem well. Each of the three major services has insisted on pressing research and development in the missile field, sometimes in the face of contrary orders from the president. The officers involved are no doubt sincerely patriotic. But they are so firmly convinced that the national welfare depends on the supremacy of their particular organization that they feel justified in defying such instructions. This is why the problem of perceptual distortion occupies a key place in understanding policy decisions. If the individual sees his action as both right and essential to the nation's welfare, and if his definition of national welfare is biased by his organizational loyalty, he will take actions which are detrimental rather than helpful.

The leaking of classified material, a serious offense against military regulations, is often practiced when it will be of advantage to a single service. Senator Clinton P. Anderson has cited a number of such cases, including the extraordinary instance of sale of Polaris submarine blueprints to a toy manufacturer. The manufacturer put out an exact scale model of the supposedly top-secret weapon and priced it at $2.98. "The navy justified the release of the information," comments Senator Anderson, "on the ground that focusing attention on this vessel helps gain public support for the Polaris submarine program."[14]

It may be that the navy officers had reason to believe that the Russians already had complete knowledge of our designs. But no official decision had been made to declassify the information. Nevertheless, in order to strengthen the navy relative to the other armed services, this material was released.

The primary motivation in such behavior is probably prestige seeking, in the sense that the individual has identified himself with his service and gets pleasure from strengthening it. He hopes to win larger navy appropriations from Congress and to expand his own power within the navy. If he is part of a growing program, his chances of promotion are improved. And he gets a great deal of satisfaction out of beating the competition in the army and air force. Need I add that similar examples can be provided for all services? The expanding ego is found in every human organization; we must learn to detect it and guard against policy decisions misguided by such distorting influences.

Economic Interests and Service Rivalries

Service rivalries are induced in part by ego motivations of officers in the three major services. It is natural that each officer will seek major importance for his own service because this will automatically increase his personal prestige. This is unfortunate in the sense that these very able men may spend more time feuding among themselves than exploring ways of protecting the long-run interests of the nation.

But there is another problem here, which is at least equally important. This is the fact that the economic motivations of supply industries become involved. The aviation industry, not surprisingly, has a vested interest in building more manned bombers. The propaganda favoring the B-70 program did not arise mysteriously out of nowhere. It sought financial advantage for identifiable firms. Such propaganda would have been reasonable if, for example, Boeing (or the Aerospace Industries Association financed jointly by Boeing, Lockheed, Douglas, and other aviation industries) had inserted full-page advertisements in newspapers explaining why they thought the B-70 was needed. The public could have related program to source and made an intelligent decision.

When armament manufacturers hide behind the military spokesmen, the citizen is confused. He sees honest, intelligent, patriotic men contradicting one another, and he cannot understand the extent to which the profit-making propensities of tank manufacturers, shipbuilders, or the aviation industry affect the content of these messages.

Obviously, we do not infer from this any malicious intent on the part of any industrial group to start a war. Most industrial executives are hard-headed, intelligent men. They know what war would mean in terms of plant destruction, if not in terms of their own personal lives. But *preparations* for war can be quite profitable, and it is only plausible that each will see the situation in such a fashion that his product merits highest priority. He then works with all the subtlety and persuasiveness available to convince the Congress, the Pentagon, or the White House that a certain program should be favored. Further, he does not gain the support of generals and admirals by crude methods of financial inducement (although he may indicate that he has a good job waiting for this man on his retirement from military duty). Each military officer can genuinely and honestly support a program because he is firmly convinced that his arm of service will make the greatest contribution to national security.

Congressmen, too, get involved in this peculiar tangle of motivations. The congressman from Detroit will be expected to look out for the interests of Detroit workers and merchants. If contracts go elsewhere, the community suffers. The same is true of areas where aviation is concentrated, or shipbuilding, or rocketry. Thus, an alliance is constructed of the military, the political, and the industrial leaders to propagandize for a certain program. The significance of this alliance will be explored in Chapter 9.

ROLE AND PERSONAL RESPONSIBILITY

If every man assigned to a given social role begins to think in terms of his limited responsibility and to exaggerate those elements in the situation which make his role more important, how can we hope to achieve rational thinking about international problems? The question is not easily answered.

One avenue which merits exploration is the reallocation of responsibilities. It has often been suggested that the USA create a Cabinet post, secretary of peace, whose task would be that of seeking opportunities to build peaceful relations with other nations. This would presumably build in mental biases directly opposed to those cited above for the defense establishment. And out of the interaction of the two might come a more sensible approach.

Another technique which is being used more widely today is that of getting working papers prepared by experts who have no direct affiliation with a government bureau or service. In this way it is hoped that some of the pressures cited above will not be operative. This technique has undoubtedly been useful, although it is still common for the contracting agencies to pick experts who are known from past performance to be sympathetic to a preferred point of view.

It would be desirable to have more research on methods of training which would help the government official to become conscious of his own biases. Some men are capable of standing outside the situation and taking a detached look in a larger perspective. We urgently need more information on how to identify such men, or how to develop such skills in individuals having the needed technical competence within their special service.

9
Group Influences
on Decisions:
The Power Elite

Perceptions of international issues, and
decisions on these issues, are affected by many
considerations other than strictly objective
data. In preceding chapters we have seen that
loyalty, hostility, economic advantage and
social role may operate to modify one's image
of other nations or of national goals. There
is still another variety of influence, which
deserves at least brief mention in this connection. This is the impact of the group of
persons with whom one comes into daily or
regular contact. Conformity to one's associates is a very strong factor affecting the
perception and decision process.

Conformity would not be an important
consideration in connection with *national*
policy decisions if the members of the national
executive came into regular contact with a
wide variety of advisors espousing divergent
policy views. This, however, is not the case.
Each executive tends to surround himself with
like-minded associates and assistants. The
individual who differs often with his superior
soon finds himself excluded from the decision-
making process, if not from government
employment. The executive consequently is
not protected from the hazard of one-sided
reports; he receives an illusory impression of

129

objectivity because his informants confirm one another.

The dangers implicit in this situation would be minimized if the top decision makers came into regular contact with diverse spokesmen for nongovernmental groups urging differing policies. Unfortunately, there is some reason to believe that even these interactions do not cover a wide range of alternatives. The basis for this development was suggested in the preceding chapter. The leading businessmen, military leaders, and diplomatic officials of a nation often share, perhaps for quite different reasons, a tough, aggressive, nationalistic policy in foreign affairs. A decision maker, if he associates mainly or exclusively with these individuals, finds that conformity pressures reinforce his strong inner motives in the direction of nationalism.

The sociologist C. Wright Mills called attention to the appearance of such a clustering of influential persons in this country and labeled it "the power elite." Other observers, also, have independently reported the existence of a power elite, and comparable groups have been described in other countries. While the effect of a power elite appears to be subsidiary to those subjective influences enumerated in earlier chapters, it merits some examination here.

THE AMERICAN ELITE

While Mills generally receives credit for first calling attention to the formation of an American power elite, the concept first drew widespread attention when President Dwight D. Eisenhower delivered his Farewell Address to the people of this country. This, in part, is what he said:

> Now this conjunction of an immense military establishment and a large arms industry is new in the American experience. The total influence—economic, political, even spiritual—is felt in every city, every statehouse, every office of the federal government. . . . we must not fail to comprehend its grave implications...
>
> In the councils of government, we must guard against the acquisition of unwarranted influence, whether sought or unsought, by the military-industrial complex. The potential for the disastrous rise of misplaced power exists and will persist.
>
> We must never let the weight of this combination endanger our liberties or democratic processes...Only an alert and knowledgeable citizenry can compel the proper meshing of the huge industrial and military machinery of defense with our peaceful methods and goals, so that security and liberty may prosper together.[1]

C. Wright Mills was even more eloquent and disturbed in describing this trend toward a concentration of power. He wrote:

> At the top of this structure [of American society] the power elite has been shaped by the coincidence of interest between those who control the major means of production and those who control the newly enlarged means of violence; from the decline of the professional politician and the rise to explicit political command of the corporate chieftains and the professional warlords; from the absence of any genuine civil service of skill and integrity, independent of vested interests.[2]

This, Mills concludes, is a relatively new development in American history.

> In the long peace of the nineteenth century, the military were not in the high councils of state, not of the political directorate, and neither were the economic men— they made raids upon the state but they did not join its directorate. During the "thirties," the political man was ascendant. Now the military and the corporate men are in top positions.[3]

The anxieties expressed by Eisenhower and by Mills explain why so many Americans have become disturbed by the expanding political activity of military men. This trend represents a real threat to civilian control of national policy, a cherished American tradition. From the point at which President Truman discharged General MacArthur for refusing to conform to policy directives, to the Senate investigation of "muzzling the military leaders" in 1962, pressures on both sides have been mounting.

The alliance of military and economic power has become considerably more explicit. General MacArthur, for example, took an appointment as chairman of the board of Remington-Rand. General Leslie Groves, of A-bomb fame, became a vice-president in the same firm. Frank Pace, secretary of the army under Truman, became board chairman of General Dynamics. Air Force General J. T. McNarney took on the presidency of Corvair. Admiral Ben Moreell went with Jones and Laughlin Steel Co. General Somervell became president of Koppers Company, a Mellon-owned enterprise in Pittsburgh. Dozens of such cases could be cited. Companies which deal daily with the military as their biggest customer want, not unnaturally, ex-military men in top posts.

This has led to repercussions. Unpleasant questions have been raised about military men setting up big contracts for their employers-to-be and about the general-become-businessman who negotiates about profit rates with his former immediate subordinates.

I am not concerned here with the possibility of mere financial self-seeking by these men. Such corruption, if it exists, is of minor importance. The real problem arises from the distortion in thinking about national needs and national problems which is likely to result from the realistic conditions under which these men operate. With full patriotism, with honest intentions, with conscious integrity, they will still tend to exaggerate threats from abroad, magnify evidences of hostility, press Congress for bigger defense appropriations. They will be blind to opportunities for tension reduction, and they will misperceive gestures of cooperation from the opponent as tricks for getting us to disarm.

Some years ago, Clemenceau observed that "War has become too important an affair to entrust to the generals." So, nowadays, is *preparation* for war. The production of armaments has now become our major industry. Too many people live on wages and salaries paid from defense contracts. The profit margin of major corporations is determined by defense spending. The unconscious pressure to maintain and increase such arms production is incalculable.

Is this an exaggeration, a distortion? We need only refer to the cases of Nazi Germany and militaristic Japan to show how close to reality we are. In Germany, the nazi leaders and the big industrialists formed a closely interwoven network. The "prosperity" of Germany from 1933 to 1939 derived from big armaments spending; the Krupp works made fancy profits by using slave labor. A totalitarian regime can keep its people in submission only by constantly emphasizing the dangers from abroad. Even if the nazis and the samurai consciously and deliberately exaggerated how they were menaced from outside, this does not mean that the same effects cannot occur unconsciously. Our American power elite is marvelously placed to produce, on request, evidence that we are in dire peril. Naturally, all good Americans subordinate their criticisms of the government under such conditions. Does this explain why the Germans tolerated some nazi policies? We cannot be sure, but obviously the nazi myths of persecution by the Jews, the western powers, the communists, and everyone else must have served a purpose in maintaining national unity and avoiding questions, criticisms, and rebellion.

A similar situation is arising in our own country. Critics of the House Un-American Activities Committee have been denounced as communists; even ex-President Eisenhower has been publicly characterized as a "conscious agent of the communist conspiracy." Critics of the military indoctrination program of General E. A. Walker were smeared as communists. The democratic freedom to object to governmental policy seems to be in for tough sledding, although it may not reach the low point seen in Soviet Russia or Nazi Germany. There is a common tendency to be in favor of "free speech for everyone who agrees with me, but not for people who disagree with me." Such a definition of free speech is, of course, meaningless.

As Mills points out, there are more factors inducing common ways of thinking among the power elite than merely their position at the top of American society. Biographical data indicate that these leaders, business, military or political, come primarily from the upper third of the population in terms of father's income status. They are college graduates, mostly from the Ivy League schools; and they are Protestants, mostly Episcopalians or Presbyterians. Thus they share common origins, common educational and religious backgrounds, and, hence, common values.

These factors are not enough to establish the power elite as a homogeneous group, but they help us to understand common ways of looking at problems. Probably, as Mills suggests, the remaining major attribute these men have in common is *success*. These are the successful business leaders, the successful generals and admirals, the successful politicians and statesmen. Their mutual admiration draws them together and makes possible smooth cooperation in guiding national policy decisions.

OTHER POWER ELITES

The existence of a select ruling group in England is rather widely recognized and requires less elaboration than has been given for the USA. There is, in the first place, a hereditary aristocracy which provides a nucleus for, although it does not determine, the elite group. Secondly, the British educational system screens out far more of the underprivileged economic groups than in this country. But even among the graduates of the famous public schools and the two great universities, there is an inner circle which, at times, has been surprisingly compact and powerful. This inner group is often referred to as "The Establishment."

A. L. Rowse, in his book *Appeasement*,[4] has noted the extraordinary status achieved, particularly within the British government, by graduates of All Souls College, one of the constituent colleges of Oxford University. He presents evidence, for example, to support the view that the appeasement of Hitler was due almost entirely to the All Souls Group. He does not interpret this as evidence that these political leaders were sympathetic to fascism but rather that they were too conservative to permit the changes necessary for effective opposition to fascism.

The tendency of Russia to develop a power elite is underscored in this description by Erich Fromm of the deviations from the ideal of the classless society:

> In terms of *control,* the Soviet Union is a society with rigid class distinctions. Aside from the managerial bureaucracy, there are the political bureaucracy of the Communist party and the military bureaucracy. All three share control, prestige, and income. It is important to note that they largely overlap. Not only are most managers and top officers members of the party, but also they often "change hats," that is, work for a time as managers, and then again as party officials. On the fringes of the three bureaucracies are the scientists, other intellectuals and artists, who are highly rewarded although they do not share in the power of the three main groups.[5]

It is not necessary for us to consider at this time the evidence that these class distinctions in the Soviet Union are tending to become hereditary (as a result of better educational opportunities for children of the elite, the use of influence in promotion to power positions, etc.). What is important is that the interests of those holding power roles may be tied in with aggressive, expansionist policies. Thus, the Communist party functionary may be focused on ideological triumph throughout the world, but he is keenly aware of the potential usefulness of the Red Army in winning or protecting power for a communist group in another nation. Similarly, he recognizes the importance of an efficient armaments industry as a source of supply for guerrilla groups as well as for protection against the menace of American attack. The frequency with which individuals change roles, as mentioned by Fromm, simply means that the psychological pressures for aggressive policies are likely to be enhanced as each individual successively becomes identified with a task force striving toward a particular national-ideological goal.

We could, of course, identify other power elites throughout the world. It has been previously pointed out that military officers in Latin America and the Middle East most often come from the wealthy land-owning class and that, consequently, the civilian governments in these countries tend to be powerless to impose sound taxation or land-reform policies. The future probably will bring some of these individuals into civilian government posts, and, hopefully, consequent coordination of policy will result from the recognition that strengthening the national economy would be more gratifying to their desires for power than protecting the interests of the land-owning aristocracy.

POWER AND SOCIAL ROLE

Some social scientists have objected to C. Wright Mills' analysis of the power elite as being phrased in such a fashion as to sound like still another devil theory of war. If the reader received such an impression, it is erroneous. Mills did not intend to imply that the individuals who comprise the power elite were bad in any personal sense. He was concerned about the high concentration of power in a limited number of social roles which are the realm of a relatively small group of individuals sharing common views of reality.

There are two kinds of power which are of concern to social scientists: personal power and the power of social roles. The former is of limited relevance. It includes the physical power to coerce others into doing your bidding (the armed thug, for example), the power of a wealthy person to bribe or bully others into doing things for economic reasons, and the power of the gifted speaker to influence people by appealing to emotion rather than reason. These make up a small fraction of the totality of power in a modern society.

The importance of the second kind of power—that adhering to a social role—can be illustrated by reference to the American presidency. Lyndon B. Johnson was the same person—with the same abilities, motives, expectancies, and prejudices—on the day after he assumed the role of president as he had been the day before. Yet there was an enormous change in the power he could wield. As vice-president he could at best offer advice. As president he could issue commands to a great federal organization, including the most potent military machine on the planet.

The key to this sudden transformation lies, of course, in the attitudes of American citizens. Because they accept the pattern of institutional structures, they accept the notion that each citizen must obey the orders of the commander in chief. This widespread acceptance carries with it the tremendous potency of conformity pressures on any rare person who may tend to deviate. The attitudes basic to the power of governmental roles are instilled early in life and are, for the most part, unconscious. Thus, it is easy to assume that "it is just natural" for power to go with a given social role.

The fallacy is revealed by looking at a few critical instances. The new nations in the southern hemisphere have written constitutions which define certain roles and assign certain powers to the occupants of these roles. However, the attitudes of the citizens do not provide adequate support for the written documents. Thus, the president or the prime minister who issues orders to the national army may, instead of obedience, encounter mutiny and death.

Even long-established societies may, under adverse conditions, reveal the fallacy of trusting to constitutions or formal governmental structures to locate power. The French monarchy had ruled for several hundred years prior to 1789, but the long tradition of obedience to royal power broke down under the stress of economic hardship and resentment of aristocratic privileges. The same process occurred in Russia in 1917.

It is a grave mistake, therefore, to assume that the study of written constitutions or of historical practice will suffice to locate the seats of power. In general, such studies will be accurate; but in crucial instances the analysis will fail. The key principle is this: *Power accrues to the occupant of a social role in so far as the persons affected by this role accept it as having power.* Such attitudes need not include the belief that the power is right or just; as the nazis and communists show, unwilling submission is compatible with maintenance of a power structure.

How is this relevant to the question of the power elite? Simply, we must avoid thinking of the individuals holding high-status positions in the military-industrial complex as warmongers. The concern expressed by former President Eisenhower was for the merger of roles, for the concentration of political, military, and economic power into fewer and fewer hands. The USA has traditionally endorsed pluralism, a variety of power roles, in order to minimize the dangers associated with absolute monarchy. The policy implications, therefore, include separation of the military from power in the civilian government and separation of economic power from both roles.

How do these considerations bear on our major concern, international relations? The inferences are indirect, but it is widely believed that the nationalistic pressures identified in preceding chapters become more intense as social roles are combined. This would mean that a military man as ambassador or secretary of defense, for example, might be more rigid in his insistence on considerations of national honor and sovereignty without regard to the impact of our policies on other nations than would a civilian. Awareness of the extensive economic repercussions of a cutback in armaments may unconsciously bias governmental officials against tension-reducing policies, and this effect would be intensified if the key decision makers have been intimately associated with the big arms-producing industries. In other words, the coalescence of two or more sets of psychological pressures upon the occupant of a single social role must be expected to have greater impact than a single set of pressures.

The ceding of power to international organizations is also rendered more difficult by the concentration of power into a small set of roles— and for the same reasons. If, therefore, the main hope of peaceful settlement of disputes among nations lies in stronger international institutions, the trend toward merger of these national power roles is a bad omen for the future.

COMMON INTERESTS OF THE POWER ELITES

On the other hand, the peaceful settlement of disputes would be facilitated if the members of the power elites found that they had major interests in common. This resembles the argument, commonly heard around the turn of the century, that the existence of an interlocking aristocracy in various European countries was a factor favoring peace. The theory was that the different aristocratic groups had a common interest in survival and, consequently, that they would seek out peaceful solutions for national disputes.

Unfortunately, the prediction proved unsound. Nationalism prevailed over kinship and other aristocratic communalities. The British may have felt regret at opposing their German relatives, but their economic and power interests were tied to the supremacy of Britain as a nation.

Recently the question has been raised, not entirely cynically, about the power elites of the USA and the USSR. Should it appear that they have common interests (the argument runs), then they will search out peaceful solutions to conflicts rather than run the risk of warfare with concomitant destruction for both groups.

Some cynics have suggested that the power elites in the USA and in Russia have already found something on which they can cooperate. This cooperation is said to be in keeping the Cold War sufficiently frightening so that nobody protests the magnitude of the defense budget. In the USA, defense budgets now run to almost 10% of gross national product, and corresponding estimates for the USSR run as high as 25%. Certainly in the latter nation, the demand for consumer goods would cut this figure drastically, if fear could be reduced. In the USA, many pressures develop when any suggestion of a cut in defense spending is offered. Cities protest closing of bases, contractors moan about ending production of obsolete arms, labor unions picket over loss of jobs when contracts expire. There are, consequently, many people who, consciously or otherwise, are disposed to magnify the dangers which face us—so that their economic security will not be endangered. Some evidence has been noted to show that the same phenomenon is developing in Russia.

This analysis, if correct, would prove that cooperation with the Russians is possible; but, at the same moment, it would suggest that this cooperation will be maintained only in the form of a nervous balance of terror, which the leaders hope to contain so that it does not explode into war. Cooperation on a more fundamental and significant level cannot be expected unless basic changes occur in this elite structure.

10
The Emerging Nations

This book is concerned with psychological factors which influence the course of international relations—particularly, conflicts between nations. I have attempted to identify ways in which the psychological states of individuals may modify the inputs of information to decision makers and may also affect the resulting policy decisions. The examples used have been drawn from the major nations of the western world. But if this mode of analysis of international conflict is valid, it should also throw light on trends in the new nations of Africa and Asia, the so-called underdeveloped or emerging nations.

In earlier chapters, the deleterious effects of nationalism received considerable attention. Nationalism, we have observed, supports delusions of grandeur with respect to one's own nation and delusions of persecution with respect to nations perceived as competitors or opponents. But nationalism also cements national unity, maintains law and order by underwriting submission to to the authority of legitimate leaders, and establishes a basis for cooperation in business and industry.

When we look at the emerging nations in light of this analysis, we realize that the psychological approach can indeed be valuable. Especially we can understand some of the crucial differences in national policy of these new nations as compared with the western powers.

There are two ideas which must be stressed. The first is that the emerging nations have a deficit of nationalism, not an excess. The talk about the revolution of rising nationalisms in Asia and Africa is mostly off the point. These nations, by and large, need a planned program for increasing nationalism without increasing it to the level where it becomes as dangerous to future history as it has been in past history in the West.

The second idea which demands our attention is that the facts as seen by leaders in these new nations do not correspond with those seen by their ostensible followers, the citizens; nor do they correspond well with the facts as seen by leaders in the developed nations.

A DEFICIT OF NATIONALISM

When Metternich said, "Italy is only a geographical expression," he referred to the complete lack of national unity in nineteenth-century Italy. Today it would be appropriate to say the same of the Republic of the Congo—it has territorial boundaries, but the citizenry has no sense of national unity, no loyalty to the central government, no identification among different tribes. The same holds to a considerable extent for India, where the divisive forces of religion, caste, and language create tremendous obstacles to unification. And we can conclude the same for Laos, for Nigeria, and even for Brazil.

Cynics have suggested that the Indians and Pakistanis cooperated to get the British out only so they could be free to attack each other. While this is an obvious exaggeration, it is clear that primary loyalties in these areas are to much smaller groups than to the nation as a whole. Bengalis are hostile to Mysore or Punjab, and Keralese are hostile to North India. Each group attempts to give economic support to its own members (this is the dynamic basis for the language riots) and is submissive to local leaders; each rejects the authority of the central government. Recognizing this cultural fragmentation is crucial for an understanding of the new nations. In the African countries, the fragmentation is based on tribal leaders and loyalties but the result is the same.

What is a nation? We might say that it is a state of mind. Or, more precisely, a nation comes into existence as individuals believe in its existence. Italy did not exist as a nation until Piemontesi and Napolitani recognized a higher organization superseding their loyalties to regional symbols. The Congo will become a nation when the Baluba and the Kasai tribesmen (and others) pay loyalty to the central government and not primarily to their tribes.

This is not to deny the importance of political apparatus, economic organization, and military forces in defining a nation. However, these institutional apparatuses function only if they provide a focus for the citizen's perception of his nation as a unit. One of the reasons for the drive to build armies in these small, obviously helpless countries (helpless against the great powers, that is) derives from the unique role of the army as a national symbol. By bringing men of all regions into a single uniform, the army communicates a sense of unity, of belonging.

Where, then, is the nationalism that set aflame Southeast Asia, the Congo, Kenya, and Nigeria? It existed, at the time of the wave of nationalist demands, primarily in the minds of a few, mostly western-trained leaders, who aspired to autonomy for their nation, in the style of western sovereignty, and to positions of power and wealth for themselves through the creation of these new political units. Much of the dynamic for the riots against the colonial powers came from resentment of western domination and from economic frustration. Only a small increment was due to nationalism as we in the West understand it.

The underdeveloped nations must be viewed as geographical aggregates, which often have not even a common language and a common culture to unite them. They are split into economic, religious, linguistic, and tribal groupings. The governing class is often small and unpopular. The splintered existence of these new nations results in even more prickly problems for us to grasp.

If we are to relate intelligently to these emerging nations, we must have a better understanding than is now common of the internal processes of change. Most of the underdeveloped areas manifest tendencies considerably more complex than a mere response to western technology or ideology.

Economists Millikan and Blackmer, in *The Emerging Nations,* suggest that the modernization process frequently stems from inner disequilibrium. This might involve, for example, one clan or class holding others in an inferior position:

> Thus social tensions may lead to the rejection of traditional attitudes by certain groups, who turn to new activities which may restore their prestige and sense of achievement. Indeed, it is virtually never the social group in control of a traditional society that leads the way to modernization. That group, which finds the traditional social order satisfactory, virtually always resists change, even if the society is threatened from without and change is necessary to resist that threat.[1]

This is one reason why the communists have had a strategic advantage over the West in dealing with the emerging nations. We have tried to deal with ruling classes, sometimes even a small ruling family, as in Iran and in South Vietnam, to bring about industrialization and democratization. But both these trends threaten the security, wealth, and prestige of the rulers. How can we expect them to cooperate wholeheartedly in their own downfall? Winston Churchill once said that he had not become prime minister to preside over the disintegration of the British Empire. But even so potent an individual as Sir Winston could not stem the tide of disintegration, and it is to the credit of the British ruling class that they adapted to the change. This is not happening in Latin America or in the Middle East.

The result, in most areas, is that profound internal tensions rip at the vital structure of the nation. An intellectual group, or even an entrepreneurial group, rebels against the domination of the rulers. Since they cannot look to us for help, they look to the communist world. We send military aid and even troops to hold them in subjection. And if the forces demanding change win despite our support of the conservatives, how can we expect them to view us with friendship?

DIFFERENCES IN PERCEIVED FACTS

There is a conflict between the traditionalist leaders and the new nationalist leaders in their differing views of the facts. The former see a happy if primitive people, devoted to their tribes and their villages and submissive to their local leaders, who care for them benevolently. The new leaders emphasize a different set of observations: lack of literacy, lack of unity, lack of export trade and the economic appurtenances of civilization, lack of status in the community of nations.

The traditional leader is likely to be hostile to communism because this ideology implies snatching away the power and the creature comforts attached to his privileged position. Thus, he finds a natural affinity with the West, which defends the status quo and sees communism as its enemy.

The rising leadership group does not view communism as a menace. When we attempt to frighten them with the notion that communism would mean a totalitarian regime with concentration of power and rigid controls over the people, these leaders are not disturbed. They identify themselves with the elite of the Communist party, with those who wield power. Regimentation of the masses is perceived as a necessary device for mobilizing the energies necessary to create a technological society, which involves building capital assets, preventing excessive consumption, and suppressing tribal dissents. Thus, to the emergent leadership of these areas, the communist example may actually be attractive because of the greater power of governing officials in a communist state. And they can realistically point to the difficulties of breaking down traditional habits of work, of superstitions, and of group barriers without a substantial degree of regimentation.

Perceptions of International Issues

It is easy to be cynical about the motivations of neutralist leaders, who are delighted to play off the USA against the USSR in order to get bigger grants from both sources. But perhaps the matter is not that simple. Taking aid from both sides relieves a leader of the accusation that he is joining the Cold War. There is good reason to believe that most of these governments genuinely desire to "remain free of entangling alliances," as Thomas Jefferson advised an infant nation many years ago.

Harrison Salisbury has offered an interesting report on the situation in Outer Mongolia, a small nation sandwiched between the USSR and Red China. He reports that the government there has welcomed Soviet aid to provide a bulwark against complete domination by the Chinese but that they openly expressed the hope that the USA would also be willing to help them. "In fact, they are most eager for United States recognition," he writes, "and would welcome American technical aid if for no other reason than to broaden the international political basis of their country."[2]

We are prone to underestimate the importance of the desire for autonomy in these small nations. Even the communist regimes, as Yugoslavia shows, may rebel against Moscow's domination. On our side, the argument for encouraging such autonomy is overwhelming. This need not mean that we pour billions into communist satellites; it does mean that we should keep contacts open and maintain some reservoir of good will against the day when this leadership group, or another, may wish to declare its independence of Russian control.

Regardless of the fanaticism which communism can inspire in many human beings, and regardless of the help which the Soviet Union has given to smaller communist countries, the desire of the local leaders for power in their own right is very great. If we in the West believe that a pluralistic communist bloc (as opposed to the monolith it allegedly was from 1945 to 1960) would be to our advantage, we should stop lumping all communists together and we should provide at least modest encouragement to leaders who strive for autonomy, power, and nationalism within their country.

It would also help if we applied such thinking to neutralist and pro-western leaders. Aid does not buy friends. Supplying even desperately needed food to India and Egypt will not purchase loyalty, perhaps not even gratitude. The desire for national power and the feeling of humiliation associated with an admission that "We cannot even feed our own people" oppose such outcomes. It is not even true that the anti-western attitudes of leaders are based on the cynical "What have you done for me recently?" A more realistic view is that the leaders are embarrassed by being forced into admitting that they cannot fulfill the power role of protecting and nurturing their people. They are thus susceptible to any position on an issue which involves asserting their pride and their independence of western support. Since they control the channels of communication, they prefer to tell their people that they have somehow obtained food, without giving credit to the giver. And in order to salve their own feelings, they attack the West as overpowering or exploitative.

The craving for nonalignment is based both on the wish of these leaders to be free of domination by either East or West and on a realistic view that national energies should be devoted to building roads, schools, and industries—not to ideological disputes. Many Americans who want the emerging nations to side with the source of gifts of food and arms forget the early phases of our own history. French military assistance was crucial in the Revolutionary War; yet our leaders at first sought to remain neutral in the conflict between France and England. And by 1798 we were threatening war against France. So much for gratitude!

Neutralist leaders support their nonaligned stance by seeing the superpowers as substantially alike. And they perceive that their advantage lies in a balance of power. Lloyd Free asked leaders in India the following question: "Which would be better in terms of India's own interests — for Russia and the other communist powers to be militarily stronger; for the USA and its allies to be stronger; or for the two sides to be fairly evenly balanced?" Only 6% preferred to have Russia stronger, and 9% preferred the US stronger; 49% chose the "balanced" solution. Most of the respondents said the real interest of India lay in seeing the great powers disarm and coexist peacefully.[3]

Remarks such as the following cast some light in Indian criticisms of the USA: "We have always expected more from the United States than from the Russians, and that is why we become more disappointed with the US when it doesn't live up to our expectations." And another significant quotation: "We cannot afford to antagonize anyone. We cannot afford to make enemies of either Russia or China." The omission of the USA in the latter quotation seems significant. The Indians were not worried about harsh treatment from this country, but they did seem to feel that antagonizing Russia or China would be dangerous. This, it seems to me, is a compliment to our nation, although others may not see it so.

Facts as Seen by Citizens

We do not know as much as we should about how these and other issues appear to the rank-and-file citizens of these new nations.[4] Far more money is spent on military force than on studying whether armed power is likely to solve our problems.

It does seem clear that the average peasant in India or Vietnam or the Congo has no knowledge of the outside world or of its implications for him. The real government is the village council or the local chief. The central government is often seen as a ruthless tax-collecting agency, which serves no useful purpose in his life.

One can deplore the apathy of these people with respect to such innovations as better plows, seed, or fertilizer — until one learns that all of the increased produce will go to the landlord and none to the person who tills the soil. At this point, the American is likely to ruminate that in such a system he too would be uninterested in improving agriculture. But indeed, the typical American would rebel against such an exploitative system — at which point our government would denounce him as a communist and perhaps send in a special counterinsurgency force to suppress his activities.

It is doubtful that the peasant in South Vietnam, in 1964, could perceive any difference between the Viet Cong and the Saigon government. Each was a source of death and taxes. He may have seen the VC in a slightly more favorable light, because the rebels promised an end to the landlord system. But it is probable that he distrusted their promises as he did those coming from Saigon. Perhaps, the international relations experts will say, the facts as seen by illiterate peasants are not relevant to policy decisions. Yet it is fairly obvious that how these peasants see facts and issues will affect the chances of life and death for American and allied soldiers involved in guerilla conflict in these areas. Conferences and treaties, after all, only confirm what has been decided by other means.

POLICY STEPS TOWARD NATIONAL UNITY

Faced with opposition from tribal or regional leaders and with apathy on the part of the rank and file, the head of any one of these new nations must search for devices that will build national patriotism and a feeling of unity. Local loyalties and linguistic barriers may make it virtually impossible to win popular cooperation for national policies. The first task facing the leader of one of these new nations is to weld it into a functioning group.

The temptation to use the heat of military adventures in this welding process is very strong. Working together on a common task is the best way to unify a group; and a military campaign provides emotional excitement and a common enemy, factors favoring the merging of factions into a unified whole. As an example, let me cite the seizure of Goa by India in December 1961. When Prime Minister Nehru was questioned about this action, he stated:

> Nothing in our fourteen years of independence has excited
> and thrilled the people of India as the liberation of Goa
> ...There is no doubt in my mind of the full justification
> for the use of force against Portugal.[5]

Military victories have always excited and thrilled the noncombatant. It may be unjustified cynicism to imply (as many Indian newspapers did) that Nehru timed the invasion of Goa to give maximum benefit to the Congress party's campaign for the 1962 election, but it would be only minimal realism to state that such actions increase national unity. And so, while Nehru may have meant "full *moral* justification for the use of force," the detached observer may suspect that the unconscious justification lay in the effects of the adventure on the Indian population. Unity was desperately needed. Pride in national achievements was urgently sought. Victory over Portugal provided a real political boon to the political leader striving to weld a fragmented population into a national citizenry. Sukarno of Indonesia similarly used a military campaign against the Dutch in New Guinea, and many other leaders of poorly integrated nations will undoubtedly be tempted to follow such tactics. The hazard to the rest of the world of course, rests chiefly upon the danger of great power involvement.

Military success also strengthens the personal position of the leader. While Nehru needed no such artificial assistance, other political figures may. It is instructive to remember that John Adams, probably our most unpopular president, received tremendous popular acclaim at only one point in his four-year term. This was when he mobilized our Navy in 1798 and gave orders to fire on French ships attempting to bar us from trading with England.

My point here is only that even weak, underdeveloped nations (like the USA in 1798) may adopt a belligerent stance and stir up great excitement in the population. The leader who takes such a strong stand increases his popularity and unites the people behind him. Thus, there is a great temptation for new nations to use this method of building national unity.

THE ECONOMIC PROBLEM

The economic problem of the emerging nations is obviously not psychological in nature. Poverty is not a matter of perceptual distortion. The unrealistic belief that independence would somehow magically end poverty was a misperception, deliberately fostered by some nationalistic, power-seeking leaders. The inability to deliver on these promises accounts for much of the instability of these new regimes, e.g., in the Congo, where many natives evidently expected to live in big houses with plenty of servants after independence. Their frustrations led to hostility directed against the political leaders.

Various experts have suggested that instead of talking about the relation of East to West, we should be concerned about the relation of North to South. For various reasons, the northern hemisphere of the earth is, on the whole, industrialized, urbanized, and literate. The southern hemisphere contains a preponderance of peoples who are agricultural, rural, and illiterate. These people, who make up over half of the human race, are stirring and demanding a better life. The underdeveloped economies of South Asia, Africa, and Latin America today represent danger points — smoldering embers which may at any time burst into flames. The West has still failed to arrive at any consensus on the manner of helping these people without starting a conflagration.

The political problem is in part one of perception. The underdeveloped nations have long been accustomed to poverty. Now their leaders see that this low standard of living is unnecessary. They see the possible gains to their people from industrialization; they see the gains to themselves in terms of power and prestige. Unfortunately, they do not see the long struggle — the slow transition from tribal, traditional societies to technologically advanced, industrial nations. If we warn them of the dangers of attempting too rapid a leap, they will not listen. They are in no mood for gradualism. They demand immediate action that will lead toward higher material standards of living.

That such demands are irrational needs little proof. We in the industrialized North know that you cannot run a mechanized society without skilled workers, that factories interlock with other factories, that a large body of educated white-collar technicians must be somehow trained. So their impatience will doubtless lead the emerging nations into many pitfalls. Unfortunately, irrationality is a common human trait; to characterize the citizens of such a nation as Ghana in this vein has little justice. The charge can be leveled with equal merit against those in the industrial North. It is, for example, quite irrational to expect people to show patient calm when their children are suffering from malnutrition while Americans allow grain to rot for lack of a market. Bandying such criticisms about achieves nothing but a macabre debate. What faces us is a set of facts — illogical, brute facts. Calling them irrational will not induce them to vanish. Somehow we of the North must deal with them.

Chester Bowles, then Ambassador to India, argued that we must expect the emerging nations of the South to seek to emulate us.

> The most powerful ideas and principles in the history of man are closely linked with the evolution of American democracy. Today it is *our* revolution for self-determination, for human dignity, and for expanding economic opportunities which is alive and marching in Burma, India, and the Philippines, in Nigeria, the Sudan, and Tunisia, indeed throughout the noncommunist world.[6]

Having set them this magnificent example, we should not scold them for imitating it. If we tell these people that they are trying to move too rapidly and refuse to help them in their efforts, they will simply turn elsewhere for aid. It may be that aid from the East will prove to be bait for a trap—but they will be desperate enough to take the chance. And if such a situation multiplies our problems, forces us to pay higher taxes for ever greater military forces, may it not appear in the long run that *we* were the irrational ones?

There are two ways of looking at the revolutionary changes sweeping the so-called backward areas of the world. One way uses the phrase "revolution of expectations" and emphasizes the notion that the peoples of Asia, Africa, and Latin America now expect the gratifications associated with living in the industrialized western countries. It could not be otherwise, of course. With easy travel, many western visitors, movies, and similar influences, these people soon learned that their poverty was not the outcome of an all-powerful fate. Thus, they are moved to desire—indeed, to demand—that the circumstances of their lives be changed.

But this process has its other facet. This is what might more accurately be called "the revolution of frustration." Even if the tremendous economic resources of the industrialized West were fully mobilized, only slow progress could be made to end this harsh mode of life in the emerging nations. Will the people wait? There is already evidence to suggest that they will not—at least, not peacefully. Frustration of these newly awakened desires leads to aggression, and aggression, generally, to violence—internal or external. This violence, if it could be contained in the form of domestic revolution against feudal landlords, might be tolerable and even desirable. But violence in the powder keg of the East-West conflict makes us all shudder. It might well be the match that ignites the explosives.

Alternatively, local leaders seeking to divert the hostility from themselves may stir up foreign quarrels. Many observers so interpret Chinese seizure of parts of India: Peasant discontent over the Chinese commune program demanded an outlet, and so these border disputes (over valueless real estate) were brought into public attention. The dangers of such aggressive acts need no emphasis.

Psychological Implications of Aid

Given these severe economic problems, the emerging nations must have aid from the industrialized world. Two kinds of pressures will insure that foreign aid programs continue. The first is simple humanitarianism. Regardless of ingratitude or of half-hearted acknowledgement of our food support, the USA will undoubtedly continue to provide substantial amounts of grain. Other nations also help in this way.

Secondly, our concern with reducing the likelihood of military adventurism will prod us into continued economic assistance. The world is simply too dangerous right now to run the risks associated with military aggression by new nations seeking to unify their people or to displace internal hostilities onto foreign foes.[7] Thus, we have a sizable stake in keeping the level of frustration in these areas below the danger point.

The problem is not a simple one. A fairly sound principle of economics is that, as incomes go up, people demand more manufactured goods and fewer raw foods and basic materials. Thus, demand pushes up prices on products from the industrialized North but drives down prices on raw materials from the agricultural South. This means that the relatively affluent northern hemisphere is creating serious problems for its poor neighbors. As Dudley Seers demonstrates,[8] the new nations must industrialize in order to share in this affluence.

But industrialization requires capital goods, and capital goods must come from somewhere. In the USA, our great transportation network and our basic industries (such as steel) were created by ruthless exploitation of immigrant labor and, in many cases, by defrauding small investors. In the USSR, the heavy industries were created by forcible seizure of grain from the peasants to pay for imported machinery and by forced labor of millions of political prisoners, prisoners of war, and those simply unfortunate enough to be available.

The emerging nations are not, by and large, in a position to attract surplus laborers from other countries, use them on capital goods programs, and then drop them to survive or starve. They do, of course, have the option to militarize the country, seize crops of food and fiber, and ship them abroad to pay for heavy equipment. This method is typical of the communist regimes, although it is likely that not even communist leaders would praise it. But is there an option?

Seymour Melman, in his vigorous book, *The Peace Race,* [9] provides an alternative: that the USA employ its millions of underutilized workers and its many idle plants to turn out great quantities of such items as lathes, grinders, and other metal-processing machines which are at the heart of any developing industrial machine. Melman argues that about 10% of our gross national product would be needed to supply Latin America, Africa, and noncommunist Asia with the capital goods they need and the trained workers they must have to get under way. He is thus talking about more than $40 billion dollars per year — a striking contrast to our recent foreign aid program of $4 billion but considerably less than our defense budget, which now exceeds $50 billion.

Melman's argument, in brief, is as follows: Making these goods available on easy terms to underdeveloped nations would open the road for their rapid development without totalitarianism. It would end the state of desperation which fosters both communism and military adventurism. It would open markets for the industrialized West, because our experience invariably is that we trade more with industrial than with agrarian countries. Finally, he believes, it would put the USSR in a pincers from which they could escape only by agreeing to steps toward disarmament, since they could not compete with the West in supplying heavy machinery while maintaining their arms program. If substantial disarmament followed, the cost to the USA would be reduced very materially. Further, the chances of war would be substantially diminished. These are all strong arguments for Melman's concept of a "peace race."

The Population Explosion

The desperate striving of the underdeveloped nations for improvements in living standards has continually been frustrated by the rapid expansion of their population. There are many problems intertwined in this case. We must remember that in most such areas children are the "social security" of the parents; how else can aged individuals be cared for? Second, their experience has been that many children die; hence, a large number must be born. The new medicines and insecticides have changed the death rate without changing cultural expectancies. Finally, techniques of contraception are neither known nor available. Some additional complications, such as the notion that a man's virility can be shown only by siring numerous offspring, may be ignored as less relevant. (An important point must be kept in mind. It would be catastrophic if efforts to reduce birth rates in the emerging nations were perceived either as devices to reduce the strength of the colored races relative to the whites or to hold these new nations in a permanently inferior status. We must always be alert to possible misinterpretations— however irrational—of our proposals.)

The USA has a large stake in the matter of population limitation. It is not very helpful to install a sprinkling system in your own house if your neighbor stores gasoline and plays with lighted matches.

Aid through International Agencies

Our bilateral aid program has run into some difficulties. One of these is the feeling, among our own citizens, that the nations we feed should be grateful and should show this by being anti-communist. Yet most of them would resent the suggestion that they would vote for the political party which gave them the largest handouts. A second difficulty is the resentment and feeling of inadequacy noted among leaders of the recipient nations. A third is the fact that implications of alignment in the Cold War are seen, even if not justified, and that political frictions within the recipient nation block efficient utilization of materials supplied.

As a technique for dealing with these problems, one suggestion is that foreign aid programs be channeled through the UN and its specialized agencies. This method would remove most of the sources of difficulty mentioned above.

A further advantage of using international agencies for aid is, in the long run, even more important. Our hopes for world peace rest on the building of international cooperation and on creating international institutions which will be respected and supported. Given our present mutual hostility vis-à-vis the USSR, it is unlikely that the UN will be allowed to build up any substantial military organ of its own. The sole remaining source of power is economic. If the UN can be assigned the job of disbursing both western and eastern aid, the result will be to build up in the new nations an image of the UN as a power center.

Secondly, we may cite the tribal legacy which says that a successful man must take care of his relatives. Employment in government bureaus and in private industry is often based on nepotism, not on efficiency. Thus, many very inept, if not actually stupid and ignorant, individuals are placed in key positions. The economic cost of this attitude-complex in the emerging nations is incalculable but enormous.

Thirdly, we must consider the resistance of the peasants to innovations in agricultural methods. Some of this resistance is understandable—for example, tenant farmers in many Asian nations would not benefit at all from a crop increase. But even on owner-tilled farms, there is a rigidity, an opposition to new ideas. We may joke about the American who votes Republican because his grandfather voted for Abraham Lincoln. But the harm done is slight compared to the Pakistani peasant who will not use fertilizer or insecticide because his grandfather did not use them.

It seems important, therefore, to recognize that changing attitudes of people in the new nations is just as much of a problem as changing attitudes in the USA toward an international police force and the ceding of sovereignty to larger groupings. In both cases, economic measures are only part—admittedly, an important part—of an effective program. It is important to develop new local resources, but it is more urgent to change those attitudes which prevent utilization of resources already known.[11]

Attitudes can be changed by studying the values held by these people and devising appeals based on their highest values. For example, in India it was found that educational materials for birth control were ineffective when based on the health of the mother. But material stressing the welfare of the child was much more successful. This kind of detailed investigation is needed in all of these areas.

Some of these problems are already being attacked, indirectly and perhaps unintentionally. It is interesting, for example, to note that our military aid missions try to teach local officers (who usually come from the upper class) the necessity of humane treatment of enlisted men. Another attitudinal change is an emphasis on promotion by merit. Many officers traditionally follow the customary pattern of taking care of their relatives, their caste, or men from their region. Military indoctrination for efficiency works in favor of promotion by merit and against nepotism. Even the expansion of the armed services has had some unintended benefits; e.g., illiterate peasants are taught some reading and writing, are required to develop habits of punctuality, become familiar with machinery, etc. All of these changes are necessary if the aid program is to work. While these indoctrination activities might go more smoothly if run by an international agency, they must be carried on by someone.

This would probably have a beneficent effect in terms of long-range policies. A very grave danger is that one or more of the emerging nations may move into a phase of aggressive national expansion. If the nation has also developed the necessary technology, it could represent a major threat to our survival. Thus, we need to balance both the need of these nations for enough nationalism to unite the people and the danger of too intense and fervent a nationalism. Building strong international institutions is a step in this balancing process.

Attitudes and Economic Development

Industrial development is not purely a matter of raising living standards, although these are desperately low in the areas under discussion. Industry also has a symbolic value. A steel mill is a crown jewel, a concrete representation of national status. Countries which have no iron ore and no coal still want this kind of installation for its prestige value.

It is reported that, at the opening of a new rolling mill built by the USA for one of these nations, the following incident occurred: Men began dancing and singing as the white-hot sheets of steel flashed through the huge conveyors. The noise and excitement increased. Suddenly, one of the men ran toward the machinery, leaped onto the white-hot metal, and was instantly incinerated. Whether or not the story is true, it reflects the mystical, quasi-religious attitude taken toward installations of this type. In the West, too, steel has been a Moloch devouring many sacrifices. But in the new nations, steel can inspire these self-sacrificing attitudes, rather than coercing them.

A steel mill, unfortunately, does not in itself guarantee a viable economy. The new nations have other problems, internal and attitudinal, as well as economic. Indeed, many observers feel that until the citizens of these countries acquire new ways of looking at reality, the building of plant facilities will be futile.

One of these problems is the pace of the work life. In many underdeveloped areas, e.g., India, a 40-hour week for office employees would be considered excessively burdensome.[10] Now we can debate whether the USA can afford a 35-hour week, but there is plenty of evidence to indicate that India cannot afford this luxury. Likewise, local capitalists cannot continue to put their profits in Swiss banks rather than expanding their facilities. Such tactics slow down the process of industrialization. The attitude toward work must be changed if the benefits of modern industry are to be reaped. The "achievement motive" must be cultivated. Certain of the Puritan values could help solve economic problems of underdeveloped nations.

The Peace Corps, the Quakers, and other volunteer groups are making important psychological contributions by breaking down the stereotype of the wealthy American who is contemptuous of the peasants. One of the best ways to break up a rigid attitude is to introduce dissonant information, i.e., stimulus inputs which cannot be fitted into the prejudiced belief. While the prejudiced person is usually adept at refusing to see such information, repeated exposure usually is effective. We must learn the stereotyped image of the American in each country and take deliberate steps to modify its undesirable aspects—not by propaganda but by actions such as those of the volunteers.

PLANNING FOR SOUND ECONOMIES

Our aid program, either run bilaterally as at present or through international agencies, should be used not only to reduce suffering and to modify attitudes but also to build desirable institutions for the future. Economists, for example, stress the possibilities of regional specialization as a method by which the emerging nations can progress faster and securely. Unfortunately, it appears that our foreign aid program has, on the whole, paid relatively little attention to the theory. This may mean that the leaders of the new nations need some education, or it may mean only that the Americans have been too much concerned with military buildups, too little interested in the long-range consequences. Further, our policies have been built nation by nation rather than for a whole region.

Let me illustrate what is possible. We are anxious not to develop the kinds of nationalisms that may induce conflicts between neighbors in these newly freed areas. Economic regionalism could encourage interdependence as opposed to self-sufficiency. Suppose, for example, that Nicaragua has a surplus of hides. Instead of exporting these to the USA, we might encourage development of a shoe industry. *Pari passu,* we might assist Panama to start a frozen food industry and Colombia to specialize in men's clothing.. Given such beginnings, these nations could initiate international exchange on a basis which would be beneficial to all and which would emphasize the importance of cooperation. This view may seem unduly naive, but perhaps the difficulty is only that, like Christianity, it has never been tried. An organizational basis—a Central American "common market"—already exists on paper.

A similar argument applies to agriculture. Every effort should be made to introduce diversification, which starts where possible, from existing local crops but exaggerates the uniqueness of each area. Duplication must be minimized. Local food production should, as far as possible, include a range of proteins, carbohydrates, and fats; but the exportable surplus must be planned to avoid direct competition with neighboring states. The Yankee "big brother" may thus avoid many future nationalistic conflicts.

There seems to be no sound reason why the vast outpourings of US aid under the Alianza para Progreso could not be used systematically to reward some kinds of behavior while not rewarding others. For example, within the Latin American area, there seems no obvious reason why the USA should not underwrite a large project, such as river development, if the OAS would simultaneously undertake a small one in the same region. In other words, instead of acting in a completely unilateral fashion, we could use our grants to elicit systematic gestures of good will.

The possibilities here are almost unlimited. They could include universities, building-materials factories, health programs focused on specific diseases, etc. The USA could underwrite technical training, fertilizer, seed, and other programs for diversified production if parallel activities were set up without our support. Here again the aim of minimizing competition is important. We want local support of the project, and we want an inter-American economy which involves mutual trade, an impossibility unless there is regional specialization. The same would apply to other areas.

The economic theorist has ideas which appear to have practical possibilities. Instead of trying to build up each small nation to be self-sufficient, our aid program should utilize economic theory to build viable and interlocking industries.

NATIONALISM: THE DILEMMA OF EMERGING NATIONS

The problem of achieving unity within the emerging nations forces us to face a dilemma which even the ardent internationalist finds uncomfortable. The dilemma is that, in the short run, a leader in one of the new nations has no choice but to be an enthusiastic nationalist. He must try to build loyalty, willingness to settle internal disputes peacefully, subordination of tribal to national goals, and so on, among the citizens. The tricks of traditional nationalism—military power, protective trade restrictions, delusions of superiority, critical attitudes toward foreign countries—are virtually mandatory.

There is, however, some encouraging evidence that at least some of these leaders see the hazards involved and wish to strengthen international institutions. The Central American "common market" and the Latin American Free Trade Area are evidence of such forward-looking attitudes. In Africa, the Organization for African Unity seeks to build a framework which will permit development of national loyalties but inhibit the tendency toward aggrandizement at the expense of neighbors.

In a survey of members of national parliaments undertaken not long ago, Lloyd Free[12] found more support for the UN in the emerging nations than in the USA. Specifically, he found that 74% of members of the parliament of India would support a policy of reliance on the UN to maintain peace, while in this country, 61% of Democrats and 51% of Republicans accepted such a policy. Enlightened self-interest, then, can be mobilized in favor of building international institutions.

This means that we shall be wise to involve leaders of the emerging nations in UN activities and to help them to win ego-gratifications through international roles. Thus, before 'they have gotten rigid conceptions of nationalistic roles, they will be assuming some tasks which induce a broader outlook. Common sense predicts that the national role will carry the greater weight in their thinking, but each quantum of internationalism that can be introduced in such a mixture will make the preservation of peace so much easier in the twenty-first century.

Implicit in this is the idea that we must continue to live with the voting system in the General Assembly, which grants equal votes to all nations. While this arrangement has wounded the egos of a few nationalistic Americans, it has done us no harm. And if it limits the adventurism and reckless assertion of sovereignty of these new leaders, it may save many lives.

There is no apparent escape from the trend of new nations to develop exaggerated and irrational nationalism. Our best chance is to limit this development and lay foundations for a future swing to an international orientation.

11
Negotiation:
The Dialogue
of the Deaf

It has become a commonplace to say that East and West are different worlds. Unfortunately, of the people who say this, very few realize how dreadfully true it is.

The externally visible differences—as between East Berlin and West Berlin, for example—are the least important. Different worlds do not result from such minor variations as the more restricted food supply, the monotonous clothing, or the absence of automobiles in the communist countries. These factors, while they contribute to the psychological gap, do not cause it.

The world of the communist is different from the world of the West because of bias and distortion in the receipt and interpretation of information. Since we can never demonstrate that reality is identical for two different observers, it would be defensible to assert that every individual lives in his own private world. But within the framework of a common culture, with similar pressures, similar roles, similar goals, and similar threats, people learn to see major situations in compatible fashion. There are, of course, divergences, even within a single country. Within the nation, however, it is generally true that each of us can predict

157

reasonably well the actions of our neighbors; we can communicate in a functionally useful fashion; we can, in short, understand one another.

The problem of settling disputes is difficult enough when the contestants have grown up in the same culture; one need only have a little experience with marital counseling to learn this. What is real to the husband is, often enough, pure fancy according to the wife. "She ignores me for the baby," he asserts. Her reply is, "He wants me to treat him as if I were his mother." The objective situation becomes distorted as it is seen by each person through fogs of emotion and frustration.

The task of negotiation with representatives of a decidedly different culture is extremely complex, mainly because the realities being discussed are quite different for the two persons or teams involved in the discussion. Words which seem to have a dependable meaning are found to be decidedly misleading. Consider the case of the Yalta agreement on "free, democratic elections" in the satellite nations after World War II. We had interpreted this phrase as referring to open elections in which various political parties could offer candidates. The Russians meant an election in which the voters could choose from a slate of candidates submitted by the Communist party.

Americans accused the Russians of bad faith for violating their promise, whereas it is at least plausible that the Russians thought it was perfectly clear what kind of election was meant. They regularly describe their one-party elections as free and democratic. As a matter of fact, the Russians could have argued that many states in the USA have the same kind of election; even now in parts of the South, voters mainly choose among candidates offered by the Democratic party. Hence, if the Russians had pledged "southern-style elections," we could have understood, even if we did not approve.

The problem of negotiating with the Russians is thus made difficult both by conflicts of interest, which are important but clearly understood, and by conflicts over what is real, an aspect which is rarely understood by participants on either side.

When two people sit down to debate a controversy, it frequently happens that each simply continues to state his own position without hearing what the contestant is saying. For this kind of colloquy the French have an excellent name: *le dialogue des sourds,* the dialogue of the deaf. Each speaks, but neither hears what is being said.

The Negro-White colloquy in the southern United States is a good example of this phenomenon. The Negro speaks of improved education, better job opportunities, the right to vote. The White speaks of violence, immorality, disease, and other social problems. Neither listens to what the other has to say.

It is possible to study this relationship experimentally. Psychologist Allen Edwards[1] conducted an ingenious experiment to demonstrate selective listening. He prepared a speech relating to Franklin D. Roosevelt's New Deal program (this was in 1939). Items in the speech were very carefully balanced so that every point favoring the New Deal was, at a later time, balanced by a critical point—or vice versa if the critical statement came first. He memorized the speech and gave it verbatim to several classes of college students. When these students were separated by political attitudes, it was found that the Democrats had heard a speech favoring the New Deal; and they could cite statements to support this assertion. Conversely, the Republicans had heard a speech attacking the New Deal, and they too could quote evidence for their view. Each had heard what he wanted to hear, or what was compatible with his preexisting bias. When the students were tested for memory three weeks later, the same trend was shown; and, especially interesting, their reports showed that many statements in the speech had been distorted to fit the respondent's prejudice. Thus, a Republican might remember that the TVA was mentioned; but, as he remembered it, the reference was hostile, whereas the original reference had been favorable.

An even more striking instance of this kind has been reported in an experiment by Herbert Shepard[2] using business executives. These men, involved in a management training program, were formed into teams and required to negotiate as if they were union and management spokesmen. The teams quickly became quite involved in their arguments and emotional in defense of their own position. At this point, each group was required to study the opposition's view until they were *sure* they understood it. Even after this deliberate effort, a memory test showed that most participants could not correctly state the opposing proposal, whereas they were virtually 100% accurate in stating the view of their own group. In a joint study, Robert Blake, Shepard, and Jane Mouton[3] concluded that in bargaining people became rigid and refused to discuss possible alternate solutions when (1) the stakes were high and (2) they saw agreement as impossible. In international negotiations, the stakes will always be high, but perhaps we can make some progress in removing the conviction that agreement is impossible.

THE DISARMAMENT NEGOTIATIONS

As we look at the long series of unproductive disarmament negotiations between the USA and USSR since 1945, we are inclined to suspect that here too is a dialogue of the deaf. Neither side seems capable of hearing, or of understanding, what the other has to say.

Spokesmen for each nation have regularly tried to devise formulas which will maintain their own advantage while weakening the opponent. The Russians, for example, during the period of American atomic monopoly repeatedly proposed banning both the use and the possession of atomic weapons. After they developed nuclear devices, they abandoned the latter point. Similarly, they have proposed that both the USA and the USSR withdraw their troops from all other countries, *former enemy nations excepted*. This would permit Russia to maintain troops in Rumania, Bulgaria, Hungary, etc., since these nations were allied with Germany and Italy in World War II.

Conversely, the Americans have insisted upon formulas calling for a percentage reduction of specified types of armaments, because a percentage cannot be computed unless the total is known. The Russians counter by offering to destroy 500 tanks or 100 bombers since this procedure reveals nothing about how many they have left.[4]

These postwar maneuverings with respect to disarmament and arms control have been boiled down to this: that the USSR wants disarmament without inspection, and the USA wants inspection without disarmament. Our representatives have acted with sufficient inconsistency to give a real sting to this aphorism. In many parts of the world, the Soviets have made considerable propaganda mileage out of our zigzag efforts in this complicated area.

The difficulties that confront our negotiating teams arise from the principle of agency and its corollary of biased perception of events. In addition, these principles are inextricably intertwined with the problems of suspicion and the image of the enemy as completely untrustworthy. In brief, our representatives have been obliged to press for specific proposals, not on the basis that they are logically sound, but on the basis that they appear at the moment to be in the national interest. And they have stressed inspection (because of suspicion) to the point that many world observers fear that the USA is developing the paranoid mentality characteristic of Nazi Germany.

One may be excused for wondering if either the Russians or the Americans have seriously wanted to reach agreement on a disarmament program. On every occasion since 1945 when one nation has made an offer involving significant concessions, the other has immediately raised new obstacles. A conspicuous example was the negotiation on nuclear test bans. In April 1959, the USA suggested that we ignore other types of tests and sign an agreement to ban atmospheric tests, which can be monitored from outside a nation's borders and thus would avoid the inspection problem. Without explanation, the USSR rejected this proposal. In 1962, the Russians proposed a test ban that relied only on existing detection systems, and the USA refused. (Since the American military insists that underground testing is not adequate to develop weapons systems, it is not clear why they made such a point of methods of identifying underground tests.)

The same kind of variation in position has accompanied talks on conventional arms. In 1952, we proposed before the UN Disarmament Commission a ceiling for Russia and the USA of 1.5 million men in military service. In May 1955, when the Russians offered to accept this limitation, President Eisenhower withdrew all our previous proposals. Then in March 1956, he offered a new plan with a ceiling of 2.5 million men for each of the superpowers.

As a third example, we can cite the 1962 negotiations for a joint declaration against "war propaganda"—an issue that would seem innocuous enough. After Mr. Zorin, the Russian delegate, had agreed to a draft statement on this topic, he publicly reversed his position and denounced the "American proposal" which he had helped prepare! Thus, both sides have shown a remarkable ability to back away from any appearance of an agreement on even relatively trivial issues.

To what extent the dialogue of the deaf has prevented us from making rapid progress toward reduction of tensions is not clear. The USA has repeatedly criticized the USSR for refusing to permit inspections and for upholding the veto on inspections with regard to disarmament steps. And yet, as early as 1955, and again late in 1961, the Soviets offered a draft treaty which specified that even in the first stage "the control organization would have the right to inspect without hindrance all undertakings, works, factories, and dockyards which had previously been engaged wholly or partly in the production of rockets, aircraft, surface warships, submarines, and any other means of delivering nuclear weapons . . ."[5]

On the surface there is only one kind of excuse for the American rejection of this proposal: The Russian offer relates to the manufacture of the means of delivering nuclear weapons, while we have focused on the manufacture of the weapons themselves. Is this a wide enough gap to justify our denunciation of the Soviets as unwilling to permit any inspection?

PSYCHOLOGICAL BARRIERS TO NEGOTIATION

Most of the psychological factors detailed in earlier chapters can provide barriers to successful negotiations between nations. Nationalistic feelings induce deafness to any communications which involve criticism of one's country. Emotions of anger may block messages which promise peace and cooperation. Persons who feel a strong economic interest in a given outcome of negotiations will fail to "hear" an offer which would damage their interests. In addition to these, there are additional psychological barriers which need to be recognized.

The Ego of the Diplomat

A nation is constantly faced with the danger that its diplomatic representative will become emotionally involved in a certain position, will be certain of his correctness, and will pass on to the public only those items which confirm his stand. Certainly such instances have occurred. The classical example from our own history is that of President McKinley, who went before Congress to ask for a declaration of war on Spain, even though he was carrying in his pocket a cablegram from the Spanish government yielding all of the points we had previously demanded.[6]

It is inevitable that in extended negotiations the personalities of diplomats will become involved. While the negotiator is acting only as an agent, he almost always finds himself ego-involved with a certain stand; and he may become blind and deaf to evidence which does not fit the views he has upheld so vigorously for so long a time. Probably, this is an argument for rotation of key members of a diplomatic team when parleys continue over a period of months. There is a loss of efficiency while the new members learn what is going on, but there is also a gain in flexibility in that the new spokesman can sometimes see possibilities to which his predecessor was blind or can adopt a new stance without admitting personal inconsistency.

A second psychological difficulty derives from the typical practice of conducting international discussions in the midst of a blare of propaganda. If the Russian press has just been denouncing the British prime minister as "the paid lackey of the American imperialists," the Briton's temper may well be so high that he cannot listen attentively to the content of a Russian proposal. His consciousness would be focused solely on his feelings and on opportunities to express them.

There is a third reason for this psychic deafness, which blocks the receipt of communications from an opponent. This is the possibility that the position presented might be justified and valid. This would mean that the listener and his side had been wrong and the "bad" antagonist was right. George Muench describes a labor-management controversy in which mutual hostility had reached an extraordinary peak. He found that communication between the parties was virtually zero. After working with them in a quasi-therapeutic fashion for some weeks, he found them developing some insight into their own refusals to listen.

The participants recognized, sometimes consciously and
sometimes not, that they tended to resist understanding the
other person because, through such understanding, the
individual found that the opposing viewpoint had more
merit than previously he would allow to emerge into
consciousness.[7]

In other, words a man who has reached a firm conclusion does not
want to have it disturbed by facts. He avoids such a distressing contin-
gency by blocking out any communications from the opposing party.

Muench found that as his talks continued, the union and management spokesmen became capable of checking their own feelings and
listening attentively to the other party. He persuaded them to restate
a point offered by the opponent before attacking it. In attempting to
restate these ideas, it often became clear that the point was misperceived.
Over a period of months, communication so improved that the company
changed from an average of three strikes a year to no strike in six years.

Obviously communication between union and management takes
place within the framework of a national culture and its commonly
recognized economic beliefs. Such foundations for understanding are, of
course, missing in international bargaining. Nevertheless, anyone who
reads accounts of discussions on disarmament at Geneva or on tariffs at
Paris must recognize that the emotional barriers to communication also
play substantial roles in preventing problem solving in these negotiations.

Our statesmen, after all, are human; they are beset by human
weakness as well as human virtue. Like the child who refuses to believe
anything good about his father—like the labor leader who refuses to
believe anything good of an employer, we run the risk of having diplomatic spokesmen who cannot recognize friendly gestures when they
emanate from the opposition. Thus, we face the danger of continuing
indefinitely this dialogue of the deaf.

Resistance to Change

Another psychological barrier to successful negotiation is the general
problem of psychological rigidity. The rigid personality is characterized
by refusal to change, by an insistence that change to reduce conflict
must come from the other side. A clear example of this mode of thinking
is given in a recent book, *A Forward Strategy for America*.[8] This book,
prepared by men allegedly close to our Department of Defense, abounds
in such gems as the following: "Fruitful negotiations on major issues
must await the day when a meaningful change *has occurred* in the Soviet

system.'' (p. 223) How the authors intend to persuade the communists to make meaningful changes in their system is unstated. What the authors would say if the USSR demanded meaningful changes in our system as a precondition of negotiations is also unclear. This is a childish refusal to face the facts of existence. If it is truly a guide to our defense policy, we are indeed in a bad way. Obviously, all of us would be happy if a meaningful change occurred over there. But the task of diplomacy is to help such changes come about, not to loll on one's axis until the change just happens to happen.

Similarly the authors say, ''Our policy must be based upon the premise that we *cannot tolerate the survival* of a political system which has the growing capability and the ruthless will to destroy us.'' This is close to saying that we must all commit suicide. Anyone who believes that the men in the Kremlin will sit quietly by and watch us destroy their power is insane. There should be no doubt that, if they are faced with a real threat of internal revolution and loss of power, they will launch a nuclear attack. Indeed, I suspect that, if our government were faced with an immediate and impending threat to our national survival, we too would resort to nuclear offensive strategy. Survival is the one ultimate goal which, when threatened, releases the maximum of aggression. This is a fact of human nature which policy makers must recognize.

WHAT IS THE BARGAINING PROCESS?

The dialogue of the deaf could be further illustrated by examples from union-management negotiations. However, I now want to redirect the argument to the positive side of negotiating. It is assumed, in international as in industrial relations, that bargaining will occur ''in good faith.'' Unfortunately, it is difficult to define this phrase. In international affairs, we can only try to bring it about, with no review board or agency to enforce it.

The essence of a bargain, of course, is that some advantages are exchanged. As the economist would put it, the limiting cases of a bargain are those in which all advantages are seized by party A or party B. Most bargaining results in a solution which yields some gains for each party in comparison with the continuation of the status quo. Because of the polarization of thinking in this country, every negotiating step that suggests the slightest concession to Russian views is likely to be denounced as treason. One may assume that the same is true in the USSR. Under such conditions, bargaining in good faith is very improbable.

Intensity of motivation is one factor which determines polarized thinking. If you want something strongly, any object which helps you achieve that goal will seem very good; and any condition which blocks you from goal achievement will look very bad. This is a function of the intensifying effect of a motive. Relatively weak impulses, such as liking classical music or enjoying bowling, do not give rise to extreme judgments of people who agree or disagree with you. On the other hand, strong motives, such as sex, money, and power, may set off such extreme reactions that murder follows.

In relation to international affairs, this means that the intensely nationalistic person is prone to overestimate his country's virtues and the enemy's evils. It also means that, as a threat to the nation becomes more highly visible, polarized thinking will spread throughout the population. Under strong pressure, we see everything as either black or white—for us or against us.

Such polarized thinking obviously interferes seriously with negotiations. As someone has remarked: When we most urgently need flexibility in thinking is when we have it least. In a crisis, when we should be creative and innovative in devising ways to resolve the problems without violence, we become polarized. Thought processes become rigid, and there is adherence to traditional ways of handling problems.

The magnitude of the stakes and the danger to survival inherent in nuclear warfare lead to intense motivation of national representatives in negotiations. Thus, they are subject to polarized thinking, and they are unwilling to take chances. They prefer to stick to traditional ways of behaving, even if these have repeatedly led to wars. Thus, we get the same old cliches from the Russians about "war-mongering imperialists"[9] and from the Americans about "insidious and imperialistic communists." The name-calling interferes with communication, and it certainly does not help in bargaining; but the underlying rigidity of thought is a far more serious matter.

It is unlikely that we can completely eliminate either polarized thinking or excessive rigidity from our diplomats. We may, however, by giving conscious attention to the matter, develop new insights, daring innovations in policy proposals, and novel tactics for approaching the Russians. Since our established tactics have not been very successful, it is time to adopt a more experimental approach.

FAILURES OF COMMUNICATION

The essence of the preceding comments is that failures of communication depend in large part upon the characteristics of the listener. To paraphrase an old proverb, none are so deaf as those who will not hear.

An instructive demonstration along this line works very effectively in a group situation. Those present in a group are asked to think of

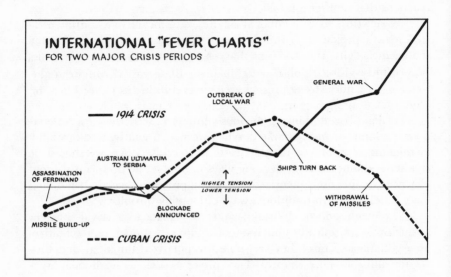

INTERNATIONAL "FEVER CHARTS"
FOR TWO MAJOR CRISIS PERIODS

Dr. Robert C. North and his associates at Stanford University are trying to introduce numerical measurement of "tension level" as it corresponds to official documents during an international crisis. If successful, such measurement would give national leaders a valuable tool for guiding decisions. (Reprinted from *Stanford Today,* Spring 1963, Series 1, No. 4, with the permission of the publishers, Stanford University. ©1963 by the Board of Trustees of the Leland Stanford Junior University.)

some instance in the recent past when they have had difficulties arising from failure of communication with people around them. Then they are asked for descriptions of these situations. In about 99% of cases, the person reports that someone else failed to understand him; only rarely will anyone mention a case in which he failed to understand the other party.

In industry this means, for example, that managers blame workers for failing to understand instructions and information given them, but that managers never blame themselves for failing to understand what the workers are trying to communicate. In race relations, Whites and Negroes blame each other for failure to receive messages; neither side accepts responsibility for failure to understand the other.

In international affairs, each nation is constantly trying to communicate to others its stand on major policy questions. These communications are frequently misunderstood. Is the defect to be found in poor transmission? Or is it rather that we do not attempt to understand what others are communicating to us? The analysis described earlier in this chapter indicates that we pay relatively little attention to what others say—unless what they say happens to fit our expectations. This would point to the conclusion that failures in international understanding result, in large part, from failure to receive and interpret messages from abroad. They do not depend primarily on failure to send messages out.

This argument does not justify reduced appropriations for the Voice of America; certainly, we have to continue trying to get our messages across. But the argument does support a different approach to the messages coming in. We must spend more time trying to figure out what given acts and statements mean *for the nation issuing them.* What are they trying to tell us? We may rationally refuse to accept the message in any event; but unless we first find out what it means, we have no intelligent basis for a decision.

Agency and Communication Problems

We must recognize that mutual understanding is hampered by the circumstances under which international negotiations occur. Each delegation comes to the bargaining session with instructions to "sell" a certain solution to the problem. This proposal may completely ignore the message transmitted by another delegation. The spokesman for his nation finds no way in which he can incorporate his instructions into a meaningful dialogue, so he simply ignores the communications from the opposition. He is acting as an agent and lacks freedom to discuss new points. He can, of course, communicate them to his superiors.

Unfortunately, the heads of governments may ignore these communications from the negotiators. A relevant illustration comes from the British, French, and Israeli invasion of Egypt after Nasser seized the Suez Canal in 1956.

When the British government was considering the proposed military expedition, many experts were called in and much material examined before a decision was reached. Nevertheless, according to R.H.S. Crossman, a Labour M.P., the key decision makers (Anthony Eden, Harold Macmillan, and Selwyn Lloyd) ignored the evidence of dangerous consequences in the USA and the UN, vetoed the virtually unanimous recommendation of the experts against the venture, and ordered the expedition. He wryly concludes that "If the free world is the place where...one may pursue the truth in politics, it is also...the place where that truth is nearly always disregarded."[10]

We do not know whether the then prime minister, Mr. Macmillan, felt that he could not yield to these adverse recommendations because he considered himself the agent of the entire nation. But it is clear that he refused to listen and that the results were unpleasant for his government.

Communication Failures within the Nation

Negotiations between nations fit the pattern I have called the dialogue of the deaf because each representative hears only what he wants to hear and ignores what does not fit into his frame of reference. The major distorting effect here derives from nationalism: Each side wants to maintain such advantages as it possesses (e.g., the Soviet resistance to inspection because secrecy is one of its military advantages.) Neither side is ready to make any concession which is perceived as weakening an established position.

Communications within the nation often show a somewhat similar pattern; but, of course, the role of nationalism is unimportant in such instances. Loyalty to an agency or an arm of the service may operate in exactly the same fashion, however. Commitment to a particular service or bureau illustrates the problem.

Murray Dyer describes a series of meetings in which representatives of the Departments of State and Defense and the CIA debated an issue of policy. The group met fruitlessly for 59 sessions, because "CIA would not budge from a position in which it was a minority of one."[11] (The Russians are not the only group to insist on a veto!) Obviously, communication was not very effective. Settlements of controversial issues within the nation cannot be achieved if each protagonist insists rigidly on his own position; and he is unlikely to change if he cannot hear (or, more precisely, does not understand) the position of his critic.

This is, of course, the point proposed above. Negotiation with the Russians is futile if they insist rigidly on their own stance, and it is equally futile if we are adamant on our own position. Further, it seems likely that at least some of this rigidity derives from a failure to understand the communication of the opponent.

COMMUNICATION WITH THE RUSSIANS

In the face of the formidable difficulties of communication between nations, one may well be surprised that success is ever achieved. To communicate successfully with an adversary calls for exceptionally careful planning.

If we decide that we want to conduct meaningful negotiations with the Russians, we shall have to abandon the familiar stance that we do not want a settlement except on our own terms. This stance is fruitless and destructive. The power of the Russians is not an illusion; it is a fact with which we must reckon. For our own survival, it is necessary that we explore ways of arriving at a mutually agreeable settlement— not exactly what we want, not exactly what they want, but a compromise both sides can live with.

We shall not achieve this by name calling. We shall not make progress by reminding the Russians of what they did in Hungary in 1956 or in Poland in 1939. The futility of such behavior is demonstrable when we note our own response to a scolding from the Russians about Cuba or about Mississippi. Heckling, in either direction, does not smooth the path to a settlement.

The skillful communicator prefers to start by finding some point of mutual agreement. If this is not available, he tells his audience something they want to hear. Thus, the politician opens his speech by coming out strongly for God, home, and country. Having gotten the audience in a receptive frame of mind, he can then try to influence them to favor his position on medical care, higher education, or the abolition of the TVA.

If we really decide to try to reach a settlement with the USSR, we shall be wise to open our communications with endorsement of an idea they like. This can be general and complete disarmament, which we all desire. It can be human welfare. It can be simply peace. We might even express admiration for their accomplishments in science, for their courageous fight at Stalingrad (now Volgograd) and for their desire to equal us in industrial production. Any such opening establishes an attitude of receptivity, a willingness to listen, which is all too rare in our negotiations.[12]

The Russian does not receive some of our messages because he believes in *his image* of the USA, rather than in our words. We must therefore attempt to modify this image. Psychological experimentation indicates that the most favorable tactic will be that of arousing dissonance, that is, introducing information which conflicts with the stereotyped picture. Our message, for example, might begin with our wish for general and complete disarmament; it might well continue with a proposal that we wish to free our productive resources for peaceful competition with the socialist bloc (as they call themselves.) The message might emphasize a desire to raise consumer standards, to end wasteful war production, to aid underdeveloped nations, etc. The purpose of transmitting such communications is to try to break up the Russian image of the war-mongering imperialist. Unexpected communications may be expected to operate in this direction.

Similarly, we can profitably stress the occasions on which we have successfully cooperated: during World War II, through navigation agreements, and in Antarctic exploration. Such cooperative exchanges and events are not as rare as many Americans believe.

In commenting upon prior Russian proposals, it would be a sound tactic to treat these proposals as offers in good faith. Our representatives seem to feel a compulsion to denounce all Russian suggestions as fraudulent, as calculated to block agreement or to stir up dissension in the West. Whether or not these charges are true, making the charges does not aid, but rather impedes, progress toward agreement.[13]

In communicating to the people behind the Iron Curtain and to their diplomats, we would find it beneficial to note the good features of the Russians proposals before pointing out what we consider to be their defects. In making counterproposals, we can give credit to them for initiating a line of discussion which we are seriously considering in spite of certain shortcomings. The principles of effective debate and persuasion are widely understood in this country; we should be able to devise tactics which will support our position in preference to theirs without stirring up additional hostility.

The use of these methods does not imply that we can deceive the Russians into accepting our policies as touched-up replicas of their own. The Russians are quite capable of defending themselves against high-pressure selling and of identifying what is to their own best interests. In later pages, I shall offer some comments on kinds of policies that would protect the legitimate interests of both nations while moving away from the tensions that beset us today.

THE PROBLEM OF CREDIBILITY

To be effective, communications must be believed. I have noted earlier that our military measures will function as a deterrent only if they are credible. Communications, whether verbal or nonverbal, must be credible or the recipient will simply ignore them.

The traditional reliance among diplomats on face-to-face communication stems in part from this question. A written note may be less ambiguous, but it may also be more deceptive. In personal conversation, an ambassador gets information from facial expression, from tone of voice, from flushing, perspiration, and gestures. He unquestionably arrives at estimations of the sincerity of a threat, the genuineness of an offer to conciliate, the honesty of a concession. Such estimations play important roles in the negotiation process.

We may speculate that this was an important factor in Premier Khrushchev's fondness for summit conferences. He apparently had confidence in his ability to judge sincerity. He also saw no point in wasting his time on subordinates, who were obligated to follow certain policies, when a chief executive might have considerably more freedom and flexibility.

Ralph Gerard[14] has offered some interesting speculations about methods for increasing credibility in negotiating situations. In brief, what he proposes is an adaptation of the lie detector for such meetings. The diplomat who is presenting an important statement and who wishes quite urgently to demonstrate the sincerity with which he holds this position may voluntarily speak with recording devices making a public record of his blood pressure, electrical skin reflexes, and the like. Experts monitoring this record for each participating nation would then be in a position to advise their chiefs as to evidence of evasion or of sincerity. We should probably note that this method does not reveal "truth" in the abstract; it reveals that the speaker *believes* he is truthful. Gerard cites the example of a psychotic who believed himself to be George Washington: While hooked up to the detector, he was asked if he were George Washington and he answered, "No." *But the lie detector showed him to be lying!* He denied his belief because he knew the investigators would not accept his identification, but the machine recorded his disbelief in his answer.)

As Gerard notes, a great deal of research would be necessary to check all possible loopholes in this procedure. It would be worthwhile to try it out on labor-management negotiations. Such usages might help to avert costly work stoppages and might also enable experts to decide what precautions must be observed to get usable—and, most important, credible—results in diplomatic situations.

Communicating with the Russians is made especially difficult (and assertions that we want peaceful coexistence especially incredible) by the high level of tension associated with our military competition. Negotiation would be easier if we could convince the Russians that our intentions are not aggressive. Mere words do not seem to be successful in putting this message across; positive actions, designed to act as communications, are required. The following chapter analyzes a specific proposal which might improve communications by reducing tension and modifying the Russian image of America.

12
An Arms Race
in Reverse

I agree with those historians and social scientists who consider disarmament to be a subsidiary issue, secondary to question of economics and strategy. None the less, arms are a highly visible aspect of strategy, and they influence the deployment of economic resources. Further, the arms race in which we intermittently compete with the Russians is a highly visible aspect of our relations with them, and it is closely correlated with the degree of tension in these relations. Since actions are inherently more credible than words, progress in making our words more believable might be facilitated by taking certain tension-reducing actions. We may therefore profit by considering whether first steps in the area of disarmament might be useful as preludes to agreement on more basic issues.

Some critics, of course, hold that this is the wrong area in which to start. The A-bomb did not start the conflict between capitalism and communism, nor would its abolition end these disagreements. In an amusing reference to the old Jewish custom of burdening a goat with the sins of a whole village and driving the goat away, Joseph Walsh and Norman Kopmeyer wrote, "If the peace movement could succeed in putting all the bombs on the back of the goat and drive it out of the village, we would still live in a nationalistic and militaristic village, and only time would stand in the way of more and larger bombs."[1] This is true if we assume that nothing is done about the nationalistic and ideological conflicts in the service of which bombs are built.

Disarmament steps have the advantage that they can be taken now and that they will tend to reduce the tension level and make other negotiations possible. If polarized thinking and threat orientation are minimized, communication about Germany, Southeast Asia, and similar topics will be facilitated.

I have noted earlier some of the difficulties in negotiation with the Russians about disarmament. They have been deaf to our proposals; and, on the whole, we seem to have been deaf to theirs. There have been multilateral sessions in the UN Disarmament Commission and bilateral sessions of our foreign ministers and our heads of state. None of these have led to any reversal of the arms race. Some observers hold that it has been slowed—that the race is no more than a rapid walk at the present time. This is a technological question irrelevant to our needs. What we must have is a reversal—a diminution in megatonnage, not a creeping inflation of destructive power.

The crucial task, as seen from our side, is that of modifying the Russian attitude. We have offered various proposals: a ceiling on conventional arms, a cutoff of nuclear production, "open skies" inspection. All of these have been rejected. As our delegates see it, the rejection is based upon Russian hostility and secretiveness.

The crucial task that the Russians find themselves facing is a modification of the American attitude. They have offered such proposals as general and complete disarmament, a ban on missile production (with inspection of missile factories), a ceiling on conventional armaments, and the denuclearization of central Europe. As the Russians see us, we have rejected their reasonable ideas because we cherish dreams of destroying the communist system and restoring capitalism everywhere.

CAN ATTITUDES BE MODIFIED?

Both sides may plausibly wonder if their task is hopeless. Perhaps, they may be ruminating, human nature is so pugnacious that efforts to remove weapons will be resisted at all costs.

Fortunately, the evidence against this pessimistic conclusion is quite strong. Man is not necessarily dominated by an inherent suicidal impulse. Further, we know that attitudes can be changed—albeit with difficulty. Teachers and advertisers change superficial attitudes easily, but other, deep-seated attitudes will yield only to two or three years of psychotherapy.

Attitudes can also be modified by actions—by changes in the physical world. There have been some spectacular examples of reduction in hostility in union-management relations in this country. The change at the Ford Motor Company in its dealings with the United Automobile Workers is a case in point. The improvement at Inland Steel and at Armour & Company can also be cited. In all three cases, the major factor in the break with a hostile tradition seems to have been a change in managerial tactics. After a period of hostility, of attempting to deny the union a foothold, management accepted the inevitable and decided to work out a way to coexist with the union. The social scientists who have observed these cases at close hand report that the change in managerial tactics brought about—after some time—a reciprocal relaxation of hostility on the side of the union.

The union-management example is not, of course, a perfect analogue for international relations. The overriding power of the government has always placed some constraints on industrial conflict. But the dramatic nature of the change within such companies as those mentioned is, nonetheless, a strong argument that the same approach might be useful in the international sphere.

We know that we can change Russian behavior by our unilateral acts, even if we have no luck in negotiating. All we have to do is announce an increase in our Polaris program, in nuclear production, or in conventional weapons and the Russians dutifully follow suit. An "escalation" of expressed hostility here induces a parallel change in the USSR. (The Russians can control our behavior by the same kind of unilateral action.)

If it is possible by unilateral action to modify Russian policy, to increase their armaments, would it be possible by unilateral action to reverse this trend? Having failed to bring about disarmament through the UN Commission or through direct negotiations, could we be more successful by taking the initiative ourselves? This is a question now being asked in many quarters.

The extreme of this proposal, which is not worth much consideration at the present time, is complete unilateral disarmament.[2] Supporters of this extreme stand include those people who want to "Ban the Bomb" in the West even if it is continued in the East and those who want to disband all of our military services. By and large, the argument here is that the Russians, not being threatened any more, would follow our example. India, after all, has not been overwhelmed by the communists,

THE BALANCE OF TERROR

"THE PROBLEM IS HOW TO TURN LOOSE WITHOUT LETTING GO"

Even with the best of intentions (which, of course, are
not always present), mutual arms and tension reduction
is difficult to achieve. Nevertheless,
we must start somewhere. (Cartoon by Mauldin, in
the *St. Louis Post-Dispatch.* Reprinted by permission.)

although India is not a member of the western alliance.

To this argument, the critics reply with the example of Czechoslovakia, which was forced to accept a communist regime in 1948 under the raw threat of military conquest. The chances of a similar fate for western Europe must not be underestimated.

Complete unilateral disarmament, then, does not seem a plausible policy for the present—even if it might be ten, twenty, or thirty years hence. We are, nevertheless, intrigued by the possibility of reversing the arms race on a smaller scale. Since we can, by taking one step forward, get the Russians to take one also, we might be able, stepping backwards, to induce a similar withdrawal by them. How might this tactic operate?

OSGOOD'S GRADUATED RECIPROCATION PROPOSAL

A means to taking the initiative in unilateral action—but toward threat reduction instead of threat magnification—has been sketched by C. E. Osgood, an American psychologist. He calls his general formulation "Graduated Reciprocation in Tension Reduction"[3]—this title being devised so that the initials spell "GRIT," a quality, he says, that will be needed to administer the program effectively.

Essentially, Osgood says, we have not succeeded in communicating to the Russians the fact that their stereotyped view of us is incorrect. They see us as bad, greedy, selfish, imperialist, warmongering capitalists. We know that this isn't so. How can we teach them to see us differently? Speeches, radio broadcasts, and printed propaganda have not been very effective. The suggestion is that we must undertake a program of action designed to break up their stereotyped picture of us and replace it with a view which will be compatible with a more peaceful type of interaction.

The following principles have been proposed by Osgood as those he considers indispensable to such a program of influencing the opponent:

1. Unilateral acts must be perceived by the opponent as reducing his external threat. Threat induces rigidity and polarized thinking; it elevates hostility; it reinforces the image of the USA as bad and, hence, not worthy of trust and cooperation. Osgood holds that there are many ways in which we can reduce by modest amounts our threat to the USSR without perceptibly decreasing our own security.

2. These acts must be accompanied by explicit invitations to reciprocate. If we make a gesture, such as closing military bases, we do not wish to appear frightened or to have been forced into the action by economic weakness. It should be made clear that this is a deliberate

policy to invite cooperation and that reciprocation by the communists will encourage us to take other similar measures.

3. The unilateral actions must be executed regardless of whether the opponent makes prior commitment to reciprocate. If we wait for a positive answer, we have simply modified slightly the verbal negotiations at Geneva. If we announce a unilateral reduction, we should take it and then remind the world that we are expecting some reciprocity.[4]

4. Unilateral acts must be planned in sequences and continued over considerable periods regardless of whether the opponent overtly cooperates. This policy, Osgood notes, is an attempt to break up a stereotyped view of the USA held by the communists (and, although he does not mention this, by many noncommunists as well). A single step is not enough, but we may choose varied areas so that we do not unnecessarily weaken ourselves in any specific theater of operations.

5. As part of a consistent policy, such acts must be announced in advance of execution and widely publicized to allied, neutral, and enemy countries. The desired psychological returns will flow from an organized, verifiable policy, not from haphazard actions without a visible pattern.

6. Unilateral initiatives must, wherever possible, focus on areas of mutual self-interest and opportunities for cooperation. While the popular view seems to be that any gain for the USSR must be a loss for us, there are actually many areas in which both sides can benefit. Scientific work—space exploration and medical research—is obviously one.

7. Acts must be graduated in risk potential to avoid excessive hazards. Unlike the absolute pacifist, Osgood recognizes that the existing hostility must be treated as reality. He therefore proposes that these arms-reducing measures be limited in scope and chosen to avoid any major weakness in our defenses.

8. The actions must be accompanied by firmness toward the opponent. If the Russians interpret the policy as weakness and begin to make forward thrusts, Osgood supports a posture of firm resistance. As far as possible, this would not interfere with the planned tension-reducing steps, and the two would be clearly separate in our public statements. Thus, the opponent would be invited to reciprocate but deterred from exploiting any advantage he thought might be opening up.

It is obvious that caution and gradualism are built into the Osgood proposal. What he proposes is a planned series of *small* changes in varied fields but with a consistent direction. Thus, we might declassify certain data derived from our space probes; on another occasion, we might invite neutral observers to inspect our missile-launching bases; or we might remove nuclear weapons from specified sites (with neutral verification).

Each such step would be widely announced ahead of time, and the Russians would be invited to reciprocate—but without our specifying *how* they must reciprocate (if we attempt to do this, we will be back to bilateral bargaining, which has not been satisfactory.) It is plausible to expect that the Russians would feel pressure from world opinion to make a similar conciliatory gesture. Further, we can assume that the Soviet Union has internal economic problems of sufficient gravity that they would like to withdraw some resources from military production for civilian purposes. Thus, if they can do so without losing face and without seeming to yield to American demands, they might follow our initiative.

The proposed program, Osgood suggests, should be combined with a "second-strike" missile strategy, which is already officially proclaimed by our defense forces. The second-strike policy is that we will not be the first to use nuclear weapons but that we will have sufficient forces (in "hardened" underground sites, in Polaris submarines, and in manned bombers) to accept a heavy blow and still deal severe punishment to an opponent. Tension reduction, therefore, would not involve steps to weaken this second-strike capacity until firm ground had been established for negotiating an *inspected* reduction of nuclear forces. The need for the program is indicated by the fact that, up to the present, we have not established mutual confidence adequate to accept a nuclear disarmament treaty. We don't trust the Russians; they don't trust us.[5] The GRIT program would seek to break the vicious circle of distrust and threat, so that it would be possible to agree on a treaty.

Osgood is not the only current proponent of small, unilateral steps toward disarmament. Amitai Etzioni, in a book called *The Hard Way to Peace*,[6] outlines a strategy which he calls "gradualism." Similarly, James Wadsworth *(The Price of Peace)*[7] thinks that we must look forward to slow rather than sudden disarmament. He differs from Osgood and Etzioni in placing more stress on negotiated moves as opposed to unilateral decisions of the USA and our allies.

Obviously, no one is in a position to say, with complete confidence, what will result from a specified tactic. The advocates of unilateral disarmament point out that we did not attack Russia when we had an atomic monopoly; therefore, we could disarm and assume that th Soviets would not exploit their military advantage. The "deterre school argues that other nations have always exploited such oppo and that we must maintain our retaliatory capacity as ?

shield. Each group can point to some bits of evidence in its favor; each can point to evidence contradicting the opposition. Hitler certainly attacked the poorly prepared West in 1939; on the other hand, prior to 1914, all the European powers had been engaging in an arms race, chiefly in the name of deterrence. Thus, the two world wars of our century suggest that neither unilateral weakness nor mutual deterrence provides a stable basis for a durable peace. This is, if not an argument for a policy of graduated unilateral steps, at least evidence that we need to explore novel alternatives instead of rigidly adhering to past strategies.

UNDERSTANDING RUSSIAN GOALS

If we wish to apply any kind of gradualist unilateral strategy in dealing with the Russians, we must consider what major goals they seek. It will not be enough to consider what actions from our point of view would be tension reducing. We have enough data that we should be able to see what will be significant in their view of world conflicts.

Perhaps the outstanding feature of Russian policy in the postwar years is fear of a reunited, revengeful Germany. This fear is not only emphasized in Russian public statements but is also perceptible behind many other maneuvers, such as the Rapacki plan for a disarmed central Europe, the opposition to the spread of nuclear weapons, and the tight control over the Ulbricht government in East Germany.

The Soviet fear has much concrete evidence to support it. Twice in the last fifty years Germany has invaded Russia and devastated large areas. The Adenauer government has repeatedly refused to recognize the Oder-Neisse line as the new eastern frontier with Poland. Substantial blocks of German votes are regularly cast for politicians who demand restoration, if not of Hitler's Reich, at least of Bismarck's Reich. Many Americans, who are by no means pro-Communist, worry about a resurgence of German nationalism and militarism.

When questions like this are raised, we find that American policy has no clear line to follow. We created the West German government as a matter of convenience because we were unwilling to maintain an occupation regime; but the Bonn government has no more legal status than that of East Germany, which we refuse to recognize. We waver in regard to how much support we will give the West Germans. At first we try to demilitarize them; then we start scolding because they do not provide troops for NATO. We exact reparations, then give them loans and grants, then demand help to ease our dollar outflow. No one should be surprised if the Russians are baffled by our German policy and fearful of what may be our long-range plan.

This analysis suggests that unilateral steps designed to make clear that we do not support any drive by Germany to regain the eastern territories (now under Polish rule) would be more useful than sending Benny Goodman to Moscow. Perhaps, we should also accept a policy of two Germanys as we have accepted two Chinas. But here we run upon a hidden American problem. We too are afraid of Germany—of a reunited Germany which would align itself with Russia. Thus, our ambivalence is due to a conflict between our desire for German support and our fear of German reunification in alliance with the opposition.

Another area of controversy is our policy toward the satellite nations—Poland, Czechoslovakia, Hungary, Romania, and Bulgaria. These countries have been set up as a buffer zone by the Russians, much as they were set up by Britain and France in 1919 as a *cordon sanitaire* to prevent the disease of bolshevism from spreading. Now the satellite nations have primarily a strategic military role, although this role is obviously far less significant today in the age of the ICBM than it seemed in 1946.

If we do not intend to provide military aid to revolts in the satellite nations—and our actions in 1953 and 1956 make it clear that we do not—then we should stop giving veiled hints of such support. It would be wiser, and more likely to succeed, if we play on the nationalism of these areas and give them some financial support when they show independence of Moscow. We must also make it clear that we do not propose to reestablish the old feudal landlords if a western-oriented regime should come to power. We must, unilaterally, change the tone of the Voice of America and Radio Free Europe and shut off aid to the governments in exile, which have been mere dreams for twenty years or more.

IMPLEMENTING A UNILATERAL PROGRAM

Taking Osgood as an example of those who have proposed this kind of approach, let me cite some of the steps he suggests and the precautions he would incorporate in implementing his unilateral program. First of all, he notes that, to be effective, a unilateral step must be perceived by our opponent as a reduction of some external threat to him. While obvious examples here would be deactivation of overseas bases or reducing our troops in Europe, there are alternative steps in this category; for example, releasing some classified scientific information or permitting neutral inspection of some of our installations.

When we are prepared to take a cautious step in this direction, we should announce it in advance and invite the Russians to reciprocate.

We can win a good deal of neutral support if we handle this wisely. But we should not specify what kind of reciprocity is expected; for if we did, we would be going back to bargaining. If the Russians do indeed take a step that we perceive to be the removal of some threat to us, we can then proceed to further steps. If the Russians do not reciprocate, we can try a new gesture in another area. Certainly, at least three or four such gestures should be attempted before the policy is abandoned.

Osgood's hypothetical program includes a timetable listing such items as the following (he offers these only as illustrations):

April 1: We announce imminent release of all medical data from our space program—reciprocation invited.

May 1: We announce removal of trade and travel restrictions affecting Communist China—reciprocation invited.

June 15: We publish plans for the denuclearization of one overseas base, and we invite UN and Russian inspection—reciprocation invited.

August 1: We announce an opportunity for Russia to "plug in" on our radar screen, which will show movement of all American bombers. Thus, we increase their warning time and prove that we do not plan surprise attack—reciprocation invited.

These are merely samples from a variety that have been or could be proposed. Note that none of these exposes us to a fatal blow, but each does remove some irritation to the Soviet bloc. The series, in fact, could be carried considerably further without endangering us or our allies in any serious way.

Will the Russians cooperate? Will they begin making tension-reducing gestures? No one can guarantee this. But there are many psychological pressures on them to cooperate in reducing tensions. First of all, both leaders and citizens in Russia know well the destruction of war and can imagine better than Americans the horror of a nuclear duel. Second, they have many urgent needs for housing, roads, and consumer goods, all of which are denied now because of the arms race. Any increase in the armament investment would mean far more hardship to Soviet citizens than to Americans.

However, it may be argued that time is on the side of the communists. Because of their remarkable strides in rocketry, they may shortly be ahead of us in destructive power. They may not wish to reduce tensions; they may prefer instead to risk the increasing hostility associated with local wars and subversive tactics. Perhaps they are confident that when, or if, the chips are down, their power could knock out the USA with tolerable destruction at home.

Etzioni argues persuasively against this view. The Russians must, he suggests, realize that if the Americans feel crowded into a corner, they can lash out with great destructive fury. The USSR might win all the preliminary battles and yet lose the major campaign. The Russians are aware of this; and, because of this awareness, Etzioni feels that the odds favor their reciprocation.

Efforts to initiate this kind of tension-reducing program will encounter, in both the USA and the USSR, the challenge that concessions are weak and cowardly. The ideal of the tough leader, who wins every time and never concedes anything to the opposition, is held in both nations.[8] Thus, if an American president set this program in motion, he would be attacked as a weakling, if not a traitor. We have some reason to believe that the same would happen in Moscow. (It is at least possible that the ouster of Premier Khrushchev was punishment for his yielding to American pressures over the Cuban missiles in October 1962. We note, however, that while the Soviet Union lost face in that encounter, the Soviet foreign policies did not seem to change much.)

The internal political implications of a policy like GRIT are interesting. Suppose an American president makes a cooperative gesture, such as removing atomic missiles from Turkey. The Russian leader may be tempted to move in and intimidate the Turks, now presumably weakened. However, if he does so, he strengthens the hands of the right-wing extremists in the USA. If he should help the American fanatics to come to power, his problems would be exacerbated. Thus, he presumably will think twice before exploiting any apparent weakening of the American defense perimeter.

This principle also operates in reverse. If the Russian government takes a step of which we approve, we should reciprocate by taking action which will make that government look good. Certainly, we should not crow that the Reds have admitted either weakness or error. If we do so, we provide aid and comfort to the right-wing Stalinists in Moscow, who, if they regain power, will make life more unpleasant for us.

These political implications of foreign tactics make it seem that there are built-in rewards for a policy of tension reduction. They are not guaranteed, but the probabilities look good enough to justify a careful experiment in this direction.

13
International
Organization

Reducing the level of armaments is only a short-term goal for us. In the long run, we must establish institutions capable of accommodating the dynamic pressures arising from human loves, hates, and ambitions by resolving disputes in a peaceful manner. The priority attached to arms reduction and tension reduction is a purely practical matter.

Vigorous efforts to ease tensions, such as those suggested in the preceding chapter, may bring about a climate for international negotiation in which other, more basic settlements can be conducted. When a high level of suspicion and hostility blocks communication between nations, and especially between the USA and the USSR, such discussions make little progress. If the tension level is lowered, we may be able to make a start on organizing a world in which nations may pursue their goals in a nonviolent manner.

Political scientists seem agreed that the two basic goals of modern nations are, first, security against military attack and, second, economic advantage. Thus, it may be stated as a minimum requirement that if individual nations are to be curbed in the use of military force, then international institutions must provide some protection for nations

STRAIGHT AND NARROW POST-WAR PATH

Just after the war, an international police force was
narrowly envisaged as merely a control over the
defeated Axis Powers. Now it appears that an
international force is needed as a restriction on
militarism anywhere on the planet. (Cartoon by Knott,
in *The Dallas Morning News*. Reprinted by permission)

against attack from outside their borders. These international institutions must also be flexible enough to provide for shifts in economic and power balances as conditions change within nations. Failure to provide military security will mean that, sooner or later, national leaders will feel impelled to resort to military action against what they perceive as a dire threat. Failure to provide flexibility will result in frustration of dynamic leadership groups and the resultant aggressive tension and violence. The UN must not seek to freeze the status quo; it must try only to insure that changes in the power balance are brought about without resort to war by those nations that are "on the make," particularly in the economic sphere.

SUPRANATIONAL CONTROL OF VIOLENCE

Individuals within a nation give up the right to carry arms at all times when they are assured of police protection. In this day of civil rights agitation, we are reminded that the police, to be effective, must be perceived as impartial. Similarly, if an International Police Force is to be created, the first psychological obstacle to be overcome is that of suspicion that the IPF will be an arm of the West (or the East) to be used in a biased fashion. This is the major stumbling block to such proposals today. The communist nations fear a strong UN military contingent because the West can still dominate voting, particularly in the General Assembly.

Human history shows that the area of peaceful cooperation is expanded as the prerogative of violence is taken over from the individual by the tribe and then the city-state and, more recently, the nation-state. An obvious next step is that some kind of supranational control be established, which will restrict the freedom of nations to resort to armed force to settle disputes.

While this step seems eminently logical, the citizens of the great powers (and many small ones too) reject it. Their rejection stems from the power of nationalism—the attitude-complex that demands complete autonomy for each nation to take such action as seems desirable in pursuing national goals. Most of these individuals readily agree that complete autonomy for individuals (including the right to use arms in pursuit of one's goals) would be utterly intolerable. No society could exist with such anarchy. Yet they cannot accept the corollary that anarchy at the level of nations is equally dangerous to the survival of civilization.

Some observers believe that this bitter opposition to any dilution of national sovereignty is weakening. An optimistic note is struck in a comment on this problem by a prominent historian, Henry Steele Commager:

Nationalism, as we have known it in the past, is too dangerously irrational for the needs of the future...It is probable that we are even now entering a new era of international relations, one in which nations may come to play on the world scene the role that states have played on the American scene, and that insistence upon all the prerogatives of national sovereignty will come to seem as outmoded and irrational as insistence upon all the prerogatives of state sovereignty in the United States today.[1]

It may be that Commager is too optimistic. Certainly, as he implies in his comparison with states in the USA, there are many conservatives who wish to maintain local sovereignty. Some southerners still believe they can defy federal control over voting by Negroes; and, similarly, there will be many who wish to deny any abdication of national sovereignty to any kind of supranational organization. Commager's hopes presumably rest on the sweep of history, which shows a gradual evolution from city-state to feudal duchy to nation-state and now to such limited supranational bodies as the European Common Market.

With respect to an International Police Force, there is a crucial question: Would the citizens of such nations as the USA and USSR[2] support such a venture? It is difficult to get any idea of public opinion from behind the Iron Curtain. But in the West, the answer is clearly affirmative. During World War II, the percentages of the American public favoring creation of such a force rose from 70% to 86%. Similar results were obtained in Britain, Canada, and Australia. These figures diminished as World War II faded into the background; but even in 1953, an Office of Public Opinion Research Survey found 56% of Americans favoring the IPF[3] (on an identical question in 1947, the figure had been 75% favorable).

The conclusion may well be that the public is ahead of the national leaders on this question. Officials are sensitive to possible abuses of an IPF, and they are probably unconsciously motivated to protect their own power. Many would be reluctant to go along with such a proposal. The best hope here seems to lie in efforts to elect leaders whose biases may favor international control of violence.

International prevention of national violence means an International Police Force equipped to take *action against aggressors*. But who is an aggressor? Hitler accused Poland of aggression in 1939. The Russians accused Finland of aggression in 1940. The Japanese in 1941 rationalized the Pearl Harbor attack by our economic aggression against them.

People will refuse to cooperate with a police force if they perceive it as biased and unjust. There must be a generally accepted mechanism for determining who is the aggressor, for guiding the police. This judicial mechanism likewise will not be trusted if it is perceived as partial. Today we have two mechanisms—the UN and the Permanent Court of International Justice—which might function in this capacity. It is well-known that the Russians refuse to be bound by either agency because they hold each to be loaded with pro-western votes. Peculiarly enough, the USA also refuses to accept decisions of the World Court. We are not sure that we would receive "justice," as we would define it, from such a tribunal.

Nations have internal revolutions if large groups feel unjustly treated. A world government would face civil war very quickly if no mechanism existed for compromising disputes and arriving at settlements which seemed reasonably fair to the participants. The American Revolution and Civil War, the French and the Russian Revolutions were all fought because no available method of resolving disputes was perceived as just by the aggrieved groups.

Two crucial problems therefore face us. How can we get people to accept the necessity of setting up a world police force that has an effective monopoly of violence? And, how can we get people to accept the justice of the decisions of an international legislative or judicial body? More specifically, can we remove the irrational, delusional attitudes that prevent effective international bodies from receiving support of both leaders and citizens?

Love of country is a noble sentiment; it is also one of the major barriers to international organization. Much of the delusional thinking that underlies both tribal war and national war is based upon blind loyalty to a group. We have seen this in the Congo, where tribal affiliations take precedence over loyalty to the entire nation. To protect tribal sovereignty, Balubas slaughter Luluas and vice versa. As westerners can plainly see, it would be in the interest of all to cooperate in building a strong, efficient, impartial central government. But the tribesmen can't see it. They see only their patriotic devotion to their kinship group.

An extraterrestrial observer could see clearly that the Americans and the Russians are just as irrational as the Congolese tribesmen. A tremendous flood of comforts and luxuries could be released to the entire human race if the arms race were ended. More importantly, the threat of imminent destruction would be relieved for all of us.

Underlying these problems of supranational control of violence, then, is a lack of mutual international identification. To us, control by our police is tolerable because "they" are also "us." But control by an international police force would seem oppressive because of the absence of this identification.

We have already noted this tendency in the mutual suspicion and distrust shown by citizens of the two great powers. Our image of the USSR and theirs of the USA carry built-in assumptions of sneakiness and violence. The anthropologists suggest that this is just about universal. In many primitive tribes, the word for "human" is also the word for "our people." Persons outside the tribe are automatically nonhuman.

People do not expect to cooperate with animals—with nonhumans.[4] The normal way of relating to an animal is by domination, by arbitrary unilateral decision, and, in some instances, by violence. This is exactly how citizens of most nations respond to symbols of other nations. The notion of bargaining, of trading our concessions for their concessions, is not seen as appropriate. Only when the other person is seen as "one of us" will cooperative methods be considered proper.

The problem of mutual identification, consequently, is at the very core of international relations. Along with the problem of perceptual distortions, it demands a solution—but gets very little attention from those who so far have been charged with the avoidance of war.

THE BASIS FOR WORLD ORDER

Whatever plan is devised for controlling national violence, there must be a sound psychological basis in the minds of the citizens affected. This includes, as a minimum, the following components: identification with others across national boundaries, loyalties that extend across national lines, and acceptance of some authority above the nation.

Mutual Identification

Mutual identification becomes possible as individuals find that they have attributes and problems in common, as they share gratifications and discomforts together, as each sees the other to be a possible source of assistance. The prototype of all identifications is that of the child with his parents. He identifies with his parents because they care for him, show him affection, gratify other needs; but this process is also facilitated as he learns that he shares their name, that he is perceived as part of their group (the family), and that he is seen as resembling them in various ways. The process of developing identification is, of course, quite complex, but these are the more important components involved.

Obviously, adults do not reinstate the parent-child relationship except in extreme cases. It is possible, however, to develop partial identifications based on profession, on hobbies, and on similarities of interest. The baseball fan who shouts for the Detroit Tigers feels that he has something in common with the others screaming alongside him.

They share a common desire (and, admittedly, a common enemy. We need to solve the problem without keeping the enemy as a symbol of unity.)

Medical men, lawyers, and others identify with a group that shares mutual professional problems. Scientists share not only an enthusiasm for a certain kind of problem but a great deal of curiosity about the work of their fellows. Religious affiliation provides a basis for identification, both in a common deity and in the sharing of rituals and beliefs.

Cross-national identifications may be cultivated by increased contacts and shared gratifications. The custom of having the American Bar Association or medical society meetings in Europe, though it may be a device for reducing income tax costs on pleasure travel, serves a valuable purpose in increasing identification with persons in the same profession overseas. International scientific congresses and other meetings help in building this attitude.

Mere tourism does not serve this purpose. There must be a feeling of common interests and shared problems. Ideally, there should be an awareness of mutual effort, as in the process of scientific research, where one man's progress may help another to complete his investigation. The tourist sometimes gets the feeling that the gratifications of persons in a foreign country come at his expense.

A wise program within the USA, calculated to develop these mutual identifications as a basis for the expansion of international institutions, would make use of many special groups within our population. The following are only some rather obvious examples:

1. American Negroes should be employed widely in Africa and, indeed, in any area where skin color is a sensitive issue. Obviously, they should go in teams with whites—we want no segregation in reverse!—but it is clear that such individuals have a communication value far beyond what they say. When Ralph Bunche and Carl Rowan visit Africa, they do not need to hand out leaflets about the growing trend toward equal opportunity for all races in our country. They exemplify in themselves the fruition of such opportunities.

2. American unionists should visit labor groups behind the Iron Curtain and, even better, unionists from those nations should be invited to the West. Hopefully, they should have an opportunity to learn about the freedom to strike (unknown in the communist world), about governmental safeguards for the individual, and so on. It is more that likely that they would go back with new ideas about the role of their own unions and probably would become a force for democratizing their governments as well as developing identification with western unionists.

3. Production experts should be used to visit the Iron Curtain countries and indicate ways in which freedom from government interference facilitates the job of increasing output. The Russian plant manager, it seems, does quite a bit of fuming about bureaucratic red tape. If he found a common ground with his western counterpart, and if he learned more about how our system works, he too could be a potent source of democratization and his group could provide a power based for policies of international cooperation.

4. Scientists of every category should be sent behind the Curtain and their opposite numbers invited to sessions in the West. Scientists place a high value on free communication, and they are intensely curious about what is going on in other laboratories. Communist scientists could profit from seeing the tangible fruits of keeping governmental hands off of research.

There are two general principles which underlie such proposals as these. First, wherever possible we should encourage individuals to identify with groups that cut across national boundaries. The greatest psychological danger from nationalism arises when there are no competing loyalties. If we wish to diminish the virulent intensity of Russian nationalism, we must get their scientists, engineers, artists, and others to feel some membership in an international community.

Second, we must improve the quality and quantity of communication across the Iron Curtain and indeed, across all kinds of boundaries that divide people. We dare not rely on printed leaflets, or radio broadcasts, or newspaper interviews. Industry learned years ago that the most effective way to communicate from management to employees was by face-to-face contact. Suspicion and hostility are more easily dissolved, and messages communicated, when personal sincerity can be clearly seen.

Attitude toward Authority

The key to an effective international organization is the public acceptance of an authority higher than that of the nation. This is going to be difficult. In the USA, any open espousal of a program to set up a supranational authority will elicit strong emotions in opposition. Our D.A.R.[5] has already taken its stand on international bodies: "Get the US out of the UN, and the UN out of the US." This, of course, agrees with Russian policy.

A strong national government is generally accepted in the United

States; few Americans would propose that we split into fifty sovereign nations, each with its own atom bombs and radar screens. The need for a supranational government, to which certain aspects of sovereignty are ceded, rests on precisely the same arguments as those used, at various times in our history, in favor of an effective central government. It is impossible to maintain meaningful international cooperation without some kind of supranational institution. As has been pointed out many times, this institution need not have comprehensive political control, such as has been centered in our federal government, but it must have a monopoly on certain kinds of military equipment.

The acceptance of such an authority by world leaders and citizens cannot be facilitated very much by such measures as were cited above. However, if cross-national identifications are built, the fear of a supranational authority will begin to diminish. Our fear results from a natural suspicion of an authority that is dominated by those we do not view as human. Once our view of humanity has been broadened, the authority problem diminishes in perspective.

The coercive nature of the military situation and the strong will to survive should provide substantial support for a move to set up international arms control and related agencies. If irrational sources of opposition can be cleared up, the task should not be excessively difficult.

Supranational Loyalties

Perhaps the most difficult phase of this problem is the development of loyalty to a unit larger than the nation. This is exceptionally difficult because about the only such unit (the UN) does not have many attributes today which foster identification and loyalty. Loyalty is encouraged if the person or group is strong enough and resourceful enough to provide some benefits, and loyalty to one's nation results from the picture of the nation as protector and provider. The UN cannot fill either role at present.

Nevertheless, it should be feasible to find some persons who are prepared to develop loyalty to the UN (those who are already internationalists) and aid them to progress along this line. Steps to involve more American citizens in UN activities—for example, in fund raising, handing out literature, educational programs—would induce a modest percentage of those so affected to develop feelings of loyalty to the UN.

Since loyalty is more readily attached to a figure that is a source of benefits, it would be desirable to channel more economic aid to new nations through the UN. This will rapidly increase the number of persons who are psychologically ready to see the UN as a powerful and beneficent figure deserving of loyal support—even if the policies adopted are momentarily unpleasant to the particular person involved.

The intent of these suggestions is not to destroy love of or loyalty to one's own nation. Our experience in the USA is an important reminder on this topic. The resident of Michigan does not love his state less because he loves his country more. But if there is a conflict, he accepts the principle that the more inclusive unit (the nation) takes precedence over the subordinate unit, the state. Similarly, Americans and Russians could continue to love their fatherlands but might still accept the rational view that the welfare of the human race takes priority over short-run advantage for their nations.

Psychologists do not know as much as they would like about the development of loyalty. In a military unit, it grows out of working together and becoming aware of mutual interdependence. If your life may depend on the cooperation of the man next to you, you are not likely to pick petty quarrels with him. It is this kind of attitude which must be somehow instilled in the minds of citizens of the world today.

Economic Cooperation

Next only to strengthening the UN and building up the authority of the World Court, peaceful dispute settlement calls for more effective economic cooperation. Disputes over trade barriers, economic monopolies within certain territories, and ownership of desirable natural resources have often set off violence in the past and will tend to do so in the future if institutions are not constructed which will foster peaceful settlements.

The psychological problems are identical with those just cited. We unhesitatingly exploit citizens of other countries because we have no identifications with them; we see them as nonhuman. We are reluctant to accept arbitration of economic disputes by a world court because we perceive such a court as unfair (any decision is unfair which favors an outsider over one of our own people!).

As has been suggested earlier, there seems clear evidence that everyone profits economically from specialization. It thus makes sense for one nation to concentrate on automobiles, another on chemicals, another on textiles. This kind of arrangement, however, implies easy trade across frontiers, and it will be tolerated only if there is general confidence that no one will take advantage of a monopoly position to exploit the other trading partners. In essence, this goes back to the notion that, if businessmen within a nation are to accept court verdicts and not resort to guns to enforce their economic position, they must have a world court that they can trust to render verdicts impartially.

Economic Aid through the UN

Steps toward building economic cooperation could be taken safely and cautiously if we began using the UN as the agency for channeling aid from the developed to the emerging nations. As already noted, the impoverished South needs massive injections of capital from the industrialized North. An international agency could route these gifts and loans in such a way as to build up complementary industries in neighboring nations. It could also encourage the advanced nations to specialize in particular forms of aid, which would automatically increase diversity and favor expansion of trade within the industrialized area.

This procedure, as noted earlier, would help to build an image of the UN as better and stronger than it is today. The citizen's devotion to his nation is based in part on his view of the nation as supporter and provider—as a source of economic blessings. Loyalty to the UN would increase if such attributes came to be associated with its image.

Both USA and USSR would benefit economically from such an arrangement. Not only would aid be handled in such a fashion as to relieve economic frustration in the new nations but also more resources within the advanced nations would be freed for consumer benefits. Thus, we need not view this kind of change in the framework of "his gain is my loss." Rather, we can see that a good bargain benefits all the participants.

A World Parliament

Because human beings, in striving to satisfy their motives, invent new ways of doing things, the world cannot be frozen into a particular kind of pattern. Instruments must be adapted to bring about change when accommodation to these dynamic human tendencies is required. This means that the world must have a legislative body, as well as the executive and judicial organs already mentioned.

We are, in fact, a little closer to the legislative idea than we are to the other organs. The General Assembly of the United Nations does not really have legislative functions, since it can only recommend to member nations; but it is at least an open forum in which grievances can be stated and social pressures exerted upon nations which disturb the peace. Some successes are credited to the UN in this respect; for example, the cessation of the Soviet pressure on Iran in 1946.

More desirable would be an arrangement by which positive actions to foster the welfare of the human race could be taken through the UN. Many individuals agree in principle that we need an agency which could pass laws effective over the whole planet, but, in practice, nationalistic feelings usually prevent any acceptance of such a legislative body.

There are many technical problems about the establishment of a world parliament—for example, how should the votes be distributed: by population, by economic wealth, by military power? These questions are not, strictly speaking, psychological in nature. If the idea of a world legislature were generally accepted, the technicalities could be worked out. Psychological factors are important because they block acceptance of the general principle.

Possible compromises between the one-nation-one-vote system now in use and the one-man-one-vote ideal have been devised by various experts. A widely debated scheme has been proposed by Professors Clark and Sohn in their book *World Peace through World Law.*[6] Their proposal calls for voting weighted by such factors as population and gross national product. It could, of course, be modified as conditions changed in the world organization or in its component nations. Freedom to negotiate changes in the rules can be built into such a plan. The important job is to win public support for some such proposal in principle—then to work out details within this atmosphere of acceptance. While each nation will support arrangements which maximize its weight in the organization, the necessity to form coalitions will facilitate compromise and the harmonizing of differences.

TECHNIQUES FOR PLANNING

Can we expect officials of present national governments to work vigorously and creatively for such plans? The answer, regrettably, must be in the negative. It is unreasonable to expect a man to develop a proposal which will diminish the importance of his role and his ego-satisfactions. There is another difficulty: that any proposal coming from a high-ranking diplomat is likely to be perceived as official government policy. If a foreign minister issues a statement criticizing the veto in the Security Council, for example, unpleasant repercussions are likely. The principle of agency seriously hampers any elected or appointed official who might wish to explore novel concepts in international affairs.

One device which has been proposed to bypass this difficulty is the "citizens' convention." Elmo Roper, for example, has proposed an unofficial meeting "...where the best minds in our country...can meet with the best minds of those democracies with whom we will inevitably share a common fate and together work out what seems to be the best way of securing close and continuing cooperation among the democracies. . . . The plan they evolved would then be submitted to the legislative bodies of their respective countries for acceptance or rejection."[7]

This technique, of course, is valuable because participants need not face the conflict between personal ethic and official responsibility; it is, by the same token, viewed as impotent and hence useless in many quarters. Ordinarily, effective policy decisions come from governmental officials. The outsider, no matter how talented, has little influence. Thus, critics of the device deprecate it as a futile exercise in debate.

History suggests that this need not be the case. From our own past we can cite the Continental Congress as a body which had little legitimate authority but which nevertheless accomplished important changes. Prior to the Continental Congress, there were the Committees of Correspondence, completely unofficial, which paved the way for revolution. Similar unofficial bodies participated in planning the French Revolution and the Russian Revolution. Indeed, only such a group could do the preparatory work for overthrowing a government. But this is not our problem. What we need is a plan for the orderly establishment of world institutions within which present national governments continue to exist—but with reduced freedom of action. It still seems likely that the citizens' convention would be a useful tactic in devising plans for such a development.

The convention, insofar as it necessarily involves people from different nations, meets another of the requirements we have laid down: the development of trust and confidence across national frontiers. A world organization cannot grow out of our present tangle of distrust and suspicion. Any procedures, therefore, which bring men together to discuss these problems in a calm and objective manner will aid in establishing this atmosphere of mutual confidence.

One further advantage of the citizens' convention can be cited. Since the men who participate in such a session are sure to be persons of prestige in their homelands, the task of winning public support for a plan is facilitated. Government officials, newspaper men, educators, and others who influence public opinion can point to the quality of the planning convention as a reason for accepting its conclusions.

Leo Szilard's Peace Lobby

While special importance must be given to planning which cuts across national frontiers, we must also consider building support for a more flexible approach within our own population. The eminent physicist, Dr. Leo Szilard, spent his last years promoting his idea for a peace lobby. Although this lobby was originally built aroung a nucleus of physical scientists who felt concerned about their social responsibilities, he also invited social scientists and political and cultural leaders to join. The whole group decided on policies which should be fostered for peace and survival. The organization collected funds for donations to the campaigns of approved political candidates and for publicity in favor of specific programs.

The peace lobby envisioned by Szilard seeks to create a counter-weight to the lobbies of manufacturers, labor unions, the AMA, farmers, veterans, and other pressure groups. Accepting the view that our government arrives at policy decisions as a result of organized pressures, Szilard wished to activate pressure for an intelligent international program. Most pressures today seek selfish advantage for some domestic interest, which often involves injury to some foreign country. At present, no one accepts any responsibility for lobbying against the harm we may do ourselves by short-sighted selfish tactics.

International Business

Another unexpected source of support for strong international institutions may come from those western business firms which have major operations in other nations. It has become apparent to the leaders of business and industry that nuclear war is no way of enforcing commercial agreements. Thus, the value of a world court and an international police force becomes apparent to them.

Many American corporations habitually send bright young men overseas for a few years to learn all parts of the firm's activities. While no systematic data are available, casual observation suggests that these executives, after they return, are more favorable to strong international institutions than they had been before.

Planners and Organizers

There appear to be two main sources of planners and organizers for an international program. One source is the volunteer group—the citizens' convention—mentioned above. An existing group, such as the United Nations Association, already provides limited pressure-group support for international initiatives.

The second, and probably more hopeful, source is the slowly expanding pool of international civil servants. This seems especially true with respect to agencies such as UNICEF, the children's fund, and SUNFED, the UN special projects fund. Members of such staffs have an excellent opportunity to get ego-expansion from strengthening international as opposed to national institutions. Certainly it would be beneficial, in terms of our long-range welfare, to increase the number and variety of social roles which involve a commitment to the welfare of people without regard to national citizenship.

Substantial benefits apparently are derived even by those persons who serve as delegates from a nation to the UN. Reports of interviews with these individuals indicate that citizens who serve on these national delegations frequently experience a broadening of their frame of reference; they become aware of the implications of policies of one nation for the citizens of another.[8]

In the long run, we must move away from reliance on volunteers and toward reliance on persons who are assigned the roles of fostering or administering international institutions. This is the way to channel individual human motives into activities supportive of world peace.[9]

14
The Long Road
to Peace

The creation of an effective international
organization will not end the problem of conflict between nations. Indeed, we have no
right to suppose that human conflicts will ever
cease—and no reason to argue that they
should cease. Most social progress has resulted
from conflict: Slavery in the Roman Empire
was not ended till the slaves rebelled; serfdom
was not ended in England until the revolt of
the serfs; women did not get the right to vote
without considerable turmoil and some violence. The list could be longer. Conflict, in
other words, has had its constructive consequences and should not be suppressed
thoroughly.

Further, even if we believed that they
should cease, group conflicts never *can* cease
completely. Human nature is dynamic.
People who are frustrated by a given set of
social rules (and all rules contain some element
of frustration) will imagine a different social
organization which provides more need
satisfaction. They will then agitate and
demonstrate for these changes. Even if they
are not frustrated at one point in time, they
may become so at another—because technological changes, such as automation, have
affected their earning power; or (as in the
communist nations today) because persons

at the top of the social hierarchy have seized special privileges (which they may have earned) to pass on to their children who have not earned anything.

Conflict, then, is a permanent and on the whole a desirable prospect. Our problem is to contain conflict within reasonable limits, minimize its destructive potential, and maximize the constructive consequences.

Within the nation our system of laws and courts provides a reasonably workable mechanism for the orderly settlement of disputes growing out of such human motives. Consequently, business competitors, unions seeking a large share of economic benefits, and racial groups protesting unfair treatment are legally restrained from resorting to violence. Implicit in the notion of an international organization (in the long run, probably a world government) is the notion that conflicts involving national interests can be similarly domesticated and settled without violence. Is this really possible? Or is it no more than a wish-fulfilling fantasy? In the following pages, I shall summarize some of the relevant variables and indicate by what means such a world of peaceful conflict resolution may be attained.

SOME PRINCIPLES OF DISPUTE SETTLEMENT

Mankind has accumulated a vast store of experience bearing on the settlement of disputes between individuals and groups; marital conflicts, parent-child difficulties, industrial disputes, racial quarrels, and national hostilities, to mention only a few.[1] I propose to offer a few generalized principles of dispute settlement derived from one or another of these various areas of experience and, in later pages, to show how the application of such ideas may guide our quest for a nonviolent solution to Cold War problems.

Beliefs about the Other

In many instances, as marital counselors can testify, the basic cause of a conflict is a difference in beliefs. Husbands may have peculiar ideas about wives (e.g., that they have no sex drive) or irrational expectations about the wife's role (e.g., that the wife should always yield to her husband's whim). Fortunately, in spite of the legend of Helen of Troy, sex does not contribute much to international controversies. Erroneous beliefs, on the other hand, provide important sources of friction. The Russians, for instance, believe—to a large extent erroneously—that we are warmongers, exploiters, colonialists, racial bigots, etc. To the

Russians, these beliefs are facts, and they behave toward us accordingly. It may be that we have some erroneous pictures of the Russians and that our distortions also contribute to the friction between our two nations.

A first principle, then, is this: *Settlement of a dispute often depends upon a change in the beliefs held by one or both parties about the other.*

Finding the Hidden Issue

Mediators in union-management disputes repeatedly express surprise at the frequency with which the manifest issue turns out to be relatively minor. A strife apparently over wages and hours turns out to be caused by the desire of a group of employers to preserve their employers' association. An exorbitant pension demand is found to be a disguised expression of discontent over work standards. Another controversy on wages has as its real basis a rumor about automation plans of the employer, leading to insecurity among the workers. Probably a number of international disputes also follow this pattern.

Men who feel threatened by some impending loss or injury may lack the ability to express their anxiety or even to name the source of their insecurity. In such cases, hostility may be manifested over some trivial but more easily verbalized issue. Mediators faced with such problems have to try to identify the hidden issue, the goal or threat which has not been clearly stated, and devise a solution that will take account of this dynamic factor.

A second principle, then, is the following: *Look for hidden goals or threats which may be eliciting hostility but which have not been explicitly stated in the dispute.* As a single example, we can cite the Russian goal of military secrecy, about which they say little but which is obviously high in their scale of priorities. Our proposals on inspection must take this goal into account even if the Russians do not openly admit its importance.

Appealing to Higher Loyalties

Two parties may be induced to settle a dispute without violence if each feels loyalty to some higher value. Ministers use the appeal to religious values as an instrument for settling many marital difficulties. Similarly, in time of war, patriotism may be invoked to persuade union and management to compromise an argument.

Thus, a third principle is this: *Peaceful settlements are facilitated if both parties feel loyalty to some grouping which includes both.* Here, however, we have difficulty in applying our experience to international affairs. The dogma of sovereignty denies that any higher loyalty can exist. "Thou shalt have no other gods before me" could have been written of the nation-state. A man who places his religion, or his ethical code, or his devotion to mankind above his obligation to the nation is denounced as a traitor. Further, he is subject to the death penalty in time of war. Few individuals, therefore, have the inner stamina to act on loyalty to ideals higher than those of patriotism.

Coercion by Greater Force

Finally, disputing individuals within the nation encounter at least the threat of greater force if violence is used. Consequently, although we still do have murders and assault cases, it seems at least plausible that the presence of the police decreases the frequency of such crimes. Likewise, we still have race riots and picket-line fighting. Since the police usually share local prejudices, they may be less than effective when violence is used against outsiders (e.g., the Freedom Riders trying to desegregate southern buses and restaurants); but the government has the power to restrain or prevent this kind of violence.

A fourth principle, then, follows: *Peaceful settlement of disputes is rendered more probable by the availability of a force which is greater than that of the disputants and which will be invoked if violence is employed.*[2]

As in the preceding case, this principle offers us relatively little help in dealing with nations. There is no *force majeure*, no policeman on the block, to suppress a riot between the USA and the USSR. However, this may not be a necessary state of affairs; as noted earlier, an International Police Force is at least a possibility.

Men have been writing plans for a lasting peace for thousands of years. So far, success has been limited, although many scholars will argue that our present institutions have saved more lives than people recognize. In any event, the fury of the violence now impending is on such a scale that peace plans are urgently needed.

Plans may aim at two sets of problems: the immediate short-run issues that may precipitate open conflict; and the long-run conditions that predispose men to resort to violence. In both categories we must consider the delusions and misperceptions which blind the participants to peaceful compromises, as well as the goals and motives which provide the dynamic energies involved. The four principles stated above suggest that there are four ways in which we may attack these problems: through modifying the way people perceive facts; through probing for hidden goals and motives and devising acceptable compromises to meet these needs; through developing loyalty—either to larger groups than nations or to higher ethical ideals than nationalism; and, finally, through development of a system in which some greater force is brought to bear on disputing nations.

MODIFICATION OF IMAGES

A Zen epigram, "The five colors blind the eye," suggests that we lose a tremendous amount of information when we classify events into a limited number of categories. An explorer of psychological bent who visited a primitive Polynesian tribe noted that they used the same word for "blue" and "green." When he gave them colored yarns to sort out, they could not correctly separate blue from green. The culturally determined classification overrode what was almost certainly an innate ability to discriminate the two sets of stimuli.

A similar culturally formed blindness may prevent us from seeing many important details of our environment. Like the highly sexed man who habitually interprets messages solely in sexual terms, we may be interpreting messages solely in terms of competition and hostility: An enemy is someone we cannot trust at any time; a friend is someone we can trust—but only if we are watching him closely. As a result, we may miss many nuances of intergroup communication and cooperation.

The perceptual problem in international relations will not be solved until we have acquired some skill in seeing a situation from another's point of view. Industry has faced this problem and made some progress. Members of management often are assigned to play the role of union spokesmen and required to present a case from the union's point of view. The process has resulted in greater flexibility in managerial views of labor problems and, often enough, in wiser approaches to union disputes. It has not ended strikes for those companies which have practiced in this vein, but the general record of such firms has been considerably more peaceful than for those which resist such innovations.

Many colleges are now using simulations of international affairs as a teaching device.[3] Teams of students are required to make decisions for hypothetical nations on arms policy, alliances, trade agreements, and domestic programs. Computers are used to determine the outcomes of such decisions, and the results are then fed back to the teams. The students thus learn to see the implications of domestic foreign policy; they incidentally find that taking a certain role means limiting the perceptual field to exclude much information. It is to be hoped that such students, as they achieve leadership roles, will remember the lessons thus acquired.

PUBLIC OPINION MAY HAVE INFLUENCE

GRIN AND BEAR IT   By Lichty

"The voters are getting mighty difficult these days! Used to be, we could promise 'em a new postoffice; now we have to promise a new world!"

Political leaders in every nation are responsive in some degree to public attitudes and motives. But to be effective, public opinion must, in some fashion, be coordinated so that it is clearly presented to statesmen. (Cartoon by Lichty. Reprinted by permission of the Chicago Times Syndicate.)

The U.S. Department of State and some other government agencies are also using simulation to explore problems. Although these agencies may not intend that those taking the role of Soviet or Chinese spokesmen will become more flexible in their views, psychologists would predict this outcome. In simulation, the individual taking an alien role must try to perceive the facts as they appear to this other person. The result almost certainly will be a better insight into the "facts" guiding the policies of other nations; and such insights will enable us to chart a wiser course in pursuit of our own goals.

Insight into the phenomenal fields of others is only one perceptual requisite of peaceful dispute settlement. We must also become aware of our own unconscious assumptions, our expectancies and biases.

An attempt has been made, in earlier chapters of this book, to note some specific instances of delusions of national grandeur and persecution. It is fairly easy to identify these in the history of other nations. However, few Americans are willing to recognize "bad" or aggressive national policies of our own nation. A teacher risks considerable punishment from local critics if he dares refer to our war with Mexico in 1848, for example, as an unprincipled seizure of territory from a weaker neighbor. By and large, we resist being made conscious of our own defects. This is an altogether human but maladaptive characteristic.

It will, of course, do little to improve the quality of international dispute settlement if we achieve insight into our own errors while the Russians and other national leaders do not. Clearly, it will *not* improve matters for us to remind others of their bad habits; we have tried this for a long time, without any positive results. Criticism from the outside, instead of increasing insight, usually raises defenses. Instead of criticism, we need informal cooperation among groups of citizens of many nations, such that each group tries to work on the decision makers (and the citizens) of its own nation.

THE SEARCH FOR HIDDEN GOALS

As noted above, the peaceful settlement of disputes is aided in many cases by the discovery that the manifest goal is trivial, whereas some concealed goal is the major dynamic factor in the conflict. In marital troubles an argument over money often is found to be merely a facade for a conflict over dominance. Such a discovery does not automatically lead to a solution, but it does make possible a rational discussion and possible compromises over who is to be boss.

This aspect of dispute settlement has been extensively explored in the field of labor relations. Mediators often encounter what looks like a head-on collision, in which the demands are completely irreconcilable. The union may demand that layoffs be based solely on seniority, and management demand that they be based on ability to do the job. Both cannot win. But closer study may reveal that the union really wants protection against favoritism and bias in layoffs—particularly, a guarantee that no one will be laid off because he has been active in the union. Similarly, management really wants protection for a few speccially valuable workers, who have not been on the job long enough to be protected by the seniority rule. When exploration reveals these deeper motives, compromise becomes possible and a solution can be worked out. Either a strictly impartial method of choosing men for layoff may be devised, or management may be given the right to keep a fixed number of men regardless of seniority. The head-on collision has been averted, and both sides feel that they have won a victory.[4]

Our relations with the Communist world, unfortunately, are not quite this simple. But the analogy is appropriate. Instead of assuming that the Russian demands represent their real motives, we need to do some exploring. There may be a basis upon which we can satisfy them without giving away our position. Conversely, perhaps we have belligerently been defending a traditional position without looking to see whether it fits current needs.

The frequency with which both USA and USSR have shifted stands on major negotiating issues is instructive. At one time, the USA refused to bargain separately on nuclear testing, calling instead for discussions of general disarmament. At another time, we resisted merging the test-ban talks with disarmament discussions. By some curious maneuvering, the Russians swapped postures with us; at first they demanded separation of the two issues, then decided they must be merged. Such shifts suggest that the real motive lies deeper. Clearly, it could not have been important to either nation that the issues be merged or separated. Policy was dictated by the way the negotiations related to other, more basic national goals.[5]

Without immediately concluding that these basic goals are mutually compatible, we can certainly conclude that analysis offers hope. Our talent for finding stands which seem utterly in opposition would be more discouraging if we were more consistent. With this degree of flexibility, we can infer that the underlying goals are separable from these bargaining points and therefore that we may find a solution that is at least minimally acceptable to both parties.

Occasionally the smaller nations, and particularly the nonaligned bloc, have attempted to mediate disputes between the great powers. The result has generally been unsuccessful. Large nations have been more successful in mediating controversies between two small countries. The reason is that the big neighbor may be able to offer inducements (rewards and punishments) to win acceptance of a solution. This lends further support to proposals for strengthening international institutions. If these are in a position to offer rewards, if not punishments, for peaceful dispute settlement, the process of mediation would receive a very considerable boost in effectiveness.

Importance of Superordinate Goals

Let me note again the importance of superordinate goals in achieving peaceful dispute settlement. Labor disputes are settled more easily when both sides recognize the need to keep the employer-firm competing effectively in the market. Marital conflicts are more easily resolved when concern for the welfare of children is seen as a higher goal than personal selfish desires.

There are undoubtedly some superordinate goals which should influence the policy decisions of nations. One of these is survival; it is unlikely that either the USA or the USSR could survive in anything like its present form if a nuclear exchange occurred. Another is the welfare of the race. Unfortunately, the tendency to perceive persons outside our nation as nonhuman interferes with the potency of this as a goal. As noted earlier, the power elites of both nations may see the preservation of their own privileged positions as a common goal toward which cooperation is possible; but this possibility is tenuous since a change in technology might induce either side to abandon cooperation in favor of attack.

Superiority of Positive Incentives

The term "international relations" covers efforts by the leaders of one nation to obtain, on behalf of and in the name of their nation, some object or behavior of value from citizens of another nation. The technique used most often is the threat of pain and suffering.

Despite their use for thousands of years, such threats are not always effective in producing the desired results. In 1940 and 1941, the nazis rained a terrifying weight of bombs on Britain but did not succeed in changing the pattern of British behavior. The French used a great military power in Algeria to no effect. Force, of course, has been successful in other instances, so we cannot discard it out of hand. But the generalization from many lines of psychological research is that it is more efficient to modify human behavior with positive than with negative incentives. Therefore, it seems wise to consider the advantages of using positive incentives for cooperation from other nations. Economic trade, for instance, involves a bargain which benefits both sides; such solutions might be devised for many international conflicts. Given the rich variety of modern production of goods, there must be many exchanges which would result in net gains for both competitors. One hopeful avenue for the future, then, is research on the use of positive incentives to bring about settlement of international disputes.

DEVELOPING HIGHER LOYALTIES

A third approach to peaceful settlement is through the development of loyalties to groups and symbols held to be more important than the national interest or national welfare. This was once held to be the role of religion; and perhaps there was, for a time, in western Europe, a period when the higher loyalty to the Catholic Church diminished the frequency of violence between city-states and feudal baronies. But this period was short and it has now vanished. The pope does not have much success in mediating disputes even between two overwhelmingly Catholic nations such as Italy and France. Moreover, the ultranationalist is likely to crusade against religious loyalties that cut across national lines. The nazis fought religion and imprisoned both Catholic and Protestant clergy. The communists have likewise downgraded religion and demanded a higher loyalty to communist ideology. These examples suggest that the nationalist recognizes the implicit danger of such a religious involvement as a possible check on the aggrandizement of the nation, and opposes it on that ground. Possibly for the same reason, internationalists have generally favored religious groupings which cut across national boundaries.

Religion is not, of course, the only possibility here. Professional and scientific groups provide a focus for loyalty which can transcend national chauvinism. Most German scientists were ashamed of the excesses of nazi converts who distorted scientific doctrines to fit nazi racist doctrines; and a few communist scientists gagged at the party-imposed orthodoxy (e.g., the Lysenko doctrine on genetics). Today the absurdities of early Soviet science are being repeated in China, where medical men doing research on burns are urged to study the writings of Mao Tse-tung as a guide in this difficult technical field.

As a result of such excesses, scientists and social scientists interested in international affairs have strongly supported informal meetings such as the Pugwash conferences —meetings that cut across national frontiers.

These meetings, including both communist and western scientists, have tried to foster mutual understanding and a loyalty to scientific research. Although it is impossible to assess the benefits of such meetings, the consensus among observers is that they have led to improved mutual understanding and that, in the long run, they may foster the kind of international loyalty that is a necessary support of international institutions.[6] On the other hand, the use of scientists as participants in actual diplomatic negotiations (as in the test-ban treaty) seems to have been of little utility. The Department of State imposed such tight controls that the scientists in the negotiating party felt they were completely unheard.[7]

THE ETHICAL PROBLEM

Considerations of loyalty, or of religion, lead us naturally to a consideration of the role of the superego (or conscience or ethics) in international affairs. As noted earlier, the power of conscience has usually ended at the national boundary. The principle of agency has been interpreted to mean that an official of the national government is justified in resorting to deceit or violence in the interests of his nation, even though he would never use such methods for advancing his personal welfare.

In this connection it is instructive to consider the changed principle of agency in corporation affairs. Not so long ago, American courts ruled that officers of a corporation must not consider the welfare of anyone except the stockholders. For instance, in the famous Ford Motor Company case in 1919 Henry Ford had instituted a policy of reducing dividends and using the retained funds to lower prices. The courts ruled that he had no right to be concerned with the welfare of the consumer.[8] Today it is generally conceded that gifts to universities, scholarships for employees' children, contributions to community-chest drives, and similar philanthropic acts are entirely within the competence of the corporation.

The principle of agency has thus been extended to comprehend acting for the welfare of a larger group (the city or the nation), of which the corporation is an inextricable part. Management spokesmen now enjoy speaking of their role as stewards for the general welfare, not as guardians of a limited ownership interest.

Could we extend the principle of agency to include the notion that governmental officials are responsible for the welfare of the planet, not just their own nation? Could we, for example, modify the reasoning underlying our foreign-aid program? Each year Congress solemnly resolves that gifts of economic and military aid outside our frontiers are in the national interest. This is probably true. But why not add that we are concerned also with world interest? After all, much of our aid program has been motivated by humanitarian considerations— to relieve hunger, as in India—and not by selfish factors.

This notion carries with it the notion that parents should instill in their children some feeling of responsibility for the welfare of people all over the world. Regrettably, psychologists know little about how this can be accomplished. Also regrettably, parents are unlikely to exert much energy to accomplish it. Child-training in western civilization, it seems, stresses the necessity to "make money, honestly if possible." Superego controls are limited mainly to the traditional negative: avoiding behavior harmful to those in the immediate vicinity (not necessarily foreigners).

To the extent that the superego represents an internalization of social rules and requirements, it should be possible to extend its coverage. The taboos of conscience once applied only to members of the tribe or to some similarly small in-group. In later years children were brought up to apply these moral imperatives to all people within the city, state, or nation. It now seems both possible and necessary that we take the next step and include all human beings within this category. Such a change, if effective, should help powerfully in bringing about peaceful dispute settlement.

Part of the problem we now face derives from the fact that citizens of one nation rarely encounter those of another. Thus the foreigner remains a shadowy, undefined figure, and it is relatively easy to categorize him as not quite human. More face-to-face contact would undoubtedly minimize this tendency.

A particularly useful approach to this problem seems to be exchange of students at the high school and college levels. They are still young enough to be reasonably plastic, and their strong desires for social approval induce them to make friendly contacts with those around them. It is not wildly optimistic to hope that these young people, as they arrive at leadership positions, will feel moral and ethical responsibilities to people of other nations more keenly than has been traditional.

MOTIVATIONS RESISTING CHANGE

The foregoing pages — indeed, much of this book — relate to changes in our ways of thinking and of organizing society so that peaceful settlement of international conflicts is fostered. In suggesting such changes, I have made the assumption that our present system of nation-states cannot continue in its present form without exposing all of us to the grave risk of destruction. The assumption seems to have support in recent history. Nevertheless, it will be rejected by many leaders and citizens of the USA and of other nations as well.

Why will it be rejected? What aspects of human nature resist change of social institutions, even when these institutions carry so much harmful potential? From the psychological point of view, at least three factors need to be considered. First, ways of perceiving reality, once established, resist modification. We label this tendency "perceptual constancy", and it takes a variety of forms, from very simple to very complex. An illustration at the simple level: As I watch a person walking away from me, I do not see him as shrinking in size, although the retinal image is constantly diminishing. An unconscious corrective factor insists that I see him as the same size, because I am sure he is the same person. At the more complicated level we may mention percepts of personalities or of groups. A daughter who has had friction with her mother during adolescence may continue to see her mother as domineering and frustrating, even after the girl has left home and the mother genuinely abandons efforts to control her daughter's behavior. Similarly, a person who has built up an image of the Japanese as cruel, bestial, aggressive, and untrustworthy, as a consequence of propaganda in World War II, may have great difficulty in changing this view, even though the behavior of the Japanese people and government has been exemplary for over twenty years. This perceptual constancy carries with it also a desire that familiar objects should not change; the average person does not want his neighborhood, his city, his state, or his nation to change.

A second psychological source of resistance to change is habit. Once we have acquired ways of behaving, we tend to continue them. The habit of using force to solve problems is a simple example. Military men spend years developing skills in the application of violence to potential foreign enemies. These habits are compatible with our ways of perceiving reality. History tells us that wars have occurred regularly (a fact about which impartial observers can agree). History also tells us that our side has always used violence only for good purposes (a "fact" about which impartial observers cannot agree). Habits and perceptions thus collaborate and reinforce one another to maintain war as an institutionalized aspect of international relations.

A third factor is motivation. Man has many kinds of motives which impel him to resist change. Psychologists use the principle of homeostasis to refer to the fact that man must maintain certain internal constancies if he is to survive. Homeostasis applies to body temperature, blood-sugar level, oxygen intake, vitamin intake, etc. If these deviate substantially from the established norm, a person dies. There is considerable evidence that, as a man grows, he unconsciously extends this homeostatic principle to his surroundings. Thus, he wants his home to be of familiar pattern (who wants to live in an igloo?). He prefers familiar foods (soldiers in training for jungle duty have a hard time learning to eat lizards, grubs, and other alien foods). The infant wants his mother to be present, the adolescent wants to stay in the protective circle of his gang, and the adult cherishes his club, his labor union, or his fraternity. Most citizens learn to value the nation as a protector and resist influences tending to bring about change. When President Franklin D. Roosevelt, irked by a Supreme Court decision, threatened to appoint new justices, the vigorous opposition was well-characterized by one politician: "God didn't give us that kind of a Supreme Court."

It seems unreasonable to blame God for our American court system; as the records show, the system was designed by men. Nevertheless, the desire to keep familiar institutions unchanged is so strong that divine support may be invoked, as European royalty many years ago claimed divine sanction for a system of arbitrary government.

The intensity of resistance to change, and the powerful emotional forces which can be mobilized to punish anyone who seeks to induce change, has been documented by James W. Silver, Mississippi historian, in his book *Mississippi: The Closed Society*.[9] Silver gives us a glimpse of the threats, economic retaliation, social ostracism, and physical brutality used to oppose those fostering Negro civil rights in the South.

Similar potent forces undoubtedly will be mobilized to oppose any meaningful efforts to modify the system of national sovereignty in favor of an effective world government. Just as chauvinistic Mississippians denounced any notion that the USA could dictate to them on racial discrimination, so patriots of every nation will do lusty battle against the idea that a world court should be given power to settle disputes between nations. State sovereignty was the rallying slogan in the South; national sovereignty will become the symbol of opposition to organization of a peaceful world.

MOTIVATIONS FAVORING CHANGE

The foregoing analysis makes things look rather gloomy. Certainly there are potent forces favoring a conservative, status quo policy—which means nationalism and power struggles between nations. Yet there are also psychological forces favoring change.

Some psychologists hold that man has an innate need to explore, to encounter new stimuli, to modify the environment.[10] At once one can think of evidence favoring this view. Young children will explore anything; they seem to lack the fear of strange situations, which develops later. Adolescents have long been known to do unusual things "just for kicks": racing, playing "chicken," sniffing model cement, taking LSD. Adults, too, show some behavior patterns which fit this description: mountain climbing, exploring, hunting dangerous game. In scientists, this desire for new experience has been domesticated and put to use in a search for new facts and principles. And the vast entertainment industry caters to man's desire for varied stimulation, for escape from his humdrum surroundings.

Which view of human motivation (as resisting change or as seeking change) is correct? This is the wrong way to ask the question. There is evidence to support both views. It is more relevant to ask "What bearing do these views of motivation have on our discussion of international affairs?"

The implications of the motives toward conservatism have already been stated. Let us take a look at implications of human motives favoring new experience and change.

Rebellion against the familiar, and desire for novelty, sparks changes in the arts. Musicians object to traditional harmony and adopt the twelve-tone scale. Some seem to abandon all rules for orderly progression of sound. Painters become bored with representational painting and develop abstract approaches. Sculptors lose interest in "pretty" romantic figures and create three-dimensional ugliness.

It seems possible that curiosity and desire for new experience might be channeled into a positive program of building international institutions. The Peace Corps, an American innovation now being widely imitated throughout the Western world, catches young people when they are curious and willing to try novel living arrangements. The broader frame of reference generated by such experiences will surely work against a rigid conservatism about national sovereignty and the superiority of a specific ideology.

Near the end of World War II there were numerous essay contests inviting people to submit ideas regarding economic planning, peace treaties, international organizations, and the like. Such devices can be used to encourage people, especially young people, to play with novel ideas and to break up traditional ways of thinking about international relations. As noted earlier, many colleges are now experimenting with simulation as a teaching device, as when teams of students may be asked to take the roles of decision makers for different nations. By the use of computers or by pre-programmed methods, the team is given feedback on the consequences (e.g., depression, tension, revolution, war) of the decisions made. The students almost invariably get a much wider view of the factors influencing policy and of the far-reaching ramifications of apparently simple choices. They frequently develop an appreciation of the viewpoint of other nations and of the need for more efficient systems of international controls than now exist.

Some of the institutes and research centers subsidized by federal funds in this country have engaged in fantastic explorations of novel ideas in the area of international affairs. Although these have unfortunately been dominated by a nationalistic approach emanating from the government itself (for example, some congressmen objected violently when they learned about a study made of the conditions under which the USA might be wise to surrender in a nuclear war), many innovative proposals have been generated, and some of them reach the eyes and ears of national leaders. Even more hopeful is the fact that some of the young scientists, teachers, and executives involved in these "think-tank" projects will later achieve roles as national leaders and may bring to bear on international problems the more flexible approaches encouraged by such programs.

The situation, therefore, is not entirely bleak. Although most people (especially those who hold posts of wealth and privilege—the so-called power elite) favor the status quo, even these individuals are conscious of the pains and frustrations associated with our present anarchic international relations. Thus they may perceive opportunities to improve the situation. And bright, alert young persons on the fringe of power situations may perceive change in institutions as an opportunity for their advancement. Thus, the motives favoring innovation and new institutional patterns may yet prove strong enough to energize programs better calculated to resolve national disputes without violence.

AN END TO WAR?

Conservatives are prone to say "We shall always have wars because you can't change human nature." If so drastic a step were required, the outlook would indeed be gloomy. Nobody knows how to change human nature, and if anyone succeeded, the outcome would be unhuman nature, perhaps much worse. Fortunately, this is not our only hope. As an alternative, we can try to adapt our institutional practices to the needs of individuals and then to adapt the behavior of individuals to these modified institutions. This sounds, and is, complicated, but the race has had several thousands of years of practice in doing just this; so we know it is possible.

In any case, peace is compatible with human nature. Very few men, even unconsciously, prefer war to peace. But they do crave gratifications, the pursuit of which leads to war. History provides ample demonstration that within the tribe, the city, or the nation, peace can become the normal way of life. If we can identify the motives and perceptions which lead men in groups to war on other groups, it seems quite feasible to devise institutions which will permit the pursuit of gratifications on a world scale without war.

The people who do not learn anything from history are those who have not listened. The record is clear. As institutions are provided for establishing laws, enforcing them equitably, and permitting change when new interest and power groups arise, peace can be maintained within the group. These institutions are supported by psychological networks involving loyalty, respect for authority, devotion to traditions, and identification with fellow citizens. There is no "instinct" which demands war as an outlet. William James erred in his famous assumption that man needs war and therefore that a struggle against nature could serve mankind as an alternative to war. Most of us have enough struggles already. Further, the average citizen has only remote influences upon decision makers. The key decisions are made by national leaders who receive direct gratifications, in power and prestige, from national expansion. Thus the crucial question becomes: What motives may influence the behavior of leaders in the direction of peaceful settlement of disputes or in a reduction of nationalist tensions? The outlook is not encouraging. A man who has reached an intensely gratifying social role as head of a great nation is hardly likely to take steps toward diminishing the power and status of that role. Nevertheless, these leaders seem to be aware that something is wrong, and that innovations should be considered. They are conscious of the great destruction and suffering accompanying war; and they may realize that another world war would probably end their prized status forever. Hence, there are strong motivational forces which may favor moves toward internationalism; the conclusion is cautious because the evidence is limited.

THE DELUSION OF HELPLESSNESS

In the face of discouraging data, we must not fall victims to the delusion of helplessness. History shows that it is possible to change institutions and modify sources of human suffering. Slavery and serfdom have largely been ended. Many manifestations of "man's inhumanity to man" have been outlawed.

Man, therefore, is not helpless in the face of his own potential for violence and cruelty. Conscience can be strengthened, laws can be framed, police can be trained to restrain such forms of behavior. To be specific, we can develop international institutions which can be used as devices for limiting and controlling international disputes; and we can instill in our children the kind of conscience which will resist the application of violence to people in other countries.

At the other extreme, we must not assume that evolution of international controls on violence is inevitable. There is no such thing as a new idea which prevails without any help from people. Karl Marx and V.I. Lenin wrote a great deal about the inevitability of communism, but both expended energy trying to organize people to bring about this so-called inevitable development.

Those who desire a peaceful world which is not dominated by communism must be willing to expend their energy likewise. History is made by human beings. The past cannot be changed, but future history can be shaped into new patterns—if enough people devote themselves to the task.

Notes

CHAPTER 1

1. Arthur M. Schlesinger, Jr. *A Thousand Days: John F. Kennedy in the White House*. Boston: Houghton Mifflin Co., 1965, pp. 211-241. On the same point, Clifton Daniels, managing editor of the *New York Times*, quotes the late President Kennedy as having said that if the *Times* had printed *all* the information it had, the Bay of Pigs expedition would have been cancelled — a clear indication that data had been withheld from him. See *New York Times*, June 2, 1966, p. 14.

2. See Chapter 3, page 44, also note 9 of that chapter.

3. A number of recent books offer contributions from the various social science disciplines relevant to the problem of international war. See, for example: Elton B. McNeil, ed. *The Nature of Human Conflict*. Englewood Cliffs, N.J.: Prentice-Hall, 1965. Herbert C. Kelman, and others, eds. *International Behavior: A Social-Psychological Analysis*. New York: Holt, Rinehart and Winston, 1965. Roger Fisher, ed. *International Conflict and Behavioral Science*. New York: Basic Books, 1964.

4. The nature of Forrestal's breakdown and the implications of his mental disturbance for decisions while he was secretary of defense are described in a sympathetic but fairly objective manner by Arnold A. Rogow. *James Forrestal: A Study of Personality, Politics and Policy*. New York: Macmillan Co., 1963. See especially pp. 122-135, 306-309, and 325-343.

5. For a good treatment of these stereotyped images as they relate to international affairs, see Otto Klineberg. *The Human Dimension in International Relations*. New York: Holt, Rinehart and Winston, 1964, pp. 33-48.

6. Joseph Frankel. *International Relations*. New York: Oxford University Press, 1964, p. 54.

7. Ross Stagner. "Psychological Aspects of Industrial Conflict." *Personnel Psychology*, 1 (1948), pp. 131-144.

8. Americans frequently express indignation over the fact that our diplomats in Moscow and other communist capitals are shadowed by plainclothes police and that our embassy is "bugged" with electronic eavesdropping devices. However, no one seems to have been alarmed by the report that "over 100 FBI agents are constantly assigned to shadowing Russian embassy personnel" in this country (*Detroit News*, Dec. 30, 1962) or that our FBI admits to having "bugged" many embassies in Washington (*New York Times*, Dec. 3, 1966, p. 1). The explanation for this double standard is quite simple. "Their" diplomats will spy at any opportunity and must be watched; but "ours" would never do such a thing, so the watching is an insult.

9. The point of view expressed here is by no means limited to psychologists. "The key to the explanation of why the state behaves as it does lies in the way its decision makers define their situation." Richard C. Snyder, H. W. Bruck, and B. Sapin. *Foreign Policy Decision-Making: An Approach to the Study of International Politics*. New York: Free Press of Glencoe, 1962, p. 51.

CHAPTER 2

1. Salvador de Madariaga. *The Blowing Up of the Parthenon*. New York: Frederick A. Praeger, 1960, p. 15.
2. H. C. Engelbrecht, and F. C. Hanighen. *Merchants of Death*. New York: Dodd Mead & Co., 1934.
3. George F. Kennan. *Realities of American Foreign Policy*. Princeton, N. J.: Princeton University Press, 1954, pp. 20-21.
4. Kennan, pp. 22-23.
5. Herman Kahn. *On Thermonuclear War*. Princeton, N. J.: Princeton University Press, 1960, pp. 144-147.
6. Mason Haire. "Role-Perceptions in Labor-Management Relations: An Experimental Approach." *Industrial & Labor Relations Review*, 8 (1955), 204-216.
7. Richard M. Brickner. *Is Germany Incurable?* Philadelphia: J. B. Lippincott Co., 1943, p. 30.
8. Brickner, p. 169, p. 171.
9. Brickner, p. 179.
10. The hazards of clinging to images based on past reality, without testing to see if conditions have changed, are eloquently stated by Senator J. W. Fulbright. *Old Myths and New Realities*. New York: Random House, 1964. See also the special issue of the *Journal of International Affairs*, "Image and Reality in World Politics," 21 (1967), No. 1.

CHAPTER 3

1. See *New York Times*, Sept. 9, 1961, p. 13.
2. Ralph K. White. "Misconceptions in Soviet and American Images." American Psychological Association, 1961; summarized in *New York Times*, Sept. 5, 1961, p. 6. For a recent report of White's continuing research on this problem, see his "Images in the Context of International Conflict: Soviet Perceptions of the U. S. and the U.S.S.R." in Herbert C. Kelman, ed. *International Behavior*. New York: Holt, Rinehart and Winston, 1965, pp. 238-276 and "Misperception and the Vietnam Way," *Journal of Social Issues*, July 1966.
3. Urie Bronfenbrenner. "The Mirror Image in Soviet-American Relations" *Journal of Social Issues*, 17 (1961), 45-46. See also *Saturday Review*, Jan. 5, 1963, p. 96; and "Allowing for Soviet Perceptions" in Roger Fisher. *International Conflict and Behavioral Science*. New York: Basic Books, 1964, pp. 161-178.
4. John Foster Dulles. *War, Peace and Change*. New York: Harper & Row, 1939, pp. 57-58. Reprinted by permission of the publisher.
5. Dulles, pp. 58-59.
6. S. E. Asch. "Studies of Independence and Conformity." *Psychological Monographs* No. 416 (1956), 70. See also *Social Psychology*. New York: Prentice-Hall, 1952, pp. 451-473.
7. Richard S. Crutchfield. "Conformity and Character." *American Psychologist*, 10 (1955), 191-198.
8. Gustave LeBon. *The Psychology of the Great War*. Trans. by E. Andrews. New York: Macmillan Co., 1916, p. 35.
9. LeBon, p. 30.
10. Joseph B. Harrison, L. A. Mander, and N. H. Engle, eds. *If Men Want Peace*. New York: Macmillan Co., 1946. See especially "Nationalism," by Mander and Harrison, p. 259.
11. Lloyd A. Free. *Six Allies and a Neutral*. New York: Free Press of Glencoe, 1959.
12. This passage was written before the break between Russia and China made the division between nationalistic communism and evangelistic communism so obvious. Regrettably, we may have to wait thirty or forty years for the Chinese communists

to quiet down; in the meantime, their actions reveal the great error of founding American policy on an assumption of communist unity.

CHAPTER 4

1. Ross Stagner, J. F. Brown, R. H. Gundlach, and R. K. White, "Analysis of Social Scientists' Opinions on the Prevention of War." *Journal of Social Psychology.* 15 (1942), 381-394.
2. Nikos Kazantzakis. *Report to Greco.* Trans. by P. A. Bien. New York: Simon and Schuster, 1965, p. 98.
3. Ross Stagner. "Studies in Aggressive Social Attitudes." *Journal of Social Psychology,* 20 (1944), 129-140.
4. United States Information Agency. "Khrushchev and Stalin as Seen by the Soviet Bloc." *Repatriate Reports,* April 10, 1958.
5. Melville Dalton. *Men Who Manage.* New York: John Wiley, 1959.
6. Charles A. Beard. *The Idea of National Interest.* New York: Macmillan Co., 1934.
7. Robert R. Sears, Eleanor Maccoby, and H. Levin. *Patterns of Child Rearing.* Evanston, Ill.: Row, Peterson & Co., 1957, pp. 362-393.
8. The argument that conscience should restrain the nation from adopting certain kinds of military strategy is cogently put by Anatol Rapoport. *Strategy and Conscience.* New York: Harper & Row, 1964. See especially pp. 284-288.
9. Edward Crankshaw. *Cracks in the Kremlin Wall.* New York: Viking Press, 1951.
10. Pryns Hopkins. *Psychology of Social Movements.* London: Allen & Unwin, 1938.
11. An interesting discussion of emotions in relation to delusions of national virtue will be found in Leonard W. Doob. *Patriotism and Nationalism: Their Psychological Foundations.* New Haven: Yale University Press, 1964.

CHAPTER 5

1. J. M. Fletcher. "Verdict of Psychologists on War Instincts." *Scientific Monthly,* 35 (1932), 142-145.
2. Nikos Kazantzakis. *Report to Greco.* Trans. by P. A. Bien. New York: Simon and Schuster, 1965, p. 111.
3. However, to consider international war as an example of hostility displaced from family disputes seems to me quite ridiculous. This view has been seriously espoused by many distinguished psychoanalysts, for example, Edward Glover: "A world war is simply an extension of a family affair." (*War, Sadism and Pacifism.* London: Allen & Unwin, 1933, p. 25.) While no one will question that basic dynamic patterns, such as readiness to resolve disputes by violence, originate within the family and may affect decisions of national leaders, there are still enormous differences between "a family affair" and a world war.
4. Carl I. Hovland, and Robert R. Sears. "Correlations of Economic Indices with Lynchings." *Journal of Psychology.* 9 (1940), 301-310.
5. James Reston. *New York Times,* April 30, 1961, p. 10E.
6. George F. Kennan. *Realities of American Foreign Policy.* Princeton, N. J.: Princeton University Press, 1954, p. 20.
7. Deterrence seldom works, even at the individual level. Speaking of his work with aggressive, destructive juvenile delinquents, psychologist Elton B. McNeil says: "Deterrence of aggression we have found always to be a part solution and an unstable one at best. Unless the basic causes of aggression are remedied, deterrence can bring only a false sense of security. Positive deterrence in the form of need satisfaction and acceptable alternative forms of behavior must be a necessary second step." See "Psychology and Aggression." *Journal of Conflict Resolution,* 3 (1961), 195-293. The quotation is from p. 288.
8. See James G. Miller. "Information, Input Overload, and Psychopathology." *American Journal of Psychiatry,* 116 (1960), 695-704.

9. It is not surprising, therefore, that various psychiatrists and psychoanalysts have called for "certificates of mental health" or psychoanalysis for all national leaders. See, for example: Alix Strachey. *The Unconscious Motives of War.* New York: International Universities Press, 1957, p. 263. George W. Kisker, ed. *World Tensions.* New York: Prentice-Hall, 1951, pp. 36-37, 311-312. Unfortunately, the belligerent neurotic who gets himself into a power role is not likely to take a year or two off for psychoanalysis; indeed, he will deny that it is needed in his case. And who could have forced Hitler or Stalin to accept psychotherapy?

CHAPTER 6

1. Jules Monnerot. *Sociology and Psychology of Communism.* Trans. by Jane Degras and Richard Rees. Boston: Beacon Press, 1953, p. 19.
2. Jules Monnerot, p. 19.
3. *New York Times Magazine,* June 5, 1966, p. 44.
4. *New York Times Magazine,* June 5, 1966, p. 44.
5. Richard Crossman. *The God That Failed.* New York: Harper & Bros., 1949. See especially the essay by Ignazio Silone, pp. 106-112.
6. Stringfellow Barr. "Comedy of Dollars." *Saturday Review,* May 27, 1961, p. 15. This is a review of T. S. Loeber. *Foreign Aid: Our Tragic Experiment.* New York: W. W. Norton & Co., 1961.
7. Robert R. Palmer. *Age of the Democratic Revolution, 1760-1800.* Vol. I: *The Challenge.* Princeton, N. J.: Princeton University Press, 1959, p. 241.
8. While the text refers for the most part only to the Russian variety of communism, it is quite feasible to substitute China without changing any general principles. At this time the Chinese show more ideological fanaticism than do the Russians; both are high on nationalism. The similarities are noted by various authors. See, for example, Arthur H. Dean. "What It's Like to Negotiate with the Chinese." *New York Times Magazine,* Oct. 30, 1966, pp. 44-59. Dean says of the Chinese chief negotiator, "Huang Hua habitually called me a capitalist crook, a rapist, thief, robber of widows, stealer of pennies from the eyes of the dead. . . .a murderer lying in the gutter with filthy garbage . . ." Unfortunately, the communists have no monopoly on such epithets. In a recent speech, an American general commented, "We have to recognize that the Russians are liars, swindlers, and cutthroats and treat them as such."—Brig. Gen. Frank L. Howley, speaking to the Michigan Education Association in Detroit. Quoted in *Royal Oak Tribune,* Oct 20, 1961, p. 20.

CHAPTER 7

1. Norman Angell. *The Great Illusion.* New York: G. P. Putnam's, 1913.
2. Kenneth E. Boulding. Personal Communication.
3. H. C. Engelbrecht and F. C. Hanighen. *Merchants of Death.* New York: Dodd, Mead & Co., 1934.
4. George Seldes. *Iron, Blood and Profits.* New York: Harper & Row, 1934, pp. 57-59, 33-35, 110-111. For a current example of the technique, see the *Saturday Review,* May 13, 1967, p. 85.
5. *New York Times,* March 11, 1962.
6. V.I. Lenin. *Imperialism.* New York: International Publishers, 1939.
7. Foster Rhea Dulles. *America's Rise to World Power.* New York: Harper & Row 1955, p. 120.
8. Ross Stagner, J. F. Brown, R. H. Gundlach, and R. K. White. "Analysis of Social Scientists' Opinions on the Prevention of War." *Journal of Social Psychology,* 15 (1942), 381-394.

9. E. E. Schattschneider. *Politics, Pressure, and the Tariff.* New York: Prentice-Hall, 1935.

10. Cordell Hull. *Papers Relating to the Foreign Relations of the United States: Japan, 1931-1941.* Washington, D. C.: Government Printing Office, 1943, Vol. II, p. 749.

11. Details of the extensive economic retaliation against the USA following the passage of the Smoot-Hawley Act can be found in J. M. Jones. *Tariff Retaliation.* Philadelphia: University of Pennsylvania Press, 1934.

CHAPTER 8

1. Regarding the Adolf Eichmann case, see Hannah Arendt. *Eichmann in Jerusalem.* New York: Viking Press, 1964.

2. See Claude Eatherly and Gunther Anders. *Burning Conscience.* New York: Monthly Review Press, 1962.

3. The famous legal authority, Blackstone, referred to national sovereignty as the "supreme, irresistible, absolute, uncontrolled authority." On this definition a well-known psychiatrist has commented: "These words—supreme, irresistible, absolute, unlimited—are reminiscent of the delusions of grandeur of the manic patient." K. E. Appel. "Nationalism and Sovereignty: A Psychiatric View." *Journal of Abnormal and Social Psychology,* 40 (1945), 355-362. (See also Brickner's comments on national delusions of grandeur, cited on pp. 27-29 of this volume.)

4. J. S. Berliner. *Soviet Economic Aid.* New York: Praeger, 1958.

5. Interesting quotations from interviews with congressmen, revealing the regional and economic pressures to which they are subjected, can be found in Charles L. Clapp. *The Congressman: His Work as He Sees It.* Washington: The Brookings Institution, 1963.

6. Subcommittee on International Organizations and Movements, House Committee on Foreign Affairs. "Behavioral Science and National Security." Report No. 4, *Winning the Cold War,* pp. 9-10R. Quoted by George E. Lowe. "The Camelot Affair." *Bulletin of the Atomic Scientists,* May 1966, pp. 44-48.

7. Norman Cousins. "The Four Centers of U. S. Foreign Policy." *Saturday Review,* July 2, 1966, pp. 16-17. In his book *The Hard Way to Peace* (pp. 104-105) Etzioni identifies various events which appear to be sabotage of U. S. foreign policy by military officers. Similarly, the arrest of Prof. F. C. Barghoorn on Oct. 31, 1963, by Russian security officers was interpreted in some quarters as an effort by Stalinists to sabotage the Khrushchev coexistence policy. See *New York Times,* Nov. 17, 1963, p. 1E.

8. John Kenneth Galbraith. Testimony before the Senate Foreign Relations Committee, April 25, 1966. Cited in *Saturday Review,* July 9, 1966. p. 14.

9. These and other alarming quotations can be found in *The Nation,* Oct. 28, 1961, p. 332.

10. Thus, any offensive action is always rationalized as being defensive in character.

11. *War/Peace Report,* May 1962, p. 7. (Italics mine.)

12. Trumbull Higgins. *Korea and the Fall of MacArthur.* New York: Oxford University Press, 1960, p. 145. But see, on the same page, MacArthur's striking remark: "You cannot control war; you can only abolish it."

13. It is interesting to note that a Russian diplomat is reported to have said: "We have a lot of trouble with our military men, too." See also: Robert H. Cory, Jr. "Images of United States Disarmament Negotiating System." *Journal of Arms Control,* 1 (1963), 654-662.

14. Senator Clinton P. Anderson. "The Test Debate." *New York Times Magazine,* Feb. 25, 1962, pp. 15, 67.

CHAPTER 9

1. *New York Times,* Jan. 19, 1961, p. 22.
2. C. Wright Mills. *The Power Elite.* New York: Oxford University Press, 1956, p. 276. See also p. 279.
3. Mills, p. 276.
4. A. L. Rowse. *Appeasement: A Study in Political Decline.* New York: W. W. Norton & Co., 1961. He says of the British government leaders in 1956: "They would not listen to warnings, because they did not wish to hear...There was a fatal confusion in their minds between the interests of their social order and the interests of their country." (p. 117.)
5. Erich Fromm. *May Man Prevail?* New York: Doubleday & Co., 1961, pp. 54-55.

CHAPTER 10

1. Max F. Millikan and D. L. M. Blackmer. *The Emerging Nations.* Boston: Little, Brown & Co., 1961, p. 10.
2. Harrison Salisbury. *New York Times.* Jan. 1, 1962, p. 1.
3. Lloyd A. Free. *Six Allies and a Neutral.* New York: Free Press of Glencoe, 1959.
4. See the articles in D. Lerner, ed. "Attitude Research in Modernizing Areas." *Public Opinion Quarterly,* 22 (1958), No. 3.
5. The Nehru quotation is from a press conference, Dec. 28, 1961, and is recorded in "Prime Minister on Goa," External Publicity Division, Ministry of External Affairs, Government of India, pp. 24, 29. One can only guess at what he would have said regarding the Chinese justification for using force in order to "liberate" territory which, they held, had been illegally seized by India.
6. Chester A. Bowles. *American Politics in a Revolutionary World.* Cambridge, Mass.: Harvard University Press, 1956, pp. 106-107.
7. Economic aid will have the effect of reducing frustration levels and, thus, of minimizing the danger of aggression by one of these new nations against a neighbor. Military aid, by contrast, facilitates aggressiveness and violence, as in the case of Pakistan's war with India, September 1965. (See note 8, Chapter 8.)
8. Dudley Seers. "Model of Comparative Rates of Growth in the World Economy." *Economic Journal,* 72 (1962), 45-78. The dilemma arises from the fact that, if agricultural production is increased, there is no domestic market for the goods; and if industrial goods are turned out, there is no market for them either. Most of these nations have a very small group (perhaps, at most, 20 per cent of the population) living in a cash economy. The further problem is that people getting above the subsistence level want industrial goods — radios, cars, TV sets — not yams or bananas. Hence supply and demand operate to force industrial prices up, agricultural prices down.
9. Seymour Melman. *The Peace Race.* New York: Ballantine Books, 1961.
10. The argument that the Indian worker is undernourished and cannot work a full 40-hour week is fallacious. The short workweek primarily applies to those who are relatively well-fed; the truly undernourished workers are those who, even now, put in more than 40 hours weekly.
11. It is not simple to find indigenous leaders who, faced by conservatism, will push these new attitudes and the new technology. Tribal leaders have power and privileges which they lose in a new modern nation. It is virtually inherent in the primitive situation that new leadership groups must be found. The interaction of

psychological, social, and economic forces in this complex is well-explored by E. E. Hagen. *On the Theory of Social Change.* Homewood, Ill.: Dorsey Press, 1962. See especially Chapters 9, 15.
12. Lloyd A. Free. (See note 3.)

CHAPTER 11

1. Allen L. Edwards. "Political Frames of Reference as a Factor Influencing Recognition." *Journal of Abnormal and Social Psychology,* 36 (1941), 35-50.
2. Herbert A. Shepard. "The Psychologist's Role in Union-Management Relations." *Personnel Psychology,* 14 (1961), 270-279.
3. Robert R. Blake, Herbert A. Shepard, and Jane S. Mouton. *Managing Intergroup Conflict in Industry.* Houston, Texas: Gulf Publishing Co., 1964.
4. Bernard G. Bechhoefer. *Postwar Negotiations for Arms Control.* Washington: Brookings Institution, 1961.
5. Bechhoefer, p. 293, on Russian offer; p. 311 on American retreat. For the reader who likes a play-by-play summary of the negotiating process, showing the concessions and compromises offered by each side and the retraction of offers during the period 1947-1960, a concise account is given by Lloyd Jensen. "Soviet-American Bargaining Behavior in the Postwar Disarmament Negotiations." *Journal of Conflict Resolution,* 7 (1963), 522-541; *Journal of Arms Control,* 1 (1963), 616-635.
6. Foster Rhea Dulles. *America's Rise to World Power.* New York: Harper & Bros., 1955, p. 41.
7. George A. Muench. "The Resolution of Conflict in Union-Management Relationships." American Psychological Association, Sept. 5, 1964. See also "A Clinical Psychologist's Treatment of Labor-Management Conflicts: A Four-Year Study." *Journal of Humanistic Psychology,* 3 (1963), 92-97.
8. Robert Strausz-Hupé, W. R. Kintner, and Stefan T. Possony. *A Forward Strategy for America.* New York: Harper & Row, 1961.
9. These distortions sometimes reach the height of absurdity. For example, in September 1966 the western creditor nations agreed to extend their loans to Indonesia, which obviously could not pay off. The Soviet Union called this "blackmail" against Indonesia! (*New York Times,* Sept. 25, 1966.) One wonders what word the Russians would have chosen had the creditors insisted on partial repayment.
10. Richard H. S. Crossman. "Reading Khrushchev's Mind." *Commentary,* December 1961, p. 503.
11. Murray Dyer. *The Weapon on the Wall.* Baltimore: Johns Hopkins University Press, 1959, p. 132.
12. This discussion benefited from a document, "A New Approach to Communicating with the Russians," prepared by a group of faculty members at Cornell University, Jan. 25, 1961.
13. The argument assumes that we are trying to negotiate. The evidence indicates that this is not always true. A concise definition of the "dialogue of the deaf" is reported by Arthur H. Dean. "What It's Like to Negotiate with the Chinese." *New York Times Magazine,* Oct. 30, 1966, p. 44: "General Harrison...gave me a sealed envelope which he told me to open in the privacy of my tent. It was inscribed: 'How to Negotiate with the Communists.' Inside was a sheet of paper with the single word: 'Don't.'" How one settles international conflict with such an approach to negotiations is not clear.
14. Ralph W. Gerard. "Truth Detection," in Quincy Wright, William N. Evan, and Morton Deutsch, eds. *Preventing World War III: Some Proposals.* New York: Simon and Schuster, 1962, pp. 52-61.

CHAPTER   12

1. The quotation is from Joseph L. Walsh, C. S. P., and Norman Kopmeyer. "Morality and Nuclear War." *Newman Review* (Wayne State University) 14 (1962), 19-21.

2. Not all experts would agree that this is too extreme for consideration. Psychiatrist Jerome D. Frank suggests that the barrier of hostility and tension which today blocks communication between East and West can be broken only by an extraordinary act, such as unilateral nuclear disarmament. For his logic, see "Breaking the Thought Barrier: Psychological Challenges of the Nuclear Age." *Psychiatry*, 23 (1960), 245-266.

3. Charles E. Osgood. *An Alternative to War or Surrender*. Urbana, Ill.: University of Illinois Press, 1962.

4. An instance in which the Russians did reciprocate, under quite tense circumstances, is cited by Charles E. Osgood. *Science and Human Affairs*. Palo Alto, Calif.: Science and Behavior Books, 1965, p. 165.

5. Some degree of mutual trust is indispensable if we are to arrive at a workable settlement of these disputes. See Morton Deutsch. "A Psychological Basis for Peace," in Quincy Wright, William N. Evan, and Morton Deutsch, eds. *Preventing World War III: Some Proposals*. New York: Simon and Schuster, 1962, pp. 380-387.

6. Amitai Etzioni. *The Hard Way to Peace*. New York: Collier Books, 1962. See especially Chapter 4. Both Etzioni and Osgood emphasize the need for a long-range plan, as against sporadic isolated gestures for tension reduction.

7. James J. Wadsworth. *The Price of Peace*. New York: Frederick A. Praeger, 1962.

8. Arthur Schlesinger, Jr., testifies to the felt pressure on governmental officials to prove that they are tough-minded and will endorse aggressive policies. Writing of the hectic conferences prior to the Bay of Pigs expedition in 1961, he says "...the representatives of the State Department failed in defending the diplomatic interests of the nation. I could not help feeling that the desire to prove to the CIA and the Joint Chiefs that they were not soft-headed idealists but were *really tough guys* too influenced State's representatives at the Cabinet table." *A Thousand Days: John F. Kennedy in the White House*. Boston: Houghton Mifflin Co., 1965, p. 231. (Italics mine.)

CHAPTER 13

1. Henry Steele Commager. "Brave New World of the Year 2000." *New York Times Magazine*. Nov. 1, 1959, p. 24.

2. And, of course, Communist China. At present the Chinese fear that an IPF would block their efforts to spread their influence through the arming and leading of "revolutions" in various emerging nations. The Russians seem to have lost some of their ideological militancy, perhaps to the point of accepting an IPF if it is not dominated by the West. The prospects regarding Chinese acquiescence are less cheerful.

3. These and other relevant figures will be found in William Buchanan, H. E. Krugman, and R. W. Van Wagenen. *An International Police Force and Public Opinion*. Princeton, N. J.: Center for Research on World Political Institutions, 1954.

4. The point was graphically expressed by Heinrich Himmler, Chief of the Nazi Gestapo, in a speech in 1943: "Whether foreign populations live prosperously or die from hunger interests me only insofar as we might need them as slaves for our own civilization...We Germans, who are the only people in the world with a decent attitude to animals, will also have a decent attitude to these human animals; but to care about their welfare would be a crime against our own blood..." Quoted by Sibylle Bedford. "The Worst That Ever Happened." *Saturday Evening Post*, Oct. 22, 1966, p. 88.

5. D.A.R.: Daughters of the American Revolution.

6. Grenville Clark, and L. B. Sohn. *World Peace through World Law,* 2d ed. Cambridge, Mass.: Harvard University Press, 1960. The authors point out that many solutions can be devised for the problem of voting rights in such a world organization; the real obstacle is the refusal of nationalists to subordinate the rights of their nation to the welfare of the race.

7. *War/Peace Report,* May 1961, pp. 5, 11. See also his remarks in "Toward a New Spirit for NATO." *Saturday Review,* April 21, 1962, p. 15.

8. See, for example, C. F. Alger: "United Nations Participation as a Learning Experience." *Public Opinion Quarterly,* 27 (1963), 411-426. On the especially important question of whether Soviet delegates learn from their UN stay, see Alexander Dallin. *The Soviet Union at the United Nations.* New York: Frederick A. Praeger, 1962. Dallin believes the Russians *do* enlarge their perspectives. Some interesting interviews are also reported by Gary Best. "Diplomacy in the United Nations." Unpublished Ph.D. dissertation, Northwestern University, 1960.

9. A more detailed psychological analysis of the International Police Force idea will be found in H. C. Kelman: "Internationalizing Military Force," in Quincy Wright et al., eds. *Preventing World War III: Some Proposals.* New York: Simon and Schuster, 1962, pp. 106-122.

CHAPTER 14

1. For a more extended analysis of dynamic similarities among these varieties of conflict, see Ross Stagner. *Dimensions of Human Conflict.* Detroit: Wayne State University Press, 1967.

2. Over forty years ago, Sigmund Freud, whose brilliant insights into psychological dynamics are yet unexcelled, took a similar stand on the necessity of yielding some sovereignty to an international authority: "Wars will only be prevented with certainty if mankind unites in setting up a central authority to which the right of giving judgment upon all conflicts of interest shall be handed over. There are clearly two separate requirements involved in this: the creation of a supreme authority, and its endowment with the necessary power. One without the other would be useless." *Collected Papers,* Vol. V. London: International Psychoanalytic Press, 1953, p. 278.

3. See, for example, Harold Guetzkow, C. F. Alger, R. A. Brody, R. C. Noel, and R. C. Snyder. *Simulation in International Relations: Developments for Research and Teaching.* Englewood Cliffs, N. J.: Prentice-Hall, 1963.

4. Ross Stagner and Hjalmar Rosen. *Psychology of Union-Management Relations.* Belmont, Calif.: Wadsworth, 1965.

5. (See note 5, Chapter 11.)

6. Scientists and technologists, organized in voluntary societies, had a profound impact on the course of history in the seventeenth and eighteenth centuries. See, for example W. H. G. Armytage. *The Rise of the Technocrats: A Social History.* London: Routledge & Kegan Paul, 1965.

7. Harold K. Jacobson and Eric Stein. *Diplomats, Scientists and Politicians: The United States and the Nuclear Test Ban Negotiations.* Ann Arbor, Mich.: University of Michigan Press, 1966.

8. *Dodge* v. *Ford Motor Co.,* 204 Mich. 459, p. 460, Feb. 7, 1919.

9. James W. Silver. *Mississippi: The Closed Society.* New York: Harcourt, Brace & World, 1966.

10. D. E. Berlyne. *Conflict, Arousal and Curiosity.* New York: McGraw-Hill Book Co., 1960.

Index